# Governing Islam

*Governing Islam* traces tl ... ... contemporary struggles between Islam and secularism in India, Pakistan, and Bangladesh. The book uncovers the paradoxical workings of colonial laws that promised to separate secular and religious spheres, but instead fostered their vexed entanglement. It shows how religious laws governing families became embroiled with secular laws governing markets, and how calls to protect religious liberties clashed with freedom of the press. By following these interactions Stephens asks us to reconsider where law is and what it is. Her narrative weaves between state courts, Islamic *fatwas* on ritual performance, and intimate marital disputes to reveal how deeply law penetrates everyday life. In her hands law also serves many masters – from British officials to Islamic jurists to aggrieved Muslim wives. The resulting study shows how the neglected field of Muslim law in South Asia is essential to understanding current crises in global secularism.

JULIA STEPHENS is Assistant Professor in the Department of History at Rutgers University, New Brunswick. Her research and teaching span the fields of modern South Asian history, law, Islam, colonialism, and gender. Her writings have appeared in *History Workshop Journal*, *Law and History Review*, *Modern Asian Studies*, and *Journal of British History*.

# Governing Islam

*Law, Empire, and Secularism in South Asia*

Julia Stephens
*Rutgers University, New Jersey*

CAMBRIDGE
UNIVERSITY PRESS

# CAMBRIDGE
## UNIVERSITY PRESS

University Printing House, Cambridge CB2 8BS, United Kingdom

One Liberty Plaza, 20th Floor, New York, NY 10006, USA

477 Williamstown Road, Port Melbourne, VIC 3207, Australia

314–321, 3rd Floor, Plot 3, Splendor Forum, Jasola District Centre, New Delhi – 110025, India

79 Anson Road, #06-04/06, Singapore 079906

Cambridge University Press is part of the University of Cambridge.

It furthers the University's mission by disseminating knowledge in the pursuit of education, learning, and research at the highest international levels of excellence.

www.cambridge.org
Information on this title: www.cambridge.org/9781107173910
DOI: 10.1017/9781316795477

© Julia Stephens 2018

First published 2018

Printed in the United Kingdom by Clays, St Ives plc

*A catalogue record for this publication is available from the British Library.*

*Library of Congress Cataloging-in-Publication Data*
Names: Stephens, Julia Anne
Title: Governing Islam : law, empire, and secularism in south Asia /
Julia Stephens, Rutgers University, New Jersey.
Description: Cambridge, United Kingdom ; New York, NY : Cambridge
University Press, 2018. | Based on author's thesis (doctoral – Harvard University,
2013) issued under title: Governing Islam : law and religion in colonial India. |
Includes bibliographical references and index.
Identifiers: LCCN 2018002368 | ISBN 9781107173910 (hardback)
Subjects: LCSH: Muslims – Legal status, laws, etc. – India – History –
19th century. | Muslims – Legal status, laws, etc. – India – History –
20th century. | Law – India – Islamic influences – History – 19th century. |
Law – India – Islamic influences – History – 20th century. |
India – History – British occupation, 1765–1947.
Classification: LCC KNS2107.M56 S84 2018 |
DDC 342.5408/529700904–dc23
LC record available at https://lccn.loc.gov/2018002368

ISBN 978-1-107-17391-0 Hardback
ISBN 978-1-316-62628-3 Paperback

To my parents, Sharman and Michael Stephens
Who gave me the freedom to wander
And a family full of love and good food to come
home to

# Contents

| | | |
|---|---|---|
| *List of Map and Figures* | | *page* viii |
| *Acknowledgments* | | ix |
| *Note on Translation, Transliteration, and Abbreviations* | | xiii |
| | Introduction | 1 |
| 1 | Forging Secular Legal Governance | 22 |
| 2 | Personal Law and the Problem of Marital Property | 57 |
| 3 | Taming Custom | 86 |
| 4 | Ritual and the Authority of Reason | 105 |
| 5 | Pathologizing Muslim Sentiment | 132 |
| 6 | Islamic Economy: A Forgone Alternative | 155 |
| | Conclusion | 184 |
| | *Select Bibliography* | 191 |
| | *Index* | 211 |

# Map and Figures

**Map**

1   India in 1947                                                                *page* xiv

**Figures**

1   On December 6, 1995 in New Delhi Muslim women
    carried scales of justice to demand compensation for the
    victims of the riots that occurred after the destruction of
    the Babri Masjid in 1992. Photograph courtesy of Doug
    Curran and Getty Images                                                           2
2   In the cartoon the "religious fanatic" declares: "If we
    commence civil disobedience, then the government
    will have to bow before us." The "somewhat-reasonable
    Muslim" replies: "Stop it. I've heard enough. Don't be a
    braggart. You save your own head by asking for forgiveness
    and want to establish your leadership by fooling and
    ensnaring others." *Milap*, July 17, 1927, 5. Image courtesy
    of the Centre of South Asian Studies, Cambridge University       140

# Acknowledgments

This book has traveled with me across multiple continents and institutions, and along the way I (and it) have acquired many debts.

Our journey began in graduate school, where I was blessed with wonderful mentors. Sugata Bose provided me with the intellectual scaffolding which undergirds my understanding of South Asian history, both in this book and for a lifetime of future scholarly endeavors. Ayesha Jalal and I share a love for argument, and we debated together through my six years of graduate school. Her critical insight pushed me to think deeper about governance, law, and Islam. Emma Rothschild has been my archival inspiration and confidante, sharing my pleasure in dusty boxes and tattered documents. She has also continually supported me through the emotional ups and downs of graduate school and the tenure track. Some of my oldest and deepest scholarly debts are to Judith Surkis. Her probing questions during the initial stages of the dissertation led me towards its central themes. I am so happy that our paths have reunited at Rutgers, where she continues to be a mentor, friend, and intellectual interlocutor.

I have been blessed with many wonderful friendships, and in the process this book has gained some of its most critical feedback. At Cambridge, Rachel Berger, Sarah Beth, Rohit De, Leigh Denault, David Lunn, Uditi Sen, and Mitra Sharafi welcomed me into the vibrant world of South Asian Studies. During my time in India, David Boyk, Rotem Geva, Riyad Koya, Daniel Majchrowicz, Durba Mitra, and Bart Scott shared with me the delights of kebabs and Urdu literature. At Harvard, Sana Aiyar, Tariq Ali, Mou Banerjee, Hannah Callaway, Antara Datta, Merih Danali, Philipp Lehmann, Erik Linstrum, Sreemati Mitter, Dinyar Patel, Mircea Raianu, Ben Siegel, Aleksandar Sopov, Josh Specht, Gitanjali Surendran, Michael and Heidi Tworek, and Jeremy Yellen listened to countless hours of intellectual musings, normally while eating and drinking in one of our kitchens. In the frantic days of finishing the book, David Lunn, who has seen this project through its entire evolution, swept in with a final act of kindness by agreeing to read the complete manuscript.

The Centre for History and Economics at Cambridge University and Trinity Hall provided a convivial community to begin the process of turning my dissertation into a book during a post-doctoral fellowship. I am particularly grateful to Tim Harper, Inga Huld Markan, Gareth Stedman Jones, William O'Reilly, and Emma Rothschild for many inspiring conversations over afternoon tea.

At Yale, as we whirled through the chaos of our first jobs, Rohit De kept me sane as I balanced teaching and writing. His deep knowledge of Indian law has profoundly shaped my work, and his friendship provided a crucial ballast during angst-filled revisions. Abbas Amanat, Dani Botsman, Naomi Lamoreaux, Karuna Mantena, and Francesca Trivellato provided much helpful advice. Steve Pincus shared his formidable intellectual energy and pushed me to be more ambitious in my arguments. I am particularly grateful to Ben Kiernan and K. Sivaramakrishnan, who read the book manuscript in full, and whose insightful comments helped immensely in my revisions. Over many cups of chai, Kasturi Gupta enlivened my time at Yale with her wit and hospitality.

Most recently, during the book's final journey towards publication, my new colleagues at Rutgers University have warmly welcomed me into their community of intellectual comradeship. Special thanks go to Seth Koven for urging me to let my enthusiasm for archives and stories shine through my wranglings with the intricacies of law and governance.

At various stops in this journey, colleagues at conferences and workshops have provided invaluable feedback. While my debts to individual scholars and institutions are too numerous to recount in full, the following colleagues deserve particular thanks for providing critical feedback at crucial stages in the development of the book: Seema Alavi, Fahad Bishara, Kavita Datla, Durba Ghosh, David Gilmartin, Manu Goswami, Janet Halley, Iza Hussin, Farina Mir, Eleanor Newbigin, Dwaipayan Sen, Uditi Sen, Mitra Sharafi, Sunil Sharma, Taylor Sherman, Mrinalini Sinha, Shabnum Tejani, Robert Travers, and Fadzilah Yahaya. I am particularly grateful to Ritu Birla and Barbara Metcalf, who read the full manuscript during a book workshop at Yale. Their comments allowed me to return to the manuscript with fresh insights during my final revisions.

The research for this book was funded by numerous institutions and grants, including the U.S. Department of Education's Jacob K. Javits fellowship, the Harvard South Asia Initiative, the Weatherhead Center for International Affairs, the Mellon Foundation, the Center for History and Economics, the Yale South Asia Council, and the Macmillan Center for International Affairs. I have benefitted enormously from the help of staff members at the British Library, Khuda Bakhsh Oriental Library, Lincoln's Inn Library, the National Archives of India, Nadwatul Ulama

Library, Nehru Memorial Library, Osmania University Library, the
Privy Council, and the Uttar Pradesh State Archives. The Interlibrary
Loan Departments at Harvard, Yale, and Rutgers have tirelessly trolled
the earth searching for materials for me. The Five College Consortium
and the University of Massachusetts generously provided library access
and intellectual community during the academic year 2012–13. In
reading and translating Urdu materials, I have received invaluable help
from Naseem Hamed Abbasi, Sayeed Ayub, Timsal Masud, and Asma
Nuzhath. Mufti Hafiz Syed Sadiq Mohiuddin of Hyderabad generously
explained various aspects of *fiqh* and provided guidance in understanding
several difficult texts. Daniel Majchrowicz has repeatedly suggested the
perfect English translation for Urdu idioms. Lucy Rhymer and Lisa
Carter of Cambridge University Press have waited patiently as I took
longer than expected to finish the book, all the while providing prompt
and cheerful responses to my many email queries.

My family has always been incredibly supportive of my scholarship.
My parents gave me the gift of freedom while always being just a phone
call away when I needed help. My sister and brother have reminded me
that there is more to life than work, and tolerated me when I have occasionally forgotten. My uncle Mel opened his flat to me in London and
enthusiastically listened to reports from the archives. Deborah, my *de
facto* elder sister, has shown me by example that it is possible to be both
a happy person and a productive scholar.

Johan has been my partner and comrade in arms through the ups and
downs of researching and writing this book. Over and over again he has
transformed my tears of frustration into cascades of laughter. I look forward to sharing a life of love and scholarship with him.

# Note on Translation, Transliteration, and Abbreviations

Unless otherwise noted, all translations are my own. When translating directly from non-English sources, I have followed the transliteration scheme employed in John T. Platts, *A Dictionary of Urdu, Classical Hindi, and English,* while omitting any diacritical accents. When citing names from primary sources, I have followed as closely as possible the actual spelling in the texts, although some standardization across sources has sometimes been necessary when referring to a single individual. For historically well-known people, places, and terms, I have tried to use common spellings to avoid confusion.

The following abbreviations are used in the text:

AIR     All India Reporter
HCPP    House of Commons Parliamentary Papers
IJE     Indian Journal of Economics
ILR     Indian Law Reports
IOR     India Office Records
NAI     National Archives of India
TOI     Times of India

Map 1. India in 1947.

# Introduction

In 1995, a group of veiled Muslim women took to the streets carrying market scales to protest the Indian government's failure to protect Muslim minorities (see Figure 1).[1] The immediate context was the third anniversary of Hindu extremists tearing down the Babri Masjid, a Mughal-era mosque. Yet the women's protest brought into a common frame two seemingly timeless and powerful symbols – scales of justice and veils. Scales of justice convey the neutrality of secular law.[2] As tools of commercial calculation, scales are also associated with the economy. The protesters' veils, in contrast, suggest Muslim piety, traditional gender roles, and communal identity. By linking Islamic veils and market scales to secular justice, these women brought into dialogue ethical discourses – about culture and economy, religion and secular law – that are often kept apart and figured as oppositional.

The women's protest was so striking because it ran against the current of contemporary coverage, which typically portrays Muslim religiosity as a barrier to secular law. These sentiments were fueled by a series of legal controversies in the 1980s, including the passage of the Muslim Women (Protection of Rights on Divorce) Act and the ban on Salman Rushdie's *Satanic Verses*. A review of the editorial pages of the *Times of India*, India's largest English-language daily, provides a snapshot of how coverage of these events opposed Islam and secularism. In 1986 the ominous title

---

[1] "Liberhan Report on Babri Demolition," photo 7 of 7, *NDTV.com*, accessed April 7, 2015, www.ndtv.com/photos/news/liberhan-report-on-babri-demolition-1039/slide/7. The use of the common balance to invoke symbolic scales of justice has reappeared as a trope in protests marking the anniversary of the destruction of the Babri Masjid. For images of this practice in other protests, see "India in Pictures," image 6 of 9, *The Wall Street Journal*, December 7, 2011, accessed April 7, 2015, www.wsj.com/ articles/SB10 00142405297020477040457708328397116516; "Revisiting Ayodhya," image 8 of 14, *Hindustan Times*, December 6, 2012, accessed April 7, 2015, www. hindustantimes.com/ photos/india/ayodhya/Article4-969382.aspx.
[2] Of course scales of justice also have been associated with images of divine justice, but today are more likely to evoke secular imaginaries. Dennis E. Curtis and Judith Resnik, "Images of Justice," *The Yale Law Journal* 96, no. 8 (July 1, 1987): 1727–72.

Figure 1. On December 6, 1995 in New Delhi Muslim women carried scales of justice to demand compensation for the victims of the riots that occurred after the destruction of the Babri Masjid in 1992. Photograph courtesy of Doug Curran and Getty Images.

of an editorial warned: "After the Muslim Bill: The Secular State in Peril."[3] In another article Girilal Jain, the editor of the *Times of India* from 1978 to 1988, lamented: "The reality ... is that liberalism does not command too many customers among the more articulate Muslims, with the result that fanatics manage to carry the community with them."[4] The destruction of the Babri Masjid by a crowd of Hindu activists in 1992 did nothing to dampen commentary singling out Muslims as especially prone to religious prejudice and resistant to legal reform. A year later Amulya Ganguli, in an article titled "Bigotry of Islam," proclaimed that, "the iron law of fundamentalism still has the community in its grip."[5]

---

[3] Prem Shankar Jha, "After the Muslim Bill: The Secular State in Peril," *Times of India* [hereafter *TOI*], May 20, 1986, 8.
[4] Girilal Jain, "Plight of Muslim Liberals: Implications for India's Future," *TOI*, May 7, 1992, 12.
[5] Amulya Ganguli, "Bigotry in Islam: The Silent Majority's Surrender," *TOI*, January 3, 1994, 14.

This rhetoric reflected the ascent of the Hindu Right in mainstream Indian politics from the 1980s onwards, culminating in the election of Narendra Modi as prime minister in 2014 after he openly engaged in anti-Muslim polemics. As this book will show, however, this pattern of opposing Islam and secularism draws on a much longer history. Almost two centuries ago, while deliberating on legal reforms in India in the early 1830s, a Select Committee of the British Parliament described Islamic law as "inconsistent with the views of enlightened Europeans." The report went on to define Islamic law as everything that nineteenth-century British legal modernizers were struggling against: fraught with "difficulties and uncertainties"; "manifestly unjust and absurd"; "inefficient"; "venal and corrupt" – rhetoric which would not be surprising to encounter today.[6]

The idea of Islam as antithetical to secular, modern, and liberal legal regimes has persisted despite the fact that South Asian Muslims, like the women protesting after the destruction of the Babri Masjid, have repeatedly refused such oppositions. Muslims, from eminent legal scholars to crowds gathered outside courts, have since the nineteenth century produced an alternative outpouring of legal commentary. In their own writings, Muslims have pushed back against colonial portrayals of Islamic law as irrational and retrogressive. For example, Maulana Rashid Ahmad Gangohi (1826–1905) defended the juristic device of taqlid – which Muslim modernists and Orientalists alike dismissed as "blind imitation."[7] Gangohi explained that taqlid "is beneficial, is the people's form of intizam [government], and ameliorates disorder and fasad o fitna [discord]."[8] For him, taqlid ensured much the same as what secular law promised: reasoned, ordered justice.

How are we to make sense of these two archives, one of which suppressed the internal logics of Islamic law by casting it as the "Other" of secular law, and another which vociferously contested this view? This question animates this book. Studies of colonial encounters often privilege one of these narratives over the other, focusing on either the

[6] Report from the Select Committee of the House of Commons on the Affairs of the East India Company, vol. IV, Judicial, 695, House of Commons Parliamentary Papers [hereafter HCPP], 1831–2 (735-IV).
[7] I prefer to translate taqlid as following an established authority. Indira Falk Gesink has argued that the Muslim modernist Sayyid Jamal al-Din "al-Afghani" (1839–97) was responsible for popularizing the idea that taqlid was "blind" following or imitation, a translation of the term which elided the juridical rationale for the practice. "'Chaos on the Earth': Subjective Truths versus Communal Unity in Islamic Law and the Rise of Militant Islam," The American Historical Review 108, no. 3 (2003): 723–5.
[8] Rashid Ahmad Gangohi, Fatawa-yi-Rashidiyah (Kamil) (Karachi: Muhammad Ali Karkhanah yi-Islami Kutub, 1987), 57.

powerful transformations wrought by colonial rule or the opportunities for native agency made possible by the limits of colonial control. In contrast, I do not present an account of native agency triumphing over the colonial state, or vice versa. Instead I show how Indians' engagements with and subversions of law co-existed in dynamic tension with a profoundly transformative, and deeply coercive, colonial legal project.

In the following pages, I unpack this puzzle by telling two interwoven narratives. The first traces the evolution of what the book terms colonial secular governance. By this I mean the constellation of legal institutions and normative discourse of law which the British used to govern Indian religions. In particular, I focus on how colonial secular governance operated through a series of parallel binaries that pitted family against economy, religion against reason, and community against the state. While British officials themselves rarely used the terms "secular," my use of the term aims at capturing the cumulative effects of their approach to governing Indian religions, including their unintended consequences.

Alongside this history, the book also traces the continuous subversions that disrupted colonial secular governance's dominant logics – seeking out historical precedents for the work done by the women's protest in 1995. I focus on Muslims' and women's encounters with the law because they were often treated by colonial officials as particularly irrational, prejudiced, and communal. Forced into the position of secularism's "Other," these subjects were exposed to its most aggressive antagonisms. This position, however, also provided unique opportunities to challenge secularism's animating oppositions. To capture these dynamics, I follow into court women like Mussammat Dowla, who sued in the early 1880s to recover the property of her fellow prostitute and adopted daughter on the grounds that the court had wrongly awarded the estate to a man under Islamic law.[9] I also step outside the courts to engage the stories of women (mostly unnamed) who looked for alternative legal remedies beyond the state by asking independent Muslim legal scholars to produce *fatwas* dissolving their marriage ties to abusive husbands.[10] While these women often did not get what they wanted, either from the courts or from the scholars, their engagements with law put new pressures on colonial patterns of secular governance. Bringing together these stories requires moving between different archives, some of which are obviously

---

[9] *Murad Baksh* v. *Mussammat Dowla* [1884] Punjab Record 19 249. This case is discussed in Chapter 3.

[10] See for example Aziz-ul-Rahman Usmani, *Fatawa Dar-ul-Ulum Deoband*, 14 vols., ed. Muhammad Zafir-ul-Din (Karachi: Shakil Press, 2002–9), 9: 64. For further discussion of similar *fatwas* see Chapter 2.

legal, others of which are not. By pointing to the ambiguity and malleability of colonial law, these braided narratives stretch our understanding of what makes law powerful. My hope is also that understanding how law operates opens up possibilities for subverting its power, and with it, the enduring legacies of colonial governance.

## Colonial Secular Governance: Religion, State, Family, and Economy

The book focuses on how religion emerged as a distinct social sphere, a process that was both global in scope and had unique, South Asian trajectories. Inspired by the work of Talal Asad, my work joins recent scholarship on Europe, the Middle East, Asia, and Africa in showing how contemporary understandings of religion emerged in dynamic opposition to new conceptions of secular governance and rationality.[11] Like these studies, I demonstrate how the modern state drove these transformations.[12]

This book also highlights the emergence of the economy as a distinct social sphere alongside and often in opposition to religion. While recent accounts of secularism have shown how modern forms of governance produced the family as the core site for preserving religious tradition, scholars have paid surprisingly little attention to the ways in which this process was entwined with concurrent economic changes. Historians of South Asia have, meanwhile, produced rich accounts of how transformations in the family were linked to changing modes of labor extraction and regimes of property control.[13] From the angle of legal history,

[11] Talal Asad, *Genealogies of Religion: Discipline and Reasons of Power in Christianity and Islam* (Baltimore: Johns Hopkins University Press, 1993); Talal Asad, *Formations of the Secular: Christianity, Islam, Modernity* (Stanford: Stanford University Press, 2003).

[12] For examples of recent work influenced by Asad, see Shabnum Tejani, *Indian Secularism: A Social and Intellectual History, 1890–1950* (Bloomington: Indiana University Press, 2008); Nandini Chatterjee, *The Making of Indian Secularism: Empire, Law and Christianity, 1830–1960* (Basingstoke: Palgrave Macmillan, 2011); Humeira Iqtidar, *Secularizing Islamists?: Jama'at-e-Islami and Jama'at-ud-Da'wa in Urban Pakistan* (Chicago: University of Chicago Press, 2011); Hussein Ali Agrama, *Questioning Secularism: Islam, Sovereignty, and the Rule of Law in Modern Egypt* (Chicago: University of Chicago Press, 2012); C.S. Adcock, *The Limits of Tolerance: Indian Secularism and the Politics of Religious Freedom* (New York: Oxford University Press, 2014); Mayanthi L. Fernando, *The Republic Unsettled: Muslim French and the Contradictions of Secularism* (Durham: Duke University Press, 2014); Saba Mahmood, *Religious Difference in a Secular Age: A Minority Report* (Princeton: Princeton University Press, 2015). For examples of an older, but still relevant, discussion of debates about secularism in the Indian context, see Rajeev Bhargava, ed., *Secularism and Its Critics* (New Delhi: Oxford University Press, 1998).

[13] Radhika Singha, "Making the Domestic More Domestic: Criminal Law and the 'Head of the Household', 1772–1843," *Indian Economic and Social History Review*

transformations in South Asia in the nineteenth century unfolded as part of a wider global emergence of what Janet Halley and Kerry Rittich have termed "family-law exceptionalism." In both colonial and metropolitan contexts, legal reforms in the nineteenth and early twentieth centuries segregated laws of market production, covering labor and contract, from laws of familial reproduction, covering marriage and in some cases inheritance.[14] Working at the intersection of these different literatures, this book shows how the laws governing religion, family, and economy evolved in tandem, mutually enveloped in transformations in state sovereignty. By focusing on how these shifts played out in South Asia, the book shows how British colonialism fostered particular mutations of these wider global revolutions.

The early chapters of the book trace these entanglements by focusing on the particular historical forces that drove the emergence in the middle decades of the nineteenth century of personal law – the structural pivot of secular legal governance in colonial India. Scholars of South Asia have long recognized the critical role of personal law as a conceptual category. Understandings of its genealogy, however, remain surprisingly blurry. Studies alternatively describe it as dating to early-modern South Asia or to the advent of East India Company rule in Bengal. Such genealogies, I argue, are either centuries or decades premature.

Equating personal law with pre-colonial legal practices has been particularly common among scholars who emphasize the "indigenous" roots of Indian secularism by tracing its origins to Mughal policies of religious toleration.[15] This narrative has been politically important for defending the legitimacy of Indian secularism, but from the perspective of legal history, it is largely anachronistic. While research on Mughal law remains

33, no. 3 (1996): 309–43; Indrani Chatterjee, *Gender, Slavery, and Law in Colonial India* (Oxford: Oxford University Press, 1999); Mytheli Sreenivas, *Wives, Widows, and Concubines: The Conjugal Family Ideal in Colonial India* (Bloomington: Indiana University Press, 2008); Rochona Majumdar, *Marriage and Modernity: Family Values in Colonial Bengal* (Durham: Duke University Press, 2009); Rachel Sturman, *The Government of Social Life in Colonial India: Liberalism, Religious Law, and Women's Rights* (Cambridge: Cambridge University Press, 2012); Eleanor Newbigin, *The Hindu Family and the Emergence of Modern India: Law, Citizenship and Community* (Cambridge: Cambridge University Press, 2013). While these works take the family as their core focus, Ritu Birla has taken the opposite approach, focusing on the emergence of market governance, but with attention to its implications for the family: *Stages of Capital: Law, Culture, and Market Governance in Late Colonial India* (Durham: Duke University Press, 2009).
[14] Janet Halley and Kerry Rittich, "Critical Directions in Comparative Family Law: Genealogies and Contemporary Studies of Family Law Exceptionalism," *The American Journal of Comparative Law* 58, no. 4 (October 2010): 753–75.
[15] Iqtidar Alam Khan, "Medieval Indian Notions of Secular Statecraft in Retrospect," *Social Scientist* 14, no. 1 (January 1986): 3–15.

underdeveloped, in part due to fragmentary archival sources, recent work has emphasized critical discontinuities between how early-modern and colonial law governed religious difference. Such scholarship describes a pattern of what Nandini Chatterjee has termed "permissive inclusion," in which state courts were one of many venues of legal adjudication.[16] When Mughal subjects, regardless of their religion, approached Mughal *qazis*, or judges, they often applied legal norms that they understood to be Islamic, although not necessarily drawing from orthodox Islamic jurisprudence or *fiqh*. At the same time, the Mughals recognized the existence of law-like forums which operated outside the control of the state, in which different Indian communities adjudicated disputes according to their own legal norms, religious or otherwise. Based on this recent, albeit still preliminary scholarship, legal pluralism in the Mughal Empire is best understood as revolving around the co-existence of different forums of state and non-state law, which drew flexibly from different normative references, ranging from Islam to local custom. In contrast, colonial courts from the mid-nineteenth century onwards treated religious laws as circumscribed normative codes, which they applied to different religious communities in select categories of cases. These preliminary conclusions echo findings by scholars working on other early-modern Muslim empires. As one historian of the Ottoman Empire has lamented, accounts of early-modern approaches to religious diversity need to avoid the powerful "tendency to telescope time present into time past."[17]

This book, however, does not reach back to the pre-colonial past to argue for the novelty of colonial patterns of secular governance. Instead it shows how the framework of personal law represented a rupture within colonial law itself. In contrast to scholars who have dated personal law to the advent of East India Company rule in the late eighteenth century, the book shows how, during this earlier period, colonial officials referenced religious laws in a wide range of areas, from criminal law to contract.[18]

---

[16] Farhat Hasan, *State and Locality in Mughal India: Power Relations in Western India, c. 1572–1730* (Cambridge: Cambridge University Press, 2004), 72–6; Nandini Chatterjee, "Reflections on Religious Difference and Permissive Inclusion in Mughal Law," *Journal of Law and Religion* 29, no. 3 (October 2014): 396–415.

[17] Benjamin Braude, "Foundation Myths of the Millet System," in *Christians and Jews in the Ottoman Empire: The Functioning of a Plural Society*, vol. 1 (New York: Holmes & Meier, 1982), 69; Najwa Al-Qattan, "Dhimmis in the Muslim Court: Legal Autonomy and Religious Discrimination," *International Journal of Middle East Studies* 31, no. 3 (August 1999): 429–44.

[18] For an example of this earlier colonial genealogy, see Elizabeth Kolsky, "Forum: Maneuvering the Personal Law System in Colonial India. Introduction," *Law and History Review* 28, no. 4 (2010): 975. A few other historians have emphasized the middle decades of the nineteenth century as crucial to the formation of personal law.

Officials were particularly interested in Islamic legal practices, which they referred to as "Muhammadan law," a potentially offensive Anglicization, which the book rephrases as "Muslim law" when flagging colonial interpretations of Islamic law.[19] Colonial officials believed that understanding Muslim law was crucial to governing India because Hindus and Muslims had both internalized many of its norms during centuries of Mughal rule.

During the middle decades of the nineteenth century, however, Britain embarked on legal reforms in India that eventually transformed Muslim law into a personal law applicable only to Muslims, and only in domestic and ritual matters. Initially appointed in 1833, the Indian Law Commission, which was tasked with writing new legal codes, gradually translated developments in European legal thought, including an emphasis on unitary, territorial sovereignty and legal historicism, into a new colonial legal order.[20] Debates about Indian law reform borrowed the framework of personal law from European scholars writing about legal evolutions between the fall of the Roman Empire and the rise of feudalism. Law, they insisted, then adhered to communities of persons rather than to territorial spaces. Projecting Europe's past onto India's present, colonial law redefined "personal law" to refer to laws that applied only to members of a particular religious community and only in a narrow field of familial and ritual matters. The Indian Law Commission solidified this new formula in 1864 when it declared that Hindu and Muslim law would henceforth only be applied

Ashwini Tambe, *Codes of Misconduct: Regulating Prostitution in Late Colonial Bombay* (Minneapolis: University of Minnesota Press, 2009), 8.

[19] When discussing legal thought and practice among Muslims, the book attempts to echo the range of language used by historical actors themselves, who sometimes used the colonial term "Muhammadan law," but also spoke of *fiqh*, or the science of Islamic jurisprudence, and *sharia*, which literally means way or path, but which often connoted a broader aspiration to live in accordance with God's will. The choice to use various different terms to refer to what today is more often simply translated as "Islamic law" aligns with the book's wider interest in tracing the multiple lives of law across state and non-state spheres of debate and adjudication.

[20] On the rise of territorial sovereignty, see Charles S. Maier, "Consigning the Twentieth Century to History: Alternative Narratives for the Modern Era," *The American Historical Review* 105, no. 3 (June 2000): 807–31; Lauren A. Benton, *Law and Colonial Cultures: Legal Regimes in World History, 1400–1900* (Cambridge: Cambridge University Press, 2002); and Lisa Ford, *Settler Sovereignty: Jurisdiction and Indigenous People in America and Australia, 1788–1836* (Cambridge: Harvard University Press, 2010). On the critical influence of legal historicism on nineteenth-century law, see Duncan Kennedy, "Three Globalizations of Law and Legal Thought: 1850–2000," in *The New Law and Economic Development: A Critical Appraisal*, ed. David M. Trubek and Alvaro Santos (Cambridge: Cambridge University Press, 2006); Duncan Kennedy, "Savigny's Family/Patrimony Distinction and Its Place in the Global Genealogy of Classical Legal Thought," *American Journal of Comparative Law* 58, no. 4 (2010): 811–41.

in cases of "succession, inheritance, marriage, and caste, and all religious usages and institutions."[21] The legal container of "personal law" empowered a new framework for understanding Indian religions as communal, domestic, and irrational.

Legal reform in India, as well as the larger patterns of colonial secular governance, simultaneously drew on, and departed from, contemporary developments in Britain. In India, the authoritarian structures of colonial rule and the absence of entrenched common-law precedents allowed Britain to introduce more radical legal innovations than could be implemented in Britain itself.[22] This British willingness to innovate in certain areas, including the drafting of new penal, procedural, and commercial codes, co-existed with a colonial worldview that portrayed Indian society as resistant to change. This juxtaposition endowed colonial law with deep internal tensions.[23] These tensions were particularly acute in the convoluted logics that animated the colonial administration of personal laws. Colonial judges, armed with theoretically rational legal procedures, were meant to decide cases involving religious laws rooted in supposedly irrational religious beliefs. In contrast, starting in the 1850s, Britain transferred jurisdiction over divorce from the ecclesiastical courts and the Houses of Parliament to a new matrimonial causes court, which applied common civil laws to all parties. In subsequent decades, legal reforms in Britain liberalized access to divorce and gave women greater control over marital property and custody of children.[24] The creation of a newly distinct field of family law in both India and Britain reflected the common influence of "separate-spheres" domestic ideology. The consolidation of uniform, secular bodies of family law and their progressive reform in Britain, however, stands in marked contrast to the religious communalization and normative stagnation of personal law in India. These diverging patterns of legal reform created an exaggerated colonial parody of secular governance, in which

---

[21] "First Report of Her Majesty's Commissioners Appointed to Prepare A Body of Substantive Law for India," 60, HCPP, 1864 (3312) XVI.359.

[22] David Skuy, "Macaulay and the Indian Penal Code of 1862: The Myth of the Inherent Superiority and Modernity of the English Legal System Compared to India's Legal System in the Nineteenth Century," *Modern Asian Studies* 32, no. 3 (1998): 513–57.

[23] On the contradictory impulses within colonial law, see D.A. Washbrook, "Law, State and Agrarian Society in Colonial India," *Modern Asian Studies* 15 (1981): 649–721.

[24] Lee Holcombe, *Wives and Property: Reform of the Married Women's Property Law in Nineteenth-Century England* (Toronto: University of Toronto Press, 1983); Mary Poovey, "Covered but Not Bound: Caroline Norton and the 1857 Matrimonial Causes Act," *Feminist Studies* 14 (1988): 467–85; Danaya C. Wright, "The Crisis of Child Custody: A History of the Birth of Family Law in England," *Columbia Journal of Gender and Law* 11 (2002): 175–270.

religious and secular spheres were cast not just as separate, but mutually antagonistic.

In contrast, in Victorian Britain, distinct religious and secular spheres emerged more gradually and with more harmonious logics.[25] In the nineteenth century most Britons saw Christian belief and reason as mutually reinforcing.[26] Even after the Darwinian revolution, most Britons remained confident that science and Christianity were reconcilable.[27] The nineteenth-century campaign for the disestablishment of the Church of England progressed in fits and starts. More radical projects, including the movement that first coined the term secularism in the 1850s, emerged at the fringes rather than in mainstream currents of British political culture.[28] Thus as a colonizing power, Britain more aggressively secularized state power and marginalized religious authority in India than it did at home.

## The Power of Instability: The "Rubber-Band" State

In tracing the history of colonial secular governance the book presents a double vision of how law operates. On the one hand, the book underlines the cumulative power of law's normative scripts in defining newly divided spheres of religious and secular governance. On the other hand, much of the book traces how, in the daily improvisations of legal practice, these divisions were plagued by incessant ambiguities and contradictions. The persistent instability of secular/religious binaries fostered a dynamic form of governance, which was strengthened through its continual contestation and reinforcement.

In the first view, a birds-eye perspective, colonial law mapped out a powerful pattern of mutually reinforcing oppositions. It aligned state law, rational governance, and the market economy by opposing them against religious tradition, irrational belief, and the domestic family. This pattern was elaborated in normative discourses articulated through legislative

[25] Peter van der Veer has also argued that colonial policies in India were more secular than their British counterparts. "The Secularity of the State," in *The State in India: Past and Present*, ed. Masaaki Kimura and Akio Tanabe (New Delhi: Oxford University Press, 2006), 257–69.
[26] John Wolffe, *God and Greater Britain: Religion and National Life in Britain and Ireland, 1843–1945* (London: Routledge, 1994).
[27] Ira Katznelson and Gareth Stedman Jones, "Introduction: Multiple Secularities," in *Religion and the Political Imagination* (Cambridge: Cambridge University Press, 2010), 15.
[28] Edward Royle, "Secularists and Rationalists, 1800–1940," in *A History of Religion in Britain: Practice and Belief from Pre-Roman Times to the Present*, ed. Sheridan Gilley and W.J. Sheils (Oxford: Blackwell, 1994), 406–22.

proceedings and legal textbooks. While religious personal laws, unlike civil and criminal law, were never formally codified, colonial courts' allegiance to upholding prior precedents imposed an aura of stasis. Ignoring their own role in propagating this logic, colonial judges often referred to Muslim law as if it were a divine code that could not be altered. They treated the divine *sharia,* which literally means the "way," and which Muslims historically had interpreted in flexible ways across varied fields of law and ethics, as a singular and immutable code.[29] Thus, at a normative level, the colonial construction of Muslim law conformed to a pattern which historians have broadly associated with the transition from pre-modern to modern law. Flexible and decentralized practices of legal mediation were cemented into rigid and centralized state law.[30]

Everyday legal encounters, in which the patterns of colonial secular governance became blurrier and rigidity morphed into incessant instability, offer a different perspective. In the place of neat oppositions, the religious/secular divide appears fraught with ambiguities. When judges were confronted with married couples feuding over their conjugal relations and their financial entanglements, courts struggled to determine where the jurisdiction of religious personal laws ended and civil contract commenced. As Moulvi Samee-Ullah Khan Bahadur, a lower-court judge in Rai Bareilly, noted, "marriage is a religious rite, although it is in its form a secular transaction."[31] Such structural ambiguities within the religious/secular binary led courts to author diverging opinions on key legal questions. This diversity of interpretation was reinforced by the federal logic of the Indian legal system. Precedents set by superior courts in each province were only binding on lower courts within that province. It was further muddled by provisions that allowed colonial courts

[29] Gregory C. Kozlowski, *Muslim Endowments and Society in British India* (Cambridge: Cambridge University Press, 1985), 186.
[30] This narrative is common to work on both Islamic law and colonial law. For examples see Bernard S. Cohn, "Law and Colonial State in India," in *Colonialism and Its Forms of Knowledge* (Princeton: Princeton University Press, 1996), esp. 73; Rudolph Peters, "From Jurists' Law to Statute Law or What Happens When the Shari'a Is Codified," *Mediterranean Politics* 7, no. 3 (2002): 82–95. For similar accounts which focus specifically on the transformation of Islamic law under British colonial rule, see Michael R. Anderson, "Islamic Law and the Colonial Encounter in British India," in *Institutions and Ideologies: A SOAS South Asia Reader,* ed. Peter Robb and David Arnold (Richmond, Surrey: Curzon Press, 1993); Scott Alan Kugle, "Framed, Blamed and Renamed: The Recasting of Islamic Jurisprudence in Colonial South Asia," *Modern Asian Studies* 35 (2001): 257–313; Elisa Giunchi, "The Reinvention of Shari'a under the British Raj: In Search of Authenticity and Certainty," *The Journal of Asian Studies* 69, no. 4 (2010): 1119–42.
[31] Moulvi Samee-Ullah Khan Bahadur, *Judgment Containing an Exposition of the Muhammadan Matrimonial Law* (Allahabad: Indian Press, 1891), 35.

to override religious personal laws in favor of local customs, introducing a third element into the otherwise binary logic of the division between religious and secular law.

Meanwhile, the colonial state's claim to exercise singular, uniform sovereignty over its Indian territories was more a matter of normative theory than practical reality. Colonial officials, for whom ruling on the cheap often mattered more than ideological coherence, turned to religious communities and local elites to accomplish many of the day-to-day tasks of maintaining social order and mediating disputes.[32] The informal nature of this tacit outsourcing of local governance, however, meant that when intra-communal disputes landed in court, colonial judges were often unwilling to recognize the right of religious communities to impose order within their ranks. Among Indian Muslims the tension between the colonial state's simultaneous reliance on "community" as a unit of governance and its unwillingness to legally invest it with sovereign mechanisms of enforcement led to proliferating, volatile sectarian divisions. These disputes were further encouraged by the spread of print, which democratized access to religious knowledge and disrupted older structures of authority.[33] In response to the challenge of both colonial sovereignty and break-away reformist sects, new institutions of religious learning, such as the *madrasa* at Deoband, looked for ways to reassert the authority of religious scholars, or *ulama*.[34] Its newly streamlined *fatwa* department, which opened in 1893, provided over a hundred thousand detailed opinions during its first three decades of existence in response to legal queries it received from across the subcontinent.[35] By underlining the critical role that non-state actors played as alternatives to court-based adjudication, this book argues that studies of colonial law must account for its dynamic interface with these spheres of "vernacular legal culture." In contrast to the normative model of Muslim law as a singular, centralized code, this second view reveals how Islamic legal authority remained poly-centric and contested in everyday practice.

---

[32] Washbrook, "Law, State and Agrarian Society in Colonial India," 677.

[33] Francis Robinson, "Technology and Religious Change: Islam and the Impact of Print," *Modern Asian Studies* 27, no. 1 (February 1993): 229–51; Nile Green, *Bombay Islam: The Religious Economy of the West Indian Ocean, 1840–1915* (New York: Cambridge University Press, 2011).

[34] Barbara Daly Metcalf, *Islamic Revival in British India: Deoband, 1860–1900* (1982: Reprint New Delhi: Oxford University Press, 2002).

[35] Usmani, *Fatawa*, 1: 49. Qari Abdullah Muhammad Tayyib, the former head of Deoband, has estimated that the first head of the *dar-ul-ifta*, Aziz-ul-Rahman Usmani, issued about 118,000 *fatwas* between 1893 and 1928. Tayyib extrapolates this number from the 37,561 *fatwas* for this period preserved in Deoband's records, which cover less than half of the time that Usmani served as head of the *dar-ul-ifta*.

How are we to make mutual sense of these two views? The first view echoes an existing historiography on South Asia and other colonial contexts that emphasizes the role of law as a tool of domination, or what Bernard Cohn has described as the "instrumentalities of rule."[36] In contrast, over the last decade, a new wave of scholarship on South Asian law, inspired by Lauren Benton's *Law and Colonial Cultures*, has shifted towards viewing law as a site of cultural contestation in which indigenous subjects actively shaped legal outcomes.[37] This debate is not unique to South Asia, or even to colonial law, but echoes wider divergences within legal scholarship. In the United States, legal historian Hendrik Hartog has described this contrast as the difference between seeing law as a "modality of rule" versus an "arena of struggle."[38] In South Asia, growing interest in the partial and uneven penetration of state law has further complicated this conceptual landscape. While historical work on these dynamics remains limited, contemporary legal ethnographies have increasingly emphasized the interface between state law and non-state mediation and enforcement, from kinship networks to vigilante violence.[39]

Elements of both positions – of colonial law as tool of domination and as porous field of contest in dynamic tension with non-state legalities – inform the picture of law that unfolds in the coming pages. Rather than seeing these views as mutually contradictory, the book focuses on how the very instability of colonial law, both in terms of its internal ambiguities and its contested operations, made it more dynamic and persistent in its effects. This understanding of colonial law draws on Foucault's concept of governmentality, or the "conduct of conduct."[40] The book

[36] Washbrook, "Law, State and Agrarian Society in Colonial India," 677.

[37] For examples of such work see Chatterjee, *The Making of Indian Secularism*; Chandra Mallampalli, *Race, Religion, and Law in Colonial India: Trials of an Interracial Family* (Cambridge: Cambridge University Press, 2011); Rohit De, "The Republic of Writs: Litigious Citizens, Constitutional Law and Everyday Life in India (1947–1964)" (Ph.D., Princeton University, 2013); Mitra Sharafi, *Law and Identity in Colonial South Asia: Parsi Legal Culture, 1772–1947* (New York: Cambridge University Press, 2014). On the predominance of the model of law as a site (or arena) of contest in recent legal histories of South Asia, see Mitra Sharafi, "South Asian Legal History," *Annual Review of Law and Social Science* 11, no. 1 (2015): 319.

[38] Barbara Young Welke and Hendrik Hartog, "'Glimmers of Life': A Conversation with Hendrik Hartog," *Law and History Review* 27, no. 3 (October 2009): 643.

[39] Thomas Blom Hansen and Finn Stepputat, "Sovereignty Revisited," *Annual Review of Anthropology* 35, no. 1 (2006): 295–315; Gopika Solanki, *Adjudication in Religious Family Laws: Cultural Accommodation, Legal Pluralism, and Gender Equality in India* (Cambridge: Cambridge University Press, 2011).

[40] Colin Gordon, "Governmental Rationality: An Introduction," in *The Foucault Effect: Studies in Governmentality*, ed. Graham Burchell, Colin Gordon, and Peter Miller (Chicago: University of Chicago Press, 1991), 5.

extends Foucault's interest in governance as processes of arranging populations and channeling resources, or what he describes as "men in their relations to that other kind of things, customs, habits, ways of acting and thinking," to the colonial production of religion as a distinct field.[41] Foucault contrasted tactics of governmentality with the juridical functions of law, which he defined as the application of sovereign force. Governmentality, however, does not replace law. Rather it reorients law towards processes of normalization as opposed to brute coercion.[42] The concept of governmentality is therefore particularly useful for legal scholars who study civil jurisdiction, whether laws governing marriage or markets, as opposed to criminal sanctions.[43]

For this study, the particular benefit of the concept of governmentality is its emphasis on power that operates through diffuse and mobile tactics. In contrast to Foucault's concept of discipline – which entails intensive surveillance of individuals in such enclosed spaces as prisons, hospitals, and schools – governmentality is less totalizing in its operation.[44] Governmentality operates in dynamic relationship with exceptions and what Foucault terms "counter conducts," which simultaneously resist its logic and open up opportunities to reassert processes of normalization.[45] A useful visual reference for these forms of governance is a rubber-band-like web of control, simultaneously wide in scope, and flexible and fragmented in application. Applying what I think of as the "rubber-band" state model to British governance in India shows that colonial law's internal contradictions and built-in exceptions made it a more malleable, and thus powerful instrument of dominance. The ability to periodically engage with non-state legalities and to allow custom to override personal laws gave British officials strategic flexibility, an asset that allowed them to rule on the cheap.

[41] Michel Foucault, *Foucault Effect: Studies in Governmentality*, ed. Graham Burchell, Colin Gordon, and Peter Miller (Chicago: University of Chicago Press, 1991), 93.
[42] Mitchell Dean, *Governmentality: Power and Rule in Modern Society*, 2nd edn (Los Angeles: Sage Publications, 2010), 140.
[43] For two studies applying governmentality to colonial law in South Asia, see Birla, *Stages of Capital*, 21–2; Sturman, *The Government of Social Life*, 5.
[44] Tania Murray Li, "Governmentality," *Anthropologica* 49, no. 2 (2007): 275.
[45] Foucault emphasized the critical role of "counter conducts" in the eighth of a series of lectures he delivered in 1977–8 at the Collège de France. These lectures, as well as those he delivered the following year on the "Birth of Biopolitics," were only published in full in French in 2004 and in English in 2007 and 2008, considerably deepening scholars' understanding of Foucault's conceptualization of governmentality. Michel Foucault, *Security, Territory, and Population: Lectures at the Collège de France, 1977–1978*, ed. Michel Senellart, trans. Graham Burchell (Basingstoke: Palgrave Macmillan, 2007); Michel Foucault, *The Birth of Biopolitics: Lectures at the Collège de France, 1978–79*, ed. Michel Senellart, trans. Graham Burchell (Basingstoke: Palgrave Macmillan, 2008).

Alongside governmentality, the book also draws on Judith Butler's framework of iterative performance. Butler explores the complex inter-dependence of power and agency by emphasizing the emergence of norms through processes of iteration. For Butler, gender is produced through its repeated performance, a process of continual construction fueled in part by "ambiguities and incoherences" within the masculine/feminine binary that necessitate its constant reassertion. The performative nature of gender gives it power, but also allows for the possibility of "a repetition of the law which is not its consolidation, but its displacement."[46] Here I extend Butler's theorization of the performance of gender binaries to the oppositions animating colonial secular governance: between reason and religion; economy and family; state and community. Like Butler, I see these binaries as "never simply or definitively *made* or *achieved*" but instead "insistently constituted, contested, and negotiated." While Butler describes this as a state of "permanent (and promising) instability," I prefer the term *persistent* instability, which captures Butler's own emphasis on the possibility of disruption and undoing.[47] The fact that courts inevitably found that domestic relations such as marriage were entangled with economic transactions such as property ownership meant that they had endless opportunities to refine and reaffirm the boundary between religious personal laws and secular civil laws. At the same time this persistent instability meant that state and non-state forums of legal adjudication produced challenges to the "domestication" of marriage, and with them alternative imaginings of the relationship between religion and secularism.

## Optics of the Margin: Colonialism, Islam, and Gender

The book traces the history of secular governance, and its constitu-tive instabilities, by focusing on subjects who inhabited its normative margins: the colonized, Muslims, and women. As argued above, Britain treated Indian religions as especially antagonistic to secular values of rationality and neutrality. Within India, the British also singled out spe-cific populations as particularly prone to irrational religious sentiment. Muslims fell into this category because the British claimed the superiority

---

[46] Judith Butler, *Gender Trouble: Feminism and the Subversion of Identity* (New York: Routledge Classics, 2006), 42–3. My reading of Butler also draws on Judith Surkis, *Sexing the Citizen: Morality and Masculinity in France, 1870–1920* (Ithaca: Cornell University Press, 2006).

[47] Judith Butler, *Bodies That Matter: On the Discursive Limits of "Sex"* (New York: Routledge, 1993), 76, 192; emphasis in original. Judith Butler, *Undoing Gender* (New York: Routledge, 2004).

of their own institutions by emphasizing the religious prejudice of prior ruling regimes, many of which were Muslim. Importing separate-spheres ideology from Britain, colonial laws and wider discourses also treated women as embodying the spiritual essence of different religious communities. Colonial secular governance therefore positioned Muslims and women (and especially Muslim women) as doubly (or triply) antithetical to secular norms that were metropolitan, majoritarian, and male by default.

The particular antagonisms between colonial secular governance and Islam were the product of shifting British attitudes towards the legal norms that they inherited from the Mughals and their successor states. During the early decades of British rule, colonial officials often borrowed from prior legal practices, which they broadly understood to be Islamic. As pressure mounted to consolidate colonial sovereignty during the early decades of the nineteenth century, however, British officials distanced themselves from this past dependence. In order to justify the superiority of new colonial laws, the British emphasized their rationality and universal applicability by contrasting them with a vision of Muslim law as irrational and only applicable to a narrow community of co-religionists. Thus the Indian Law Commission in 1841 described Muslim law as "so interwoven with religion as to be unfit for persons professing a different faith." In contrast, the Commission praised English law as "not surpassed in the qualities for which substantive law is admired by any of the various systems under which men have lived."[48] The historical contingencies of colonial conquest in South Asia were therefore responsible for defining Islam and secular governance in mutual opposition to each other, creating antagonisms that are often assumed to be primordial.

This framework has proved highly adaptable. During the early decades of the twentieth century, an ascendant Hindu majority redeployed colonial stereotypes about Muslim fanaticism to emphasize its members' right to dominate anti-colonial agitation and new democratic institutions. In one of the earliest uses of the term secularism by an Indian politician, Lala Lajpat Rai urged Hindus to embrace secularism as an anecdote to "religionism ... the weapon of the Muslim intelligentsia."[49] Figures like Rai simultaneously claimed that their own religious sensibilities were fully compatible with Indian secularism and marginalized Muslim

---

[48] Indian Law Commissioners to Governor General, October 31, 1840, Indian Legislative Consultations, January 11, 1841, no. 16, IOR/P/207/14.
[49] Lala Lajpat Rai, "'Religionism' *vs.* Secularism," *The People*, September 8, 1927, in *The Collected Works of Lala Lajpat Rai*, ed. Bal Ram Nanda, 15 vols. (New Delhi: Manohar, 2003–10), 13: 280–4.

concerns by describing them as religiously motivated, or in the parlance of the day, "communal."[50]

If Muslims were forced first by colonial officials and later by Hindu nationalists to define secular neutrality and rationality by standing in for its opposite, Muslim women were doubly subjected to this process of "Othering." The global spread of separate-spheres ideology transformed the domestic household into the symbolic "Other" of the capitalist market: cooperative as opposed to self-interested; emotional as opposed to rational; and religiously or culturally distinctive as opposed to secular or universal. As the protectors of the home, women were expected to symbolically embody all of its virtues and its vices. Actual women, however, continually traversed these conceptual binaries. In the fields, Indian women grew the raw materials that fueled British imperial markets. Muslim women, who were not subject to marital coverture, owned and managed property.

Colonial courts in many cases constructed the unstable legal edifice of colonial secular governance on the foundational ambiguities that these women embodied. Over and over again, judges had to grapple with the disjuncture between the imagined female legal subject and the actual women who streamed into their courtrooms. Judges, working in tandem with bourgeois Indian reformers, responded to these challenges by marking out women's economic activity as suspect. They were unable to believe that Muslim women were subject to more progressive laws than their English counterparts, who only gained the right to marital property during the late nineteenth century. Emerging case law therefore invented new legal principles which treated any woman who observed *pardah*, a term used in South Asia to refer to different forms of religious and cultural seclusion, as presumptively unable to act as a fully independent economic agent. Meanwhile penal provisions and labor regulations curtailed women's ability to sell their labor on the market by conflating recruiting women laborers with pimping prostitutes. While women of all religions were at risk of such economic marginalization, the burden of these laws fell disproportionately on lower-class, lower-caste, and Muslim women, who occupied the margins of a domestic ideal that was distinctly middle-class, upper-caste, and Hindu.[51] By blaming the ongoing entanglement

---

[50] On the use of the language of communalism to marginalize Muslims, see Ayesha Jalal, "Exploding Communalism: The Politics of Muslim Identity in South Asia," in *Nationalism, Democracy, and Development: State and Politics in India*, ed. Sugata Bose and Ayesha Jalal (Delhi: Oxford University Press, 1997), 76–103.

[51] Charu Gupta, *Sexuality, Obscenity, Community: Women, Muslims, and the Hindu Public in Colonial India* (Delhi: Permanent Black, 2001); Sturman, *The Government of Social Life*, 148–95.

of domestic and economic relations on either poverty or Islam, these normative discourses diverted attention away from structural ambiguities within colonial secular governance and thus enabled it to assume a fictive coherence.

It was a dangerous thing to exist at the margins of secular governance. Occupying this position exposed colonial subjects, Muslims, and women to moral condemnation and physical violence. This marginal position did, however, offer opportunities to subvert the binary oppositions that animated colonial secular governance. This book continually returns to these disruptive performances, whether of women fighting for money in court or Muslim scholars insisting on the rational foundations of ritual law. I am also particularly interested in how these disruptive performances unfolded within and in dialogue with colonial law. My approach therefore parts ways with recent works on secularism and Islamic law that have expressed deep pessimism about the possibility of confronting secularism's failings by engaging with legal institutions. Scholars such as Saba Mahmood and Hussein Ali Agrama have focused on the possibilities that exist outside of secular, liberal law to foster alternative "cultural and ethical sensibilities" or methods of "care of the self."[52] This pessimism about engaging with the law, however, is often animated by a view of modern law that sees it as rigid, centralized, and top-down in its operation.[53] In contrast, I draw on a very different understanding of legal governance that recognizes it as diffuse, dynamic, and participatory, if still deeply coercive. I therefore find more room for creative subversion to occur when marginal subjects engage with courts or build law-like institutions in competition, but also often in dialogue with colonial law. By attending to law's own role in constructing and contesting sensibilities, the book looks to such engagements as offering, in Butler's words, "not freedom" but strategies "to work the trap that one is inevitably in."[54]

## Plan of the Book

In order to capture both the cumulative impact of legal governance and its daily improvisations, the structure of the book combines chronological

[52] Saba Mahmood, "Religious Reason and Secular Affect: An Incommensurable Divide?," in *Is Critique Secular?*, ed. Talal Asad, Wendy Brown, Judith Butler, and Saba Mahmood (Berkeley: University of California Press, 2009), 67, 89; Agrama, *Questioning Secularism*, 184.
[53] This understanding of modern law animates Wael Hallaq's argument about the impossibility of forging an Islamic version of the modern state. Wael B Hallaq, *The Impossible State: Islam, Politics, and Modernity's Moral Predicament* (New York: Columbia University Press, 2013).
[54] "The Body You Want: Liz Kotz Interviews Judith Butler," *Artforum* 31, no. 3 (November 1992): 84.

and geographical scope, stretching from the late eighteenth century to the 1950s and across different regions of India, with episodic depth. I explore specific legal issues – including marital property, customary inheritance, ritual, and censorship – in detail as they circulated across various fields of state and non-state adjudication and debate. The flipside of this selective depth, however, is that other issues, including religious endowments and non-Sunni, Muslim sects, receive more cursory treatment, although in some cases I have been able to draw on the research of other scholars to bring these topics into the book's overarching narrative.[55]

The opening chapter surveys the shifting relationship between colonial law and Islam during the first century of colonial rule. The chapter shows how the term "personal law," absent from earlier discussions in the late eighteenth and early nineteenth centuries, became entrenched as a core organizing principle of colonial law between the 1830s and the 1870s. The chapter shows how global revolutions in law, including territorial sovereignty and legal historicism, were inflected by specific developments in India, including the channeling of evangelical enthusiasm into projects of "secular conversion," which looked to law as a civilizing influence.

The following four chapters turn from a top-down view of legal change towards a zoomed-in exploration of how the religious/secular divide was adjudicated in everyday legal practice. This approach combines detailed studies of specific colonial cases with explorations of vernacular legal culture, from *fatwas* issued by scholars at the *madrasa* at Deoband to cartoons mocking Muslims who demanded legal protection from religious insult.[56] Chapter 2 explores how inherent structural ambiguities in the divide between laws governing the family and the economy led to persistent disputes among colonial judges and Muslim legal scholars about the relationship between marriage and women's property. Rather than undermining colonial secular governance, the chapter shows how the instability of the family/economy divide provided colonial courts with ongoing opportunities to reaffirm the boundaries between religious personal laws and secular laws governing economic transactions. Chapter 3 turns to the role of custom as a complement to religious personal laws. Focusing on the selective use of custom in cases involving women's participation in markets, whether as owners of property or as laborers, the chapter shows how courts systematically favored patriarchal

[55] For excellent studies of these two issues, see Kozlowski, *Muslim Endowments*; Teena Purohit, *The Aga Khan Case: Religion and Identity in Colonial India* (Cambridge: Harvard University Press, 2012).
[56] In its focus on studying case law, as opposed to a narrower emphasis on legislation, the book builds on a recent shift in the field. Sharafi, *Law and Identity in Colonial South Asia*, 9.

economic structures. Pushing back against the idea that secular governance is good for women, the chapters together show how colonial law
contributed to women's economic marginalization.

The fourth and fifth chapters turn to exploring how structural ambiguities in the oppositions between state and community and reason and
religious belief led to escalating religious tensions, both among Muslims
and between Muslims and Hindus. Chapter 4 looks at how the colonial
state and Muslim communities policed disputes over ritual practice, a
key source of escalating tensions between proliferating sects of Sunni
Muslims. In contrast to its intensive involvement in governing marriage
and inheritance, the courts took a more hands-off approach to inter-
vening in disputes over ritual. At the same time, however, they prevented
Muslims from imposing ritual conformity within their own communities
by ignoring the legal logics undergirding the Islamic principles of *taqlid*,
or the obligation to follow an established legal authority. Chapter 5
moves forward chronologically to trace how patterns of colonial secular
governance were remade by an ascendant Hindu majority during the
decades leading up to independence. It uses a famous censorship case in
the 1920s, which involved a pamphlet attacking the Prophet, to explore
how Muslim concerns about their minority status, from assaults on
their religious sensibilities to underrepresentation in the judiciary, were
dismissed as religious fanaticism.

The final chapter of the book looks at how challenges to colonial
secular governance, which percolated throughout the nineteenth and
early twentieth centuries, coalesced into a broad effort to theorize
Islamic forms of economy and social justice during the decades immediately before and after independence. Traversing fields from academic
research to popular politics, Muslims began to insist on the relevance
of religious ethics to material concerns, arguments undergirded by
theorists' emphasis on the rationality of Islam. Yet efforts to translate
these ideas into concrete political reforms foundered. During debates
over the Muslim Personal Law (Shariat) Application Act of 1937,
a focus on religious identity sidelined earlier efforts to use the bill to
promote greater economic equality among Muslims, and especially
Muslim women. Similarly, Pakistan's first constitution exempted economic matters from its Islamic provisions. The chapter concludes by
considering how the political demise of movements for Islamic social
justice was linked to a broader failure to rethink forms of legal sovereignty that undergirded colonial patterns of secular governance.

The Conclusion looks towards the present to show how colonial
patterns of governance have adapted to new political contexts in independent India, Pakistan, and Bangladesh. Despite fierce debates about

the meaning and place of religion and secularism in postcolonial societies, many features of colonial secular governance, including its focus on gender and its uneven effects on different religious communities, remain strikingly similar. Yet against this arc of continuity, the conclusion points to how creative engagements with the law might as yet unsettle secularism's persistent antagonisms.

# 1    Forging Secular Legal Governance

In 1798 officials in Calcutta commissioned John Baillie, a young British officer with a passion for Arabic and Persian literature, to complete a project started by William Jones, the famous Orientalist. Jones had compiled a collection of Arabic texts on the Shia law of contracts and inheritance, but he never completed their translation into English. The manuscript included materials on sale, debt, pawns, bail, partnership, deposits, loans, hiring, gifts, and wills. Baillie seized on the opportunity to complete his esteemed predecessor's work.[1] His finished volume, *A Digest of Mohummudan Law* (1805), included chapters on commerce, debt, pawns, insolvent debtors, inhibition, sureties, composition, partnership, "*mozarubut*" (a partnership of stock and labor), and "*mozaraut*" (a compact of cultivation).[2] Six decades later, another *Digest of Moohummudan Law* appeared, this time prepared by John Baillie's relative and executor Neil Baillie. Neil Baillie's version included one volume on Hanafi law (1865) and a second volume on Shia law (1869).[3]

[1] Lieutenant Baillie to the Committee appointed by Government for inspecting the Translation of a Digest of Mohummeedan Law, July 23, 1801, Extract Bengal Public Consultations, Board's Collections, Indian Office Records [hereafter IOR]/4/135, file 2445, 24–36, quoted on 24–5.

[2] John Baillie, *A Digest of Mohummudan Law According to the Tenets of the Twelve Imams, Compiled, under the Superintendence of the Late Sir William Jones. Extended, so as to Comprize the Whole of the Imameea Code of Jurisprudence, in Temporal Matters, and Translated; from the Original Arabic, by the Order of the Supreme Government of Bengal* (Calcutta: Hon. Company's Press, 1805).

[3] Neil Baillie, *Digest of Moohummudan Law on the Subjects to Which It Is Usually Applied by British Courts of Justice in India, Comp. and Tr. from Authorities in the Original Arabic. Part Second, Containing the Doctrines of the Imameea Code of Jurisprudence on the Most Important of the Same Subjects*, xxvi–xxvii. The first volume of the work, published in 1865, covered Hanafi law, *Digest of Moohummudan Law on the Subjects to Which It Is Usually Applied by British Courts of Justice in India, Comp. and Tr. from Authorities in the Original Arabic, With an Introduction and Explanatory Notes* (London: Smith, Elder & Co., 1865). Interestingly, when Baillie published the second edition of the first volume on Hanafi law, he added a supplement on sale, loan, and mortgage. Neil B.E. Baillie, *Digest of Moohummudan Law on the Subjects to Which It Is Usually Applied by British Courts of Justice in India. Compiled and Translated from Authorities in the Original Arabic, with an Introduction and Explanatory Notes. Part First Containing the Doctrines of the Hanifeea Code of Jurisprudence.*

But while the younger Baillie published his work under the same title as his dead relative, his *Digest* of Shia law included markedly different contents. Baillie included chapters on marriage, divorce, pre-emption, gifts, alms, wills, and inheritance. He limited his text to areas in which the British courts presently applied Islamic law, or what he described as the "domestic relations of persons to each other, or with the transfer of property *inter vivos*, or from the dead to the living."[4] References to transactions that might broadly be termed economic – sales, contracts, debts – were notably absent.

This chapter traces the evolutions in colonial legal governance that separated the two *Digests*, a period in which Muslim law narrowed to a newly restricted domain of personal law. This process of narrowing, which also saw the exclusion of Muslim law from criminal jurisdiction, unfolded gradually between the 1820s and 1860s, and was spurred by global transformations in legal thought, including the rise of territoriality and legal historicism. More locally in India, it unfolded as part of the "Age of Reform," the period from the 1820s to the 1840s in which British officials, influenced by an evangelical mindset, set out to transform Indian society. Although officials were skeptical that many Indians would be converted to Christianity, they embraced legal reform as part of a broader program of what this book refers to as secular conversion. By this, I mean that colonial officials sought to minimize the influence of Indian religious traditions to clear the way for Britain's civilizing influence.

While much of the intellectual work for the narrowing of Muslim law occurred during the second quarter of the nineteenth century, its actual implementation awaited the judicial overhaul which accompanied the transfer from Company to Crown rule after the Rebellion of 1857. In 1864 the Indian Law Commission for the first time explicitly specified that Hindu and Muslim laws would be limited to "succession, inheritance, marriage, and caste, and all religious usages and institutions."[5] This transformation in the understanding of Muslim law directly contributed to the formation of secular legal governance. It domesticated religious laws, by associating them primarily with the family, and communalized them, by limiting their applicability to a narrow group of co-believers.

---

*Second Edition, Revised, with Some Additions to the Text, and a Supplement on Sale, Loan, and Mortgage* (London: Smith, Elder & Co., 1875), xi.

[4] Baillie, *Digest* [1865], xxiii.

[5] "First Report of Her Majesty's Commissioners Appointed to Prepare a Body of Substantive Law for India," 60, HCPP, 1864 (3312) XVI.359.

In theory, this limited jurisdiction applied to all Indian religious laws. As the following discussion will show, however, the narrowing was particularly dramatic in the case of Muslim law. Because of the prior history of Mughal rule in much of the subcontinent, Islamic legal traditions and norms had widely influenced legal governance in early-modern India, and they continued to play a broad role during the early decades of Company rule. Beginning in the 1820s, however, Britain evinced a new drive to exercise a more unified, territorial sovereignty over its Indian territories. At the same time, these officials, influenced both by on-the-ground experience in India and the broad currents of historicist legal thought, did not believe that Indian religious laws could be entirely eliminated. They thus sought a compromise that preserved, but also diminished, religious laws by containing them within a new domestic and communal sphere. The result was a precarious balancing act between unity and diversity that would remain a central feature of secular legal governance for the remainder of the colonial period.

### Early Colonial Legal Developments and Muslim Law

During the first half-century of colonial rule, Company officials expressed a commitment to preserving Indo-Muslim legal structures and traditions. In practice, however, this principle was often violated, both with intent, and without. One of the most important legal changes that the Company made, in comparison to its Mughal predecessors, was to expand the judicial authority of the state. As part of this process, colonial officials commissioned English translations of Arabic and Persian legal texts, which allowed colonial judges to administer bodies of law with which they had little familiarity. These translations were fraught with errors, reified textual sources of authority over oral traditions, and discounted the diversity of everyday religious practice.[6] In certain areas Company officials began to limit the application of Islamic legal traditions to Muslims, beginning the long-term process of "communalizing" Muslim law.[7] Driven by the practical necessity of imposing order and extracting profit, Company officials also introduced significant revisions to laws governing land rights and crime,

---

[6] On the transformative impact of English translations of Islamic law, see John Strawson, "Islamic Law and English Texts," *Law and Critique* 6, no. 1 (1995): 21–38; Anderson, "Islamic Law and the Colonial Encounter," 174–5; Kugle, "Framed, Blamed and Renamed," 271–4.

[7] For a more detailed discussion of the "communal" nature of British legal reforms, see Chatterjee, *The Making of Indian Secularism*, 75–108.

jettisoning older Indo-Muslim legal practices when they conflicted with the Company's strategic interests.[8] Yet despite these significant changes, Muslim law remained a point of reference for Company law across a range of areas that extended well beyond domestic matters in the first half-century of British rule.

In 1764 the Company defeated the armies of the Nawabs of Bengal and Awadh and the Mughal emperor at the Battle of Buxar. In the treaty that followed, the Mughal Emperor Shah Alam ceded the *diwani* rights in Bengal to the Company, which included the power to collect revenue and administer civil justice. Charged with standing forth as the *diwan*, Warren Hastings issued a plan in 1772 to assume control over the judicial administration of Bengal while maintaining the Nawab of Bengal as a symbolic ruler. Hastings set up two systems of justice: the *diwani*, or civil courts; and the *faujdari*, or criminal courts. Company officials staffed the *diwani* courts, while the Nawab administered *faujdari* courts, although the Company had the power to amend *faujdari* decisions. Hastings's judicial plan of 1772 specified that "in all suits regarding inheritance, marriage, and caste, and other religious usages or institutions," in the *diwani* courts, "the laws of the Koran with respect to Mahomedans, and those of the Shaster with respect to Gentoos, shall be invariably adhered to."[9] The Company courts consulted Muslim *maulvis* and Hindu Brahmins to ascertain the appropriate religious laws.

This judicial plan emerged out of complex negotiations between Hastings's government in Calcutta and the advisers of the Nawab in Murshidabad, leading to a system that mingled their varied interests. As Robert Travers has noted, Hastings most likely inserted the clause relating to marriage and inheritance because of his communications with Muhammad Reza Khan, the Nawab's deputy.[10] In response to the Company's proposal to submit civil matters to arbitration, Reza Khan insisted that "all matters relative to Inheritance, Marriages & other Disputes, which can be determined by the Express Dictates of the Mahomedan Religion, should be decided by a Magistrate, the Religious Officers and Men of Learning."[11] Muhammad Reza Khan also objected to provisions in the plan for consultations with Brahmins in

---

[8] Radhika Singha, *A Despotism of Law: Crime and Justice in Early Colonial India* (Delhi: Oxford University Press, 1998).

[9] "Seventh Report from the Committee of Secrecy appointed to Enquire into the State of the East India Company," 343, HCPP, 1772–3 (Secret Committee Reports, vol. IV).

[10] Robert Travers, *Ideology and Empire in Eighteenth Century India: The British in Bengal* (Cambridge: Cambridge University Press, 2007), 119–23.

[11] Representation on the Subject thereof delivered in by the Naib Duan, March 26, 1772, Moorshedabad Factory Records, IOR/G/27/6.

cases of Hindu marriage or inheritance. Hindus were free to decide such disputes among themselves, he argued, but if they brought them before the courts, Reza Khan insisted that, "in a Country under the Dominion of Mussulman Emperor it is improper, that any Order should be issued inconsistent with the Rules of his Faith."[12]

Read as a literal description of the mechanics of the Mughal courts, Reza Khan's statement conflicts with historical research suggesting that Mughal governors often accommodated Hindu customs.[13] Recent research, however, has confirmed his assertion that the Mughal courts sometimes applied Muslim legal norms in cases involving Hindus, including in relation to domestic disputes.[14] This seeming tension between accommodating diversity and appealing to Islam as a universal legal norm is best understood within the wider context of early-modern legal pluralism. The Mughal Empire and its successor states, like many other early-modern empires, allowed diverse alternative legal forums to operate independently from the state, even while claiming ultimate sovereignty.[15] Through arrangements that Nandini Chatterjee has termed "permissive inclusion," litigants could, regardless of their religion, approach Mughal *qazis* (judges) to adjudicate in commercial or familial disputes. The decision of the *qazis* in such cases were often informed by Islamic legal principles.[16] Much of the time, however, disputes were mediated through alternative legal structures, whether through local notables, *panchayats* (village councils), or extended families. By fostering pluralistic, and non-monopolistic, forms of legal governance, the Mughals were able to assert the universal moral authority of Islam while accommodating diverse religious practices.[17]

The Company broke with these patterns by striving to create a more state-centered legal culture. This approach subordinated other forms of adjudication to the state's overarching authority.[18] By rejecting Reza Khan's assertion that the courts should apply Muslim law in cases

---

[12] Translation of the Naib Soubah's Representation in reply to the Honble the President of Council's Letter regarding the administration of Justice, May 4, 1772, Moorshedabad Factory Records, IOR/G/27/7.

[13] Richard Maxwell Eaton, *The Rise of Islam and the Bengal Frontier, 1204–1760* (Berkeley: University of California Press, 1993), 179–83.

[14] Hasan, *State and Locality*, 72–6.

[15] Lauren Benton, *Law and Colonial Cultures: Legal Regimes in World History, 1400–1900* (Cambridge: Cambridge University Press, 2002).

[16] Chatterjee, "Reflections on Religious Difference and Permissive Inclusion in Mughal Law."

[17] Ayesha Jalal, *Partisans of Allah: Jihad in South Asia* (Cambridge: Harvard University Press, 2008), 26–35.

[18] Travers, *Ideology and Empire*, 100–41.

involving Hindu inheritance and marriage, the Company also favored a more "communal" understanding of law rooted in defined religious identities.[19] Nonetheless, when the Company began administering criminal law in 1790, it continued to administer Muslim criminal law to all Indians.[20]

The potentially transformative impact of the Company's legal interventions was constrained by the difficulties that officials faced in ascertaining the substance of the "native" laws that they claimed to administer. British administrators could consult eighteenth-century English translations of Sanskrit, Arabic, and Persian texts, including Charles Hamilton's *The Hedaya* (1791) and William Jones's *Al Sirajiyyah* (1792).[21] In theory, these translations were meant to free Company officials from the expertise of Indian scholars and legal professionals.[22] In practice, as Jon Wilson has recently argued, it is unclear how extensively these texts were used. This scenario seems particularly unlikely for lower court judges, who often lacked any formal legal training, let alone specialized study of Hindu or Muslim law. Instead, during the early decades of Company rule, judges were more likely to trust their instincts to arrive at rough-and-ready justice, often with the influence of Indian intermediaries.[23]

A company regulation issued in 1781 gave official sanction to this approach. Judges were instructed to act according to "justice, equity, and good conscience" in cases that were not covered by explicit Company legal regulations. The reference to "equity and good conscience" might seem to invite jurists to rely on English legal principles, and in fact later nineteenth-century decisions that disregarded Hindu and Muslim law often appealed to the phrase. As J.D.M. Derrett has argued, however, colonial judges in the eighteenth and early nineteenth centuries more often understood the phrase as an injunction to apply indigenous norms of justice.[24] In ascertaining these norms, Company officials continued

---

[19] Chatterjee, *The Making of Indian Secularism*, 75–108.

[20] The use of Muslim criminal law did not officially end until the introduction of the Indian Penal Code in 1862. On reforms made to the criminal law, see Singha, *A Despotism of Law*; Jörg Fisch, *Cheap Lives and Dear Limbs: The British Transformation of the Bengal Criminal Law, 1769–1817* (Wiesbaden: F. Steiner, 1983).

[21] Charles Hamilton, *The Hedaya, or Guide; a Commentary on the Mussulman Laws: Translated by Order of the Governor-General and Council of Bengal* (London: T. Bensley, 1791); William Jones, *Al Sirajiyyah: Or the Mohammedan Law of Inheritance, with a Commentary* (Calcutta: Joseph Cooper, 1792).

[22] Strawson, "Islamic Law and English Texts," 109–26; Anderson, "Islamic Law and the Colonial Encounter," 174–5; Kugle, "Framed, Blamed and Renamed," 271–4.

[23] Jon E. Wilson, *The Domination of Strangers: Modern Governance in Eastern India, 1780–1835* (Basingstoke: Palgrave Macmillan, 2008), 75–103.

[24] J.D.M. Derrett, "Justice, Equity and Good Conscience," in *Changing Law in Developing Countries*, ed. J.N.D. Anderson (London: Allen & Unwin, 1963), 114–53.

to rely on native judicial personnel, despite their stated desire to lessen their dependence on such intermediaries. As late as 1831, Rammohun Roy, the distinguished Bengali scholar and reformer, argued that only the Muslim law officers who worked alongside British judges in the local courts truly understood their day-to-day operations.[25]

The Company's continued reliance on Muslim legal personnel ensured that Islamic legal traditions broadly informed how commercial, as well as familial, disputes were adjudicated. Much of the overt discussion of religious laws during the early decades of Company rule related to cases involving marriage and inheritance. Commercial law appears less regularly in such discussions, but this absence may be explained by the fact that the Company dealt with many of these cases through processes of arbitration, aided by Muslim legal personnel. Hastings's plan of 1772 provided that "in all Cases of disputed Accounts, Partnerships, Debts, doubtful or contested Bargains, Non-performance of Contracts, and so forth, it shall be recommended to the Parties to submit the Decision of their Cause to Arbitration."[26] In 1793 Company regulations clarified that *qazis*, along with native landholders and merchants, should be appointed as arbitrators in petty cases.[27] Even in the field of property law, which was of particular concern to the Company given its interest in maximizing agrarian revenue collection, Muslim legal personnel continued to play a critical role in daily legal governance. Thus in 1793, when Lord Cornwallis, then governor of Bengal, introduced a radical new scheme for collecting revenue referred to as the Cornwallis Code or the Permanent Settlement, it assigned significant administrative and recording tasks to *qazis*.[28]

The Cornwallis Code demoted *qazis*, who had previously enjoyed prestige as general supervisors of public morality under the Mughals and their successors, to the diminished role of native assistants.[29] Nevertheless, their duties remained extensive. The Code tasked *qazis* with "preparing and

[25] Rammohun Roy, "Questions and Answers on the Judicial System of India," in *The English Works of Raja Rammohun Roy: With an English Translation of "Tuhfatul Muwahhiddin"* (Allahabad: Panini Office, 1906), 261.

[26] "Seventh Report from the Committee of Secrecy," 350.

[27] A.D. 1793 Regulation XL, "A Regulation for granting Commissions to Natives, to hear and decide Civil Suits for Sums of Money, or Personal Property of a value not exceeding Fifty Sicca Rupees, and prescribing Rules for the trial of the Suits, and enforcing the decisions which may be passed upon them," Bengal Regulations of 1793 and 1794, IOR/ V/27/120/57.

[28] On the Permanent Settlement more broadly, see Ranajit Guha, *A Rule of Property for Bengal: An Essay on the Idea of Permanent Settlement* (New Delhi: Orient Longman, 1963).

[29] J.S. Grewal, "The Qazi in the Pargana," in *Studies in Local and Regional History*, ed. J.S. Grewal (Amritsar: Guru Nanak University, 1974), 1–10.; C.A. Bayly, *Rulers, Townsmen, and Bazaars: North Indian Society in the Age of British Expansion, 1770–1870* (Cambridge: Cambridge University Press, 1983), 310–5.

attesting deeds of transfer and other law papers, celebrating marriages, and performing such religious duties or ceremonies prescribed by the Mahomedan Law ... and also for superintending the sale of distrained property, and paying charitable and other pensions and allowances."[30] These assignments drew on *qazis'* expertise reading complex property records, whose Persian lexicography often baffled Company officials.[31] The provisions governing the duties of *qazis* also reflected the close relationship between property ownership, hereditary pensions, and family relations. The mediating role of Muslim legal personnel in all of these areas worked against drawing firm boundaries between the legal administration of domestic and economic transactions.

The shifting position of Muslim legal personnel, at once downgraded to assistants but nonetheless critical to the functioning of the colonial courts, reflected the more general balance between change and continuity during the first half-century of British rule. The Company's early legal policies disrupted legal governance in India, but the changes came in spasms. Company legal texts and courts distorted and refashioned Indo-Islamic legal traditions to fit their own conceptions of law and to serve their own purposes. The Company's ongoing dependence on native intermediaries, however, worked against a systematic program of legal reform. In the 1820s, officials began to sponsor the publication of new textbooks of Hindu and Muslim law, which, by referencing previous case law rather than translating Arabic, Persian, or Sanskrit texts, marked a critical turn towards streamlining, and Anglicizing, the administration of religious laws.[32] It was not until the late 1820s, however, that officials began contemplating a more sweeping project of legal codification that would eventually narrow Muslim law to a distinct religious-domestic sphere.

## The Problematic Narrative of the Eighteenth-Century Origins of Personal Law

It is worth reflecting for a moment on how shifting the crucial period of transformation in Indian legal governance from the late eighteenth

---

[30] A.D. 1793 Regulation XXXIX, "A Regulation for the appointment of the Cauzy ul Cozaat, or Head Cauzy of Bengal, Behar, and Orissa, and the Cauzies stationed in the several Districts, and prescribing their respective Duties," Bengal Regulations of 1793 and 1794, IOR/V/27/120/57.

[31] On the role of native intermediaries in Company documentation practices more generally, see Bhavani Raman, *Document Raj: Writing and Scribes in Early Colonial South India* (Chicago: University of Chicago Press, 2012).

[32] Wilson, *Domination of Strangers*.

century to the mid-nineteenth century departs from existing accounts of the origins of personal law in colonial India. With some exceptions, historians and legal scholars generally credit Hastings's 1772 plan with creating the system of personal law that continues to function in South Asia today.[33] The term personal law itself appears nowhere in Hastings's plan. But historians nonetheless cite as its origins the clause specifying that Hindu and Muslim law would be applied in "all suits regarding inheritance, marriage, and caste, and other religious usages or institutions."[34] Focusing narrowly on this section of Hastings's plan obscures other facets of Company law that extended the application of Muslim law into additional areas.

The 1772 Plan applied only to Bengal. The regulations put in place for courts in other regions of British India and for the Supreme Courts, which operated in the cities of Calcutta, Madras, and Bombay, treated domestic and commercial matters as part of an undifferentiated category of "civil" law. Instructions issued in 1799 for the courts in Bombay specified that religious laws should be applied to "all suits of a civil nature that respect the succession, to, and inheritance of, landed and other property, mortgages, loans, bonds, securities, hire, wages, marriage, and caste, and every other claim to personal or real right and property."[35] Similarly, the Supreme Courts, which operated under royal charters, were instructed to apply religious laws to cases involving "inheritance and succession to lands, rents, and goods, and all matters of contract and dealing between party and party."[36] Viewed in the context of these other provisions, the more narrow application of religious laws provided for by Hastings's plan seems to be an exception. The fact that this formula was not repeated when setting up courts elsewhere suggests that it resulted from the particular conditions surroundings negotiations with the Nawab's government and the wide provisions in the plan for the use of arbitrators. Contrary to existing accounts, the 1772 Plan did not result in a systematic narrowing of the application of religious laws to domestic matters.

---

[33] See, for example, Kolsky, "Forum: Maneuvering the Personal Law System," 975. For an alternative account that, like this book, emphasizes the middle decades of the nineteenth century, see Tambe, *Codes of Misconduct*, 8.

[34] "Seventh Report from the Committee of Secrecy," 343.

[35] Section XIV, A.D. 1799 Regulation IV, "A Regulation for receiving, trying, andd [sic] eciding suits in complaints declared cognizable in the civil Courts of Justice of Salsette, Caranja &c," Bombay Regulations, 1799–1814, IOR/V/8/22.

[36] 21 Geo.III.c.70. Almost identical language was included in the acts governing the supreme courts in Madras and Bombay. "An act for the better administration of justice at Calcutta, Madras, and Bombay," (1797), 37 Geo.III.c.142.

Early British texts on Muslim law also show the wide range of matters to which it was deemed relevant, extending well beyond the domestic sphere. Francis Gladwin published one of the earliest texts on Muslim law for the guidance of Company officials in 1786, a translation of a Persian text originally prepared for the Mughal Emperor Muhammad Shah (1702–48).[37] The text was divided into two parts: a short chapter on spiritual matters, chiefly concerned with the Muslim profession of faith; and a longer section titled "temporals," which covered marriage, divorce, criminal law, slavery, partnership, pious dedications, buying and selling, debt, gifts, rent, and agriculture. The division between spiritual and temporal law, which Gladwin borrowed from the Persian text, appeared in many early British accounts of Muslim law. Although Gladwin only dealt with the profession of faith under the heading of spiritual law, other authors also included fasting, prayer, pilgrimage, and alms – together composing the five pillars of Islam. British authors generally only briefly discussed this spiritual domain, although some works included longer sections on *zakat*, the Islamic charitable tax on wealth, due to its perceived relationship to property.[38] Under the heading of temporal law, British authors included topics ranging across criminal, commercial, and domestic law, often interspersing these headings in combinations that defy modern legal classifications.

Gladwin's text was closely followed by Hamilton's publication of his translation of *al-Hidaya*, a massive work that was one of the most frequently cited legal texts during the colonial period. Translated at Hastings's request, the twelfth-century Arabic commentary on Hanafi jurisprudence was first translated into Persian by four Muslim scholars before Hamilton rendered it into English.[39] The massive four-volume work covered an amazing range of topics, although Hamilton left out most of the original text related to *ibadat*, or worship.[40] Hamilton included, among others, sections on marriage, divorce, slavery, punishments, war, partnership, *waqf* (endowments), sale, debts, evidence, loans, gifts, hunting, fines, and wills. This wide-ranging study of different areas of Muslim law continued until the 1860s, with the publication of Neil Baillie's *The Moohummudan Law of Sale, According to the Huneefeea Code* (1850) and *The Land Tax of India, According to the Moohummudan*

[37] Francis Gladwin, *An Epitome of Mohammedan Law* (Calcutta: William Mackay, 1786).
[38] For example, Hamilton omitted spiritual law with the exception of *zakat*. Hamilton, *The Hedaya*, liii–lxii.
[39] Ibid., xliii–xlv.
[40] Metcalf, *Islamic Revival*, 20, footnote 9.

*Law: Tr. from the Futawa Alumgeeree* (1853); F.E. Elberling's *A Treatise on Inheritance, Gift, Will, Sale and Mortgage* (1844), which focused on Muslim law; and Standish Grove Grady's *A Manual of the Mahommedan Law of Inheritance and Contract* (1869).[41]

Given his role in preparing the second, narrowly domestic, *Digest of Moohummudan Law* in 1875, the appearance of Neil Baillie on this list is notable. As late as 1850, Baillie considered Muslim law an important point of reference for British judges because of its general relevance to determining the "usage of the country." In the introduction to the 1850 text, Baillie explained that, in cases in which judges were forced to rule according to "justice, equity, and good conscience," they might need to consider the Muslim law of sale because it continued to be a common point of reference for Indians in their dealings with each other. Most strikingly, Baillie emphasized that this was true regardless of whether the parties were Muslim or Hindu. He explained:

It is only in cases where an appeal is made to the Moohummudan law as the usage of the country, that it can now be applied to the cases of Hindoos in civil matters, by the courts of justice in the British territories in India. It is possible, however, that it may still be referred to by the Hindoos themselves in their ordinary dealings, and it is most probably the source from whence have been derived their principal notions of right and liability connected with particular contracts. If such be the case, the Moohummudan law must afford to the judge the readiest means of ascertaining the meaning of even Hindoo parties to a contract, where it has not been sufficiently expressed, or cannot be implied from the circumstances of the case.[42]

Published in the middle of the nineteenth century, Baillie's *The Moohummadan Law of Sale* marked a transition point in British conceptions of Muslim law. It is, of course, difficult to ascertain the relevance of texts such as this to the daily operation of the Company courts. Legal historians of the late eighteenth and early nineteenth centuries come up against the limitations of the archive, which contain relatively few legal records compared to the late nineteenth century. Regularized law reporting, on which detailed case-law studies depend,

---

[41] Neil B.E. Baillie, *The Moohummudan Law of Sale, According to the Huneefeea Code: From the Futawa Alumgeeree, a Digest of the Whole Law* (London: Smith Elder, 1850); Neil B.E. Baillie, *The Land Tax of India: According to the Moohummudan Law* (London: Smith Elder & Co., 1853); Francis E. Elberling, *A Treatise on Inheritance, Gift, Will, Sale and Mortgage: With an Introduction on the Laws of the Bengal Presidency* (Serampore: Serampore Press, 1844); Standish Grove Grady and W.H. Macnaghten, *A Manual of the Mahommedan Law of Inheritance and Contract, Comprising the Doctrines of the Soonee and Sheea Schools* ... (London: W.H. Allen, 1869).

[42] Baillie, *The Moohummudan Law of Sale*, x.

only commenced after the passage of the Indian Law Reports Act of 1875.[43] In and of itself, the absence of standardized record-keeping indicates the limited role of judicial precedent and the expansive independence exercised by individual British judges in early Company courts.

One rare source for studying the workings of the early Company courts is William H. Macnaghten's *Principles and Precedents of Moohummudan Law* (1825). This work suggests that the Muslim law was applied widely during the early Company period. Instead of translating Arabic or Persian texts, Macnaghten based his text on the proceedings of the Company courts. His text simultaneously documented the actual workings of the courts while also trying to standardize their future operations. Drawing on the access he had to court records as a court registrar, Macnaghten cited about three dozen *zila*, or local lower-level, court cases involving sales, debts, and property transfers.[44] Unfortunately, since his goal was to present generally applicable principles, Macnaghten does not describe individual cases. Nevertheless, his passing references to these sorts of cases suggest that lower-level courts applied Muslim law in commercial areas.

The broad application of Muslim law during the early years of Company rule suggests that "personal law" is an anachronistic term before the nineteenth century. As the following discussion will show, the term itself migrated into discussions of law in India during the 1820s in the wider context of new theories of European legal development. When first introduced, the term largely functioned to communalize Muslim law by suggesting that it only applied to a particular group of people. Between the 1840s and 1860s, the term also came to imply a limited domestic jurisdiction. The existence of language in Hastings's 1772 plan that foreshadowed these later parameters helped facilitate the later naturalization of the category. For nineteenth-century colonial officials as well as for present-day historians, the ability to project personal law back into the eighteenth century made the category seem self-evident, masking the critical transformations that propelled its formation between the late 1820s and 1860s. Having set aside this largely erroneous origin story, I now return to the particular historical forces that *did* propel its formation.

---

[43] Mitra Sharafi, *Law and Identity in Colonial South Asia: Parsi Legal Culture, 1772–1947* (New York: Cambridge University Press, 2014), 46.
[44] The list of *zila* cases appears in an appendix to the first edition, printed in Calcutta at the Church Mission Press in 1825, but not in subsequent printings.

## Changing Landscapes of Law and Sovereignty: Territoriality and Historicism

In the 1820s the patchwork legal landscape that prevailed in British India came under acute ideological pressure. A new generation of British administrators, steeped in a global revolution in legal thought, sought to impose a new order. These administrators partook of a global trend that interpreted sovereign power through the lens of territoriality, redefining sovereignty as the ability to exercise a jurisdictional monopoly within a bounded geographical space, whether colonial or national. The roots of this legal revolution stretched back at least to the seventeenth century.[45] Over the course of several decades in the early nineteenth century, however, these prior ideological currents rapidly crystallized into practical programs of legal reform from Europe to Australia. From the radical simplification of the map of European polities after the end of the Napoleonic Wars in 1815, to the assertion of settler sovereignty over the indigenous peoples of Upper Canada, colonial administrators replaced overlapping, plural legal orders with unified, territorially defined legal jurisdictions.[46] A second major current in early-nineteenth-century legal thought, the rise of legal historicism, emphasized the organic connections between law and the *Volksgeist*, or national spirit, of a given community.[47] In India, the co-mingling of territoriality and historicism would have profound effects on the eventual shape of secular legal governance.

In India, this global legal revolution corresponded to the same time period that historians often refer to as "The Age of Reform," which commenced with the appointment of Lord W.C. Bentinck as governor general in 1828.[48] Bentinck discarded the preservationist ethos that had animated Company policy for over a half-century in favor of openly

---

[45] Charles S. Maier, "Transformations of Territoriality 1600–2000," in *Transnationale Geschichte: Themen, Tendenzen und Theorien*, ed. Gunilla Budde, Sebastian Conrad, and Oliver Janz (Göttingen: Vandenhoeck & Ruprecht, 2006), 32–55.

[46] Benton, *Law and Colonial Cultures*; James J. Sheehan, "The Problem of Sovereignty in European History," *The American Historical Review* 111, no. 1 (2006): 1–15; Lisa Ford, *Settler Sovereignty: Jurisdiction and Indigenous People in America and Australia, 1788–1836* (Cambridge: Harvard University Press, 2010).

[47] Michael H. Hoeflich, "Savigny and His Anglo-American Disciples," *The American Journal of Comparative Law* 37, no. 1 (January 1989): 17–37; Duncan Kennedy, "Three Globalizations of Law and Legal Thought: 1850–2000," in *The New Law and Economic Development: A Critical Appraisal*, ed. David M. Trubek and Alvaro Santos (Cambridge: Cambridge University Press, 2006), 25–8; Duncan Kennedy, "Savigny's Family/Patrimony Distinction and Its Place in the Global Genealogy of Classical Legal Thought," *American Journal of Comparative Law* 58, no. 4 (2010): 836–7.

[48] The best survey of this period remains Eric Stokes, *The English Utilitarians and India* (1959; Reprint Delhi: Oxford University Press, 1982).

interventionist reforms, particularly in the spheres of education and law. Among other reforms, Bentinck's government criminalized *sati*, or the Hindu practice of widow burning, in 1829; significantly curtailed the use of Islamic law officers and *fatwas* in criminal trials, in 1832; and abolished the use of separate religious oaths in courts, in 1840.[49] Under Bentinck's tenure, the Company also removed the image of the Mughal emperor from its *rupee* coin, an important symbolic break from the Company's prior policy of staging its own political claims as complementing, rather than replacing, Mughal sovereignty.[50] (While marginalized, the Mughal emperor officially remained in place in Delhi until after the Rebellion of 1857.)

Bentinck's legal-reform projects showed the clear impress of territoriality, an approach nurtured in the quotidian channels of correspondence that circulated between officials located within and between different colonial territories.[51] The willingness of colonial officials to engage in legal theorizing is apparent in a series of letters that Bentinck exchanged with the judges of the Calcutta Supreme Court in 1829 and 1830 as he prepared to implement a series of legal reforms. What started as a discussion of recent clashes over jurisdiction involving several courts in Bengal quickly expanded into a broad diagnosis of what they decried as the state of legal chaos prevailing in India. The judges explained that this unacceptable state of affairs resulted from the Company's choice to graft its own judicial institutions onto the existing landscape of overlapping local and Mughal jurisdictions:

the Mahomedan and Hindu inhabitants of those provinces, like the clients under Roman law, or the vassals of the feudal system, and indeed the common people under every other state of government in which numerous chieftains or heads of political or religious classes exist, had been accustomed to think more of their fealty to the immediate chief upon whose land, or under whose protection or patronage they lived, than of the allegiance due to a common and supreme sovereign. The country was in a state in which the people ranged themselves under different flags, rather than according to boundaries of territory.[52]

[49] Lata Mani, *Contentious Traditions: The Debate on Sati in Colonial India* (Berkeley: University of California Press, 2007); Singha, *A Despotism of Law*, 295–7.

[50] John S. Deyell and R.E. Frykenberg, "Sovereignty and the 'Sikka' under Company Raj," *Indian Economic and Social History Review* 19, no. 1 (January 1982): 1–26.

[51] Lauren Benton and Lisa Ford, *Rage for Order: The British Empire and the Origins of International Law, 1800–1850* (Cambridge: Harvard University Press, 2016), 21.

[52] Letter from the Judges of the Supreme Court to the Secretary of the Board of Commissioners for the Affairs of India, "Appendix to the Report on the Affairs of the East India Company. V. On the Establishment of Legislative Councils, – A New system of Courts of Justice, – A Code of Laws, in British India," 121, HCPP, 1831 (320E) VI.465.

The judges were unanimously of the opinion that these arrangements, which once seemed acceptable, were now incompatible with Britain's well-established political presence in India.[53] For Britain to claim sovereignty over its Indian territories, no other political or legal power could hold an overlapping jurisdiction within those same spaces.

The judges' references to Roman and feudal law also suggest that growing interest in the historical development of law in Europe was shaping debates about legal reform in India. The so-called historical school emerged in part as a reaction against attempts to import Napoleonic civil codes into other European jurisdictions. In opposing alien legal imports, the historicists insisted that law only functioned when it aligned with local customs and norms, a claim that spurred new interest in researching the history of legal development in different regions. The historical school is often associated with Continental thinkers, including the German historian and jurist Friedrich Carl von Savigny, who published *The History of the Roman Law during the Middle Ages* in six volumes in Germany between 1815 and 1831. Von Savigny secured a wide reputation in the Anglophone world through English translations of such works, which first appeared in 1829.[54]

Legal historicism also had a more local genealogy in India. In the early nineteenth century, a circle of administrators sometimes referred to as the "Romantics" began to emphasize the need to preserve the organic integrity of local institutions. These officials, who were particularly influential in shaping the administration of law in the regions surrounding Bombay and Madras, wanted to minimize the introduction of new sources of law that would destabilize India's largely agrarian peasant communities.[55] Officials in Madras and Bombay were increasingly skeptical that these village communities, which they believed (sometimes erroneously) to have been isolated from outside influence,

---

[53] The judges' description of early-modern India corresponds to a considerable extent with contemporary historiography which describes early-modern India as characterized by layered forms of sovereignty. Burton Stein, *Vijayanagara* (Cambridge: Cambridge University Press, 1989), 63, 105. On the impact of British colonialism on concepts of sovereignty, see Sugata Bose, *A Hundred Horizons: The Indian Ocean in the Age of Global Empire* (Cambridge: Harvard University Press, 2006), 25–6, 40–3; Mridu Rai, *Hindu Rulers, Muslim Subjects: Islam, Rights, and the History of Kashmir* (Princeton: Princeton University Press, 2004), 27, 111–12.

[54] Friedrich Karl von Savigny, *The History of the Law during the Middle Ages*, trans. E. Cathcart (Edinburgh: Adam Black, 1829). Hoeflich, "Savigny and His Anglo-American Disciples," 17–37; Duncan Kennedy, "Savigny's Family/Patrimony Distinction and Its Place in the Global Genealogy of Classical Legal Thought," *American Journal of Comparative Law* 58, no. 4 (2010): 836–7.

[55] Stokes, *The English Utilitarians and India*, 9–25; Metcalf, *Ideologies of the Raj* (1994: Reprint Cambridge: Cambridge University Press, 2008), 25–7.

adhered to the dictates contained in orthodox Sanskrit, Arabic, and Persian legal texts. The colonial officials instead argued that many local communities followed unwritten customs, which should be given official legal sanction by Company courts. As early as 1800 in Madras and after 1827 in Bombay, the courts provided for customary law to operate alongside Hindu or Muslim law.[56] The Romantics' influence faded somewhat in the 1820s, marginalized by the more interventionist approach advocated by reformers such as Bentinck. But in the 1840s their resurgent views played an important role in shaping the administration of newly acquired territories in the Punjab. In setting up the legal administration in the Punjab, colonial administrators made extensive concessions to custom, with long-term implications for its large Muslim population.[57]

Between the 1820s and 1840s, the ideological influence of territoriality, with its emphasis on unifying law, and historicism, which valued preserving diverse local customs, pushed legal administration in India in potentially diverging directions. Yet these dueling influences increasingly converged around the shared use of the terminology of personal law. Historicists, including von Savigny, argued that the Germanic tribes that invaded parts of Europe after the fall of the Roman Empire allowed the inhabitants to retain their own laws, fostering a legal system in which laws attached to persons, rather than to territory.[58] In this evolutionary narrative, personal law became a pre-modern form which preceded, and was therefore developmentally inferior, to territorial law. During the 1830s, commentators on Indian law, like the Calcutta judges, increasingly compared Europe's medieval past with India's present, suggesting that India's ongoing need for personal law was a mark of its civilizational immaturity.[59] The merging of territoriality and historicism allowed commentators on Indian law to hold up unified, territorial sovereignty as an ideal form. It also, however, allowed for the potential recognition of legal diversity, through the simultaneous recognition of personal laws, as a possible concession to India's inferior stage of legal development. In future deliberations on Indian law this formula of merging territorial and personal jurisdictions proved a powerful means of reconciling conflicting ideological pushes towards uniformity and diversity.

---

[56] George Rankin, "Custom and the Muslim Law in British India," *Transactions of the Grotius Society* 25 (January 1939): 100–1; M.P. Jain, "Custom as a Source of Law in India," *Jaipur Law Journal* 3 (1963): 96–130.

[57] Stokes, *The English Utilitarians and India*, 9–25; Metcalf, *Ideologies of the Raj*, 25–7.

[58] von Savigny, *The History of the Law during the Middle Ages*.

[59] *Foreign Quarterly Review* 13, no. 26 (1834): 434–5.

## Evangelicalism and Secular Conversion

Bentinck's correspondence with the Calcutta judges spotlights another critical force in debates about legal reform: evangelicalism. From abolishing *sati* to diminishing the role of Islamic law officers, Bentinck's reforms often specifically targeted practices and authorities that officials associated with Indian religions. The judges voiced a broad discomfort with the ongoing importance of Muslim law in the Company's judicial administration. As Judge Edward Ryan, quoting Charles Metcalfe, a member of the Governor General's Council, argued: "That Christian Judges ... should try Hindoo prisoners according to Mahomedan law, seems sufficiently absurd; but that Christian Judges of British blood should try Christians of British extraction by Mahomedan law, seems, if possible, still more strange."[60]

The judges' aversion to having Christian judges administer Muslim law stemmed from the diffuse influence of evangelical thought on the Age of Reform.[61] British evangelical Christianity, although highly diverse and difficult to define, emphasized the direct relationship between the individual believer and God and stressed that the only route to eternal salvation was through faith in Christ's atonement on the cross. In its emphasis on the emotive dimensions of religious faith, evangelicalism stood in opposition to Enlightenment rationalism; in its emphasis on individual belief, evangelical Christianity shared with Enlightenment thought a belief in the fundamental uniformity of human nature and the systematic design of the universe.[62] Although individuals shaped by evangelicalism viewed reason alone as an insufficient guide to understanding the world, they believed in the fundamental harmony between the evidence provided by empirical observation and by Christian divine revelation.[63]

---

[60] Minute, by the Hon. Sir E. Ryan, October 2, 1829, "Appendix to the Report on the Affairs of the East India Company," 93.

[61] On the wide-ranging influence of evangelicalism within Britain itself, see Ford K. Brown, *Fathers of the Victorians: The Age of Wilberforce* (Cambridge: Cambridge University Press, 1961); Boyd Hilton, *The Age of Atonement: The Influence of Evangelicalism on Social and Economic Thought, 1795–1865* (Oxford: Clarendon Press, 1988); D.W. Bebbington, *The Dominance of Evangelicalism: The Age of Spurgeon and Moody* (Downers Grove: InterVarsity Press, 2005); Joseph Stubenrauch, "Faith in Goods: Evangelicalism, Materiality, and Consumer Culture in Nineteenth-Century Britain" (Ph.D., Indiana University, 2011). I have chosen not to capitalize "evangelical" to differentiate between evangelicalism as a broad intellectual and cultural influence and individuals who self-identified as Evangelicals.

[62] Hilton, *The Age of Atonement*, 7–8.

[63] Brian Stanley, *The Bible and the Flag: Protestant Missions and British Imperialism in the Nineteenth and Twentieth Centuries* (Leicester, England: Apollos, 1990); Brian Stanley, ed., *Christian Missions and the Enlightenment* (Grand Rapids: W.B. Eerdmans Publishing, 2001).

Many British reform projects in India were undergirded by the belief that Christianity, civilization, and commerce would act as mutually reinforcing vehicles for transforming Indian society.[64] The Company lifted an earlier ban on missionary activities in its territories in 1813. Already by the 1820s missionaries were noting the considerable challenges they faced in securing converts among Indians, who were largely unreceptive to their Christianizing message. Missionaries therefore looked for alternative, more gradual vehicles for influencing Indian society, some of which were based on the idea that Indians required prior training in rational modes of analysis before they would embrace Christianity. In Calcutta in the 1830s and 1840s, Alexander Duff set up missionary schools that offered elite education in English, which he believed would facilitate the spread of the gospel.[65] Duff's college was the first institution to teach political economy to Indians, also suggesting the close association during the period between "secular" education and missionary efforts.[66]

Most missionaries remained fiercely committed to the idea that Christianity, commerce, and civilization had to be introduced in tandem. Many other British commentators, however, increasingly advocated English education, free trade, and legal reform as more effective tools for spreading Christian civilization, and eventually Christianity, than outright proselytizing. Supporters of this strategy believed that introducing English civilization would awaken the conscience of individual Indians by exposing them to rational bodies of thought. These individuals would then spur a broader social revolution that would undermine Indian religious traditions. While downplaying direct missionary activity, these reformers retained key principles of evangelical thought. They emphasized individual conscience and associated reason with Christian morality while viewing Indian religions as bastions of unreasoning superstition. This vision, here termed "secular conversion," would deeply shape the trajectory of legal reform in colonial India.[67]

---

[64] Stokes, *The English Utilitarians and India*, 47–8. See also Andrew Porter, "'Commerce and Christianity': The Rise and Fall of a Nineteenth-Century Missionary Slogan," *The Historical Journal* 28 (1985): 597–621; Brian Stanley, "'Commerce and Christianity': Providence Theory, the Missionary Movement, and the Imperialism of Free Trade, 1842–1860," *The Historical Journal* 26 (1983): 71–94.

[65] Ian Douglas Maxwell, "Civilization or Christianity? The Scottish Debate on Mission Methods," in *Christian Missions and the Enlightenment*, ed. Brian Stanley (Grand Rapids; Richmond, Surrey: William B. Eerdmans Publishing and Curzon Press, 2001), 137–40.

[66] George Smith, *The Life of Alexander Duff* (New York: American Tract Society, 1879), 135.

[67] Gauri Viswanathan has made a similar argument about the role of English literary education in British India. *Masks of Conquest: Literary Study and British Rule in India* (New York: Columbia University Press, 1989).

The workings of the idea of secular conversion can be seen in the biography of Thomas Macaulay, who in 1833 was appointed the first chairman of the Indian Law Commission, charged by Parliament with codifying India's laws. Macaulay was the son of Zachary Macaulay, a prominent anti-slavery crusader and member of the Clapham Sect, the leading intellectual wing of the evangelical movement in Britain.[68] Privately, Thomas rebelled against his father's religious guidance, even while he maintained a public image of Christian respectability. Given his ambiguous personal beliefs, he transferred his father's evangelical devotion to his own faith in the ennobling power of "English civilization, liberty, and progress."[69] Macaulay opposed any direct government involvement in the propagation of religion in India, yet he derided the backwardness of Indian religions and framed Britain's presence in India as serving Christian purposes. In a review of Gladstone's *The State in Its Relations with the Church* (1839), Macaulay argued, "There is assuredly no country where it is more desirable that Christianity should be propagated. But there is no country in which the Government is so completely disqualified for the task."[70] Macaulay argued that direct government involvement with religion "would inevitably destroy our empire, and, with our empire, the best chance of spreading Christianity among the natives."[71] He preached instead moral uplift through the spread of English language, British commerce, and Western law.

Macaulay's enthusiasm for reform captured the appeal of secular conversion to colonial administrators. Framing Britain's purpose in India in terms of spreading a broadly defined ethos of Christian civilization sidestepped the nuances of religious divisions in Britain itself. It also pragmatically avoided the political opposition overt missionary activities often provoked within India.

### Marginalizing Muslim Law: *Lex Loci* in British India

As the president of the first Law Commission, Macaulay set out to overhaul what he viewed as the chaotic legal mishmash prevailing in India. He described the situation as "not law, but a kind of rude and

---

[68] Catherine Hall, "Macaulay's Nation," *Victorian Studies* 51 (2009): 507.

[69] Robert E. Sullivan, *Macaulay: The Tragedy of Power* (Cambridge: Belknap Press, 2009).

[70] Thomas Babington Macaulay, "Gladstone on Church and State (1839)," in *Critical and Historical Essays: Contributed to the Edinburgh Review* (London: Longmans, Green, Reader, and Dyer, 1883), 499.

[71] Ibid., 486. Sugata Bose, "Nation, Reason and Religion: India's Independence in International Perspective," *Economic and Political Weekly* 33, no. 31 (1998): 2091.

capricious equity."[72] Macaulay, like many commentators on Indian law, acknowledged the need to provide some accommodation for India's diverse religious laws. He nonetheless felt confident that law reform could provide India with a modified version of the unitary, territorial forms of law that were becoming the global standard. He thus explained: "Our principle is simply this: uniformity where you can have it; diversity where you must have it; but in all cases certainty."[73] Early in its tenure, the First Law Commission channeled these wider ambitions into its deliberations on declaring a *lex loci*, or territorial law for British India – a discussion that merged questions of territoriality, historicism, and evangelicalism. In the early 1840s, when the Law Commission set about its work, its members expressed shock that the question remained unanswered, despite over six decades of judicial administration in India. To provide an answer, they found themselves setting out a new theory of British legal sovereignty that virtually rewrote the history of British judicial power in India. In an attempt to consolidate colonial sovereignty, the Commission's report argued that English law was the universal territorial law of India unless modified by specific legislative provisions. The report demoted Muslim law to an essentially religious body of law that could only be applied to people of a particular faith.

Historians have downplayed the importance of the Commission's report because its recommendation that English law be declared the *lex loci* was never enacted. Instead, the government passed the less ambitious Caste Disabilities Removal Act of 1850, which protected converts from being disinherited under Hindu and Muslim laws. By the mid-1850s, when the Second Law Commission revisited the question of India's territorial law, the Commissioners were uninterested in the "retrospective question" of whether English law became the *lex loci* with the advent of Company rule.[74] Instead, its members proposed a more ambiguous and forward-looking legislative plan that would construct a civil code for India *de novo*, although referring to English law as the principal foundation. The ease with which the Second Law Commission

---

[72] Thomas Babington Macaulay, "A Speech Delivered in the House of Commons on the 10th of July, 1833," in *Speeches of Lord Macaulay, Corrected by Himself* (London: Longmans, Green, and Co., 1866), 76.

[73] Thomas Babington Macaulay, "Government of India," in *The Complete Works of Thomas Babington Macaulay: Speeches and Legal Studies*, University edn (New York: Sully and Kleinteich, 1900), 164.

[74] "Second Report of Her Majesty's Commissioners Appointed to Consider the Reform of the Judicial Establishments, Judicial Procedure, and Laws of India, &c.," 7, HCPP, 1856 [2036] XXV.259.

passed over the question of the relative status of English, Muslim, and Hindu law, however, suggests that the 1840 *Lex Loci* Report is no historical dead end. In the 1820s it remained possible, if increasingly controversial, to refer to English and Muslim law as parallel bodies of law, either of which could be applied beyond the narrow confines of a defined religious community. By the close of the 1840s, administrators and judicial officials regarded this as an increasingly untenable position. Instead, drawing on the framework of territorial and personal law, officials juxtaposed colonial laws, which drew on English frameworks, against Muslim law. They emphasized that colonial laws, because they were founded on rational principles of jurisprudence could be applied to different populations, while Muslim law, which was based on irrational beliefs, must be restricted to the community professing those beliefs. This shift prepared the ground for secular legal governance to take root.

Despite the sweeping questions that the *Lex Loci* Report posed about the nature of British sovereignty in India, its origins were far humbler, spurred by a series of local petitions submitted to the Government of Bengal.[75] In these petitions a group of East Indians (the contemporary term for people of mixed European and Indian origin) and Armenians complained of their uncertain status with regards to civil law and their subjection to Muslim criminal law.[76] The petitioners echoed concerns initially raised by British missionaries in Calcutta about the legal status of Christian converts, including their right to inherit property.[77] In 1832 a new regulation in Bengal provided that in cases involving parties of different religions, Hindu and Muslim law "shall not be permitted to operate to deprive such party or parties of any property to which, but for the operation of such laws, they would have been

---

[75] Benton and Ford, *Rage for Order*, 56–84.

[76] Indian Law Commissioners to Governor General, October 31, 1840, Indian Legislative Consultations, January 11, 1841, no. 16, IOR/P/207/14 [hereafter abbreviated *Lex Loci* Report.], 1. Although most of the Law Commission's reports were published as Parliamentary Papers, I have only been able to locate a manuscript copy of the *Lex Loci* Report. The pages of the report are unnumbered, but I have included page numbers counting from the first page of the report. Sections of the report were printed as part of the first report of the third Law Commission, although much of the discussion concerning Muslim law was not included. "First Report of Her Majesty's Commissioners Appointed to Prepare a Body of Substantive law for India, &c.," Appendix B, 59–65, HCPP, 1864 (3312) XVI.359.

[77] On the legal issues raised by the act of conversion, see Gauri Viswanathan, *Outside the Fold: Conversion, Modernity, and Belief* (Princeton: Princeton University Press, 1998), 75–117. On the role of Indian petitioners in raising these issues, see Chatterjee, *The Making of Indian Secularism*, 92–4.

entitled."[78] The regulation, however, was sporadically enforced and limited to Bengal.[79]

In their response to these concerns, the Law Commissioners transformed the question of the legal position of a relatively small number of anomalous Indians into a sweeping discussion of legal jurisdiction. They opened the report with the question, "What is the law to which all persons in British India for whom no special provision has been made or who are not excepted on account of special circumstances, are subject or in other words, what is the *lex loci* of British India?" The Commissioners suggested, "this is a question which we believe has never been fully discussed."[80] They noted with surprise that Bentinck's earlier correspondence with the Calcutta judges implied that India did not possess a *lex loci*, but instead administered separate bodies of law to different groups. The Commissioners insisted that "a country governed by one of the civilized nations of modern Europe, and yet having no *lex loci*, would be a Phenomenon without example in jurisprudence."[81]

The territorial push of the Commissioners' firm conviction that India must have a singular, overriding *lex loci* clashed with the Company's repeated promises to preserve Hindu and Muslim law in India – raising the question of how to balance unity and diversity. To resolve this tension, the Commissioners set out boundaries that differentiated the limited forms of authority allowed to religious laws from the overarching sovereignty of English law. In this context, they classified Hindu and Muslim law as bodies of law that could only be applied to people professing these religious faiths. They asserted that Hindu and Muslim law "are so interwoven with religion as to be unfit for persons professing a different faith. The Hindoo and Mahomedan religions are not part and parcel of the law. But the law is part and parcel of the Hindoo and Mahomedan religions. The character of a *lex loci* seems therefore to be utterly unsuited to the genius of such systems."[82] While the Report itself did not use the term personal law, in a memo debating the Report's recommendations, C.H. Cameron, a member of the Commission and its president from 1843 to 1848, clarified that

---

[78] Application of Missionaries to Remedy the Disabilities of Native Christians, "Copies of the Special Reports of the Indian Law Commissioners," 346, HCPP, 1843 (300) XXXVI.1.
[79] "Report from the Select Committee of the House of Lords, appointed to inquire into the operation of the act 3 & 4 Will. 4, c. 85, for the better government of Her Majesty's Indian territories ...," 349, HCPP 1852–3 (41) XXX.1.
[80] *Lex Loci* Report, 3.
[81] Ibid., 27.
[82] Ibid., 6.

the native laws of India consisted exclusively of "religious and personal Laws."[83]

In the case of Hindu law, the Commissioners supported their claim by quoting European and Hindu authorities that described Hindu law as having always been restricted to people belonging to that religion. The Commissioners had a more difficult time dismissing Muslim law's claims to territorial sovereignty. Commentators who had previously claimed that India had a *lex loci* assumed it to be Muslim law, following the legacy of the Mughal Empire. The Commissioners devoted some space to this view before rejecting it, quoting a recent publication by Archibald Galloway, a director of the East India Company, that argued that the British should consult Muslim law as the general reference point for framing laws for India. As Galloway explained:

The Moohummudan law … is the law which has prevailed throughout India for seven or eight hundred years; the law of the government to which we succeeded; the law which, in one instance, at least, we became bound to administer, by the acceptance of the solemn grant which gave us the country from the fallen emperor, whom we now chuse [sic] to represent.[84]

Galloway's claim that Muslim law, as administered by the Mughals, was the territorial law in British India dovetailed with established doctrines governing the legal status of conquered territories. Common-law principles dating to the seventeenth century differentiated between territories acquired through conquest, where laws were already in place, and territories acquired through the settlement of Englishmen into previously empty or uncultivated lands. In the former case, the existing law in a conquered territory remained in force unless specifically modified by the king or Parliament. In the latter case, the settlers brought English law with them, and it thus automatically became the law of the land.[85]

The Commissioners, however, rejected Galloway's reasoning, arguing instead that Muslim law could not be the territorial law of British India because it was founded on unalterable and irrational religious beliefs. They drew on *Calvin's Case* (1608), in which Edward Coke had

---

[83] Minute by the Honble C.H. Cameron, Indian Legislative Consultations, August 2, 1845, no. 35, IOR/P/207/36.

[84] *Observations on the Law and Constitution of India: On the Nature of Landed Tenures, and on the System of Revenue and Finance, as Established by the Moohummudum Law and Moghul Government; with an Inquiry into the Revenue and Judicial Administration, and Regulations of Police at Present Existing in Bengal* (London: Kingsbury, Parbury, and Allen, 1825), 262–3. Galloway published the first edition anonymously; he included his name on the title page of a second edition published in 1832.

[85] Gavin Loughton, "Calvin's Case and the Origins of the Rule Governing Conquest in English Law," *Australian Journal of Legal History* 8 (2004): 143–80.

specified an exemption to the above principles for countries conquered from an "infidel" because their laws were "against the law of God and of nature."[86] The Commissioners argued that Muslim law could not be recognized within the system of international jurisprudence because it did not recognize the right of a conquering power to introduce new laws. The Commissioners concluded that, "The English law, as it does not profess to be a revelation from God, may be changed by Parliament in the way of legislation and by the Courts of law ... But the Mahommedan Law ... assuming to be the revealed commands of God, is, upon its own fundamental principles absolutely immutable."[87]

The Commissioners nevertheless had a difficult time reconciling their description of Muslim law with the actual history of its development in India. As noted earlier, the Mughals allowed non-Muslims considerable leeway in administering their own law, contradicting the Commission's description of the immutability of Muslim law. Yet, for the Commissioners, these actual policies of religious tolerance only further reinforced their conviction that Muslim law could not serve as a *lex loci*. As the Commissioners argued: "there is *lex loci* in their Country, but they consider it as practically suspended with regard to unbelievers, until they shall be converted to the faith, or shall appeal to a Mahommedan Court."[88] Thus rather than finding in Indian history evidence of a Muslim government's ability to adapt religious laws to local conditions, the Commissioners created an analytical trap in which either the flexibility or the inflexibility of Muslim law was evidence of its lack of territorial sovereignty. They therefore refuted the legitimacy of *sharia* as it had actually been practiced in the subcontinent in favor of their own conceptions of Muslim law as an immutable body of divine commands.

The Commissioners contrasted this supposedly immutable law with English law, which they described as possessing a core set of analytical principles that could be extracted and applied in various temporal and geographical contexts. The Commissioners acknowledged that certain aspects of English law, including elements of property law and judicial procedure, were cumbersome and ill-suited for export. They also suggested that some elements of English law might be unacceptable to non-Christians, but they limited these areas to marriage, divorce, and adoption. The report concluded by extolling the superiority of English law, which they praised as "not surpassed in the qualities for which

---

[86] *Calvin's Case* Eng. Rep. 77 [1608] 398.
[87] *Lex Loci* Report, 13.
[88] Ibid., 24–5.

substantive law is admired by any of the various systems under which men have lived."[89] The Commission therefore recommended that English law should immediately be declared India's *lex loci*, applicable to all groups except Hindus and Muslims, and expressed its future plans to draft three codes of substantive law which would govern Hindus, Muslims, and all other groups. In a final act of historical revisionism, the Commissioners argued that the legislation they proposed was in fact merely "declaratory," since it would only give "an express sanction to that which ought to have taken place tacitly according to the analogy of the general principles of international jurisprudence."[90]

The Commission's recommendations made a significant step towards a modern conception of the division between religious and secular law. It associated religious law with immutable traditions and personal beliefs, while positing that a *lex loci* based on English law was capable of being adapted to different circumstances and peoples. The Commissioners created a hierarchy between these two forms of law, asserting that legal systems, like English law, which were based on rational political deliberation, could serve as universally applicable territorial laws. In contrast, religious laws had to be restricted to people sharing a common faith. Yet the report, while distinguishing between the nature of territorial and religious law, still allowed for significant areas of overlap between them. By specifying their intention to draft three codes of law, including a *lex loci* and separate codes for Hindus and Muslims, the Commissioners suggested that the areas covered by English, Hindu, and Muslim law were roughly equivalent. Within the provisions for declaring English law the *lex loci*, however, the Commissioners began to set off a sphere of domestic relations that could not be governed by a rationally formed set of universal laws. They specified that for groups that came under the *lex loci*, they would still have separate laws for marriage, divorce, and adoption. Yet, the exclusion of inheritance from this list provides an important reminder that the eventual boundaries between secular and religious law developed slowly, with debates continuing about their respective domains into the mid-nineteenth century.

The *Lex Loci* Report more overtly referenced new conceptions of territorial sovereignty than evangelical Christianity. Yet, the Commissioners, like the Calcutta judges, found the idea of applying Muslim law to Christians virtually unthinkable. Their insistence on the immutability and irrationality of Muslim legal traditions also carried an evangelical hue. Yet, more than these overt religious references, the report evinced the

[89] Ibid., 63.
[90] Ibid., 69, 74.

broader ideological impulses of secular conversion. The Commissioners largely sidestepped the question of Christianity by substituting in its place a set of legal norms that they posited as religiously neutral. The Commissioners could have satisfied the complaints of the petitioners by legislating that Christian converts would be governed by Christian law, but doing so would have acknowledged an essential congruence between Hindu, Muslim, and Christian law. Instead, by arguing that they could simultaneously provide legal provisions for Indian Christians and a universal territorial law for India, they differentiated between Christianity and Indian religious traditions. While the Commissioners viewed Muslim and Hindu law as inseparably tied to specific religious beliefs, they presented English law, with the exception of a few areas, as based on reason. The three legal systems therefore were different in nature, allowing the Commissioners to set up English law as having a unique claim to territorial sovereignty in India. The report essentially secularized English law by translating its Christian norms into the language of rational universalism – in effect rendering invisible English law's own religious underpinnings.

Yet despite this secular glossing, when the Commissioners were forced to defend their proposal from critics, they revealed that Christian conversion, or at least a weakening of Indian religious traditions, remained an implicit goal of legal reform. Supporters and critics of the draft legislation agreed about the need to transform India's religious life, but they proposed different methods for accomplishing this end. During debates over the Lex Loci Act, C.H. Cameron, the president of the Law Commission, defended its provisions by arguing that India was not yet ready for a single uniform civil law, but that declaring English law the *lex loci* would spur further social, and religious, transformation. While Cameron described himself as skeptical of missionary efforts, he praised "instruction of the Natives in the Science, Literature and Morality of Europe" as "the only safe and effectual road to conversion."[91] Like education, providing native converts with an exemplary body of law founded on rational principles of jurisprudence would, in Cameron's opinion, serve as an indirect incentive to conversion:

For suppose a Hindoo or a Mahomedan to lose his religious attachment to the Law derived from his sacred books, and to become desirous of living under a Law framed, solely upon considerations, of justice and utility; under the present system he must either remain as he is, or plunge into a mere unorganized Chaos of Equity and good Conscience ... But now let us suppose the Lex Loci enacted, comprised in a written Digest, and from time to time amended by

[91] Minute by the Honble C.H. Cameron.

the Legislature, and we will have a real object of attraction to a rational mind. It is good to live under the same system of law as one's more civilized fellow subjects. It is good to live under a system of Law in which the principle of justice and utility are unencumbered by theological dogmas, and these advantages to the Hindoos and Mahomedans, as their prejudices gradually drop off, may be expected to perceive.[92]

Although Cameron did not refer to Christian conversion directly, instead emphasizing the universal principles of "justice and utility" and the workings of a rational mind, the provisions of the proposed Lex Loci Act necessitated that an individual convert to Christianity in order to come within its provisions. Thus in Cameron's view the act of conversion still served as the gateway to a system of rational and universal justice, reflecting the evangelical view of the interdependence of Christianity, reason, and civilization.

The Lex Loci's most vocal critic, T.H. Maddock, then deputy governor general of Bengal, presented a different view of social transformation. He argued that by dividing civil and religious law into separate domains, the colonial state could foster social transformation on a broader scale. Maddock argued against narrow reforms targeting Indian converts, positing that legal reform should embrace a more ambitious strategy. Foreshadowing the route that the Law Commissions would eventually take in the 1850s, Maddock insisted that in large areas a uniform code could be extended to all Indians, regardless of their religion. As Maddock explained:

When we shall have given to all men, who choose to avail themselves of it, a plain and intelligible code of substantive law, providing for the easy decision of all ordinary disputes regarding rights and obligations, people in general will learn to be satisfied with the administration of such a law, and will in time cease to refer to authorities in which civil and religious duties are jumbled together, in a manner so confused and intricate as to render them unintelligible, and oftentimes contradictory, excepting in those matters to which the prejudices of sect and caste attach some degree of religious importance. In all the ordinary transactions of the world, as between man and man, people will learn to prefer submission to a known and intelligible code, made familiar to them by multiplied copies in the vernacular dialects, and by the daily practice before their eyes in the Courts of Law, to references to Pundits and Moolvees for interpretations of the hidden mysteries, or the ambiguous import of the text of the Shasters or the Koran.[93]

[92] Ibid.
[93] Minute by the Hon. Sir T.H. Maddock, Knt., August 26, 1845, "Report from the Select Committee of the House of Lords, appointed to inquire into the operation of the act 3 & 4 Will. 4, c.85, for the better government of Her Majesty's Indian territories ...," Appendix A, 357, HCPP, 1852–3 (41) XXX.1.

Maddock complained about the mixing of civil and religious law, highlighting a new sensibility among British officials that differentiated between a sphere in which universal principles of political economy were applicable, and a sphere governed by the "prejudices of sect and caste." While distinguishing between civil and religious law, however, Maddock still saw a connection between these two spheres. He expected civil law, while supposedly framed around religiously neutral, rational tenets, to help diminish the influence of Hindu and Muslim religious traditions. Far from endorsing a policy of religious neutrality, Maddock specified a clear if indirect role for legal reform in spurring religious transformation. Maddock's comments revealed that in creating a separate domain of religious personal law, British legal experts intended not to protect Indian religious traditions but to create legal structures that would gradually diminish their importance. The contours of a modern system of personal law thus emerged not out of the spirit of preservation, however misinformed, that animated early Company rule, but out of the interventionist and evangelical impulses of the Age of Reform.

Conceptually the groundwork for secular legal governance was falling into place by the 1840s, particularly with respect to the "communalization" of Muslim law as only applicable to a narrow group of co-believers. Case law from the 1840s shows the percolation of the new vocabulary of territoriality and personal law into parallel discussions about the recognition of customary law. These discussions were spurred by growing recognition among British officials in India that Muslims and Hindus were not two distinct, monolithic communities, but a complex mixture of many different sub-groups.

In 1847 Sir Erskine Perry, an influential judge in the Bombay Supreme Court, used the framework of territorial and personal law to decide a case which allowed for custom to be observed in the place of Muslim law. A year after the case, Perry published a translation of von Savigny's work on the law of possession, and his concurrent interest in legal historicism informed his deliberations in the Bombay case.[94] The case involved several young women who belonged to two Muslim trading communities based in Western India, the Khojas and the Memons. The women claimed a portion of their fathers' estates under the Quranic mandate that they receive a half share. Members of the Khoja and Memon communities, however, argued that they did not follow these Quranic provisions and instead by custom excluded daughters from inheriting. In his decision

---

[94] Friedrich Karl von Savigny, *Von Savigny's Treatise on Possession: Or, The Jus Possessionis of the Civil Law*, trans. Erskine Perry (London: S. Sweet, 1848).

Perry explained that the girls' representatives had argued that since this custom directly contradicted the textual provisions laid out in the Quran that "it is equivalent to a custom in England which conflicts with a subsequent act of Parliament ...." Perry, however, like the Law Commission rejected any such comparison between Muslim and English law. Instead he explained that Muslim law, as enforced by the courts in India, was a personal law, akin to the permissive legal pluralism that the German conquerors allowed to prevail after the fall of the Roman Empire in Europe. He clarified that it could not be compared to the territorial jurisdiction of European bodies of law because the notion of a *lex loci* was an "altogether modern growth, and peculiar to Christendom." According to Perry, the British in India had therefore wisely preserved aspects of Indian personal laws. But as a system of personal law, the application of Muslim law was circumscribed by the common usage within a particular community. In cases where custom contradicted scripture, Perry therefore resolutely favored custom, concluding that, "it would be a monstrous thing that an English Court of justice should be obliged to reverse such a time-honoured custom, and almost to revolutionise the internal economy of two whole casts [sic], out of some supposed obligatory force in a text called Divine, which neither the Judge nor the parties to the suit believe in."[95]

Perry's decision shows how framing Muslim law as a religious personal law contributed to its narrowing jurisdiction, excluding its application both to non-Muslims and to Muslims who claimed alternative customary practices. His decision also hinted at the emerging "domestic" contours of the eventual application of personal laws, noting that at a minimum they would be applied to cases involving "marriage, divorce, succession, and, possibly, adoption." His decision was nonetheless marked by a continuing ambiguity about the parameters of this domestic sphere, and its relation to other private transactions between persons. At various points in the decision he described the "internal economy" of a community and its "domestic usages" in parallel terms. He also noted that, "How far the peculiar laws of such non-Christian

---

[95] Sir Erskine Perry, *Cases Illustrative of Oriental Life and the Application of English Law to India, Decided in H.M. Supreme Court at Bombay* (London: S. Sweet, 1853), 110–29, quoted on 125–6. On the legal history of the Khoja and Memon communities, see J.C. Masselos, "The Khojas of Bombay: The Defining of Formal Membership Criteria during the Nineteenth Century," in *Caste and Social Stratification among the Muslims*, ed. Imtiaz Ahmad, 1st edn (Delhi: Manohar Book Service, 1973), 1–20; S.T. Lokhandwalla, "Islamic Law and Ismaili Communities (Khojas and Bohras)," *Indian Economic and Social History Review* 4, no. 2 (April 1967): 155–76.

aliens would be recognized it may not be very easy, nor is it necessary, to define beforehand."[96]

The Law Commission likewise found the problem of defining the precise parameters of personal law a persistent challenge. In 1856 the Second Law Commission abandoned the plan to draft separate codes of Hindu and Muslim law, a decision that further marked them off as distinct in nature from the rest of colonial law. The Commissioners explained that, "The Hindoo Law and the Mahomedan Law derive their authority respectively from the Hindoo and the Mahomedan religion. It follows that, as a British Legislature cannot make Mahomedan and Hindoo religion, so neither can it make Mahomedan or Hindoo law." The decision not to codify Hindu and Muslim law was tempered, however, by the Commissioners' increasingly ambitious plans to craft a uniform civil code, which would apply to all people resident in India, regardless of their religion. The Commissioners were confident that "on very many important subjects of Civil Law" there was no need for separate bodies of law. They allowed, however, that in "certain kinds of transactions among themselves" different classes of Indians would require separate laws. But the Commissioners also felt that it was "premature to attempt now to define either the exceptions or exclusions."[97] With the groundwork in place, the final push towards clarifying the exclusively domestic jurisdiction of personal law would come with the transition from Company to Crown rule in the aftermath of the Rebellion of 1857.

## The Rebellion of 1857 and the Domestication of Personal Law

The Rebellion of 1857 shook the foundation of British rule in India, leading to the end of Company rule and the introduction of direct rule by the British Crown. The consolidation of colonial administration under Crown authority included an overhaul of the Indian judiciary.[98] The consolidation of the government of India under Crown control in 1858 cleared the way for a reinvigorated agenda of legal reform. In the 1860s the process of judicial appeal was streamlined, creating a single system of high courts.[99] The Penal Code drafted by Thomas Macaulay in

---

[96] Perry, *Cases Illustrative of Oriental Life*, 117.
[97] "Second Report of Her Majesty's Commissioners," 8–9.
[98] Stokes, *The English Utilitarians and India*, 239–43.
[99] Sharafi, *Law and Identity in Colonial South Asia*, 46.

1835 was finally enacted in 1862.[100] In 1864, the government abolished the office of the *pandit* and *qazi* as official advisers to colonial courts.[101]

This program of legal reform also had major implications for the consolidation of personal law. The Rebellion increased pressure on the Law Commission to demarcate the boundaries between religious and secular legal domains. The British believed that religious opposition to Company rule, heightened by the evangelical initiatives commenced during the "Age of Reform," had fueled the Rebellion.[102] At the same time, the newly consolidated Crown government desired to modernize India's economy. Drawing an increasingly bold line between religious laws governing the family and economic laws governing the market allowed the Raj to combine potentially contradictory commitments to preserve India's traditions and cultivate its progress. To facilitate these ends, the Law Commission in 1864 clarified for the first time that religious personal laws would be maintained in matters involving "succession, inheritance, marriage, and caste, and all religious usages and institutions."[103] At the same time, the Law Commissions in the 1860s and 1870s drafted and enacted a massive body of new codes placing various facets of commercial life, including contracts, insurance, negotiable instruments, transfer of property, and trusts, squarely under standardized legal codes. As Ritu Birla has argued, these new codes effectively created the market as "a new object of sovereign management."[104] The simultaneous decision to apply uncodified bodies of Hindu and Muslim law to cases involving marriage and inheritance solidified the domestic–economic division, a core structuring binary for secular legal governance.

The significance of these post-1857 reforms for solidifying a distinctly colonial pattern of secular legal governance is apparent when contrasted with contemporaneous developments in Britain. During the same period in Britain, legal reform moved in the opposite direction by bringing domestic areas of law under secular, civil jurisdiction. In 1857 the Matrimonial Causes Act shifted jurisdiction over marital separation and divorce from the ecclesiastical to civil courts. The act also endowed the legislatures with the power to amend these laws in

---

[100] Skuy, "Macaulay and the Indian Penal Code of 1862."

[101] U. Yaduvansh, "The Decline of the Role of the Qadis in India, 1793–1876," *Studies in Islam* 6 (1969): 155–71.

[102] Thomas R. Metcalf, *The Aftermath of Revolt: India, 1857–1870* (Princeton: Princeton University Press, 1964), 92–110.

[103] "First Report of Her Majesty's Commissioners Appointed to Prepare A Body of Substantive Law for India," 60, HCPP, 1864 (3312) XVI.359.

[104] Birla, *Stages of Capital*, 4.

response to changing social conditions.[105] This vehicle for progressive adaptation was, at least in theory, absent in India. After 1856, the Indian Law Commission took the stance that, because of their religious origins, Hindu and Muslim law were largely beyond the scope of legislative intervention. In subsequent decades colonial courts did in fact reshape Hindu and Muslim law through growing bodies of case law, but they did so under the guise of "nonintervention," an approach that largely precluded overtly progressive legislative or judicial reform.

These diverging patterns in Britain and India were rooted in different understandings of the relationship between reason and religion. The ability to "secularize" marriage in Britain depended on a general consensus that reason and Christian religion were largely compatible, minimizing the perceived threat of moving marriage from ecclesiastical to civil jurisdiction. Caroline Norton, whose desire to rid herself of an abusive husband helped power marriage reform in Britain, could thus describe the goal of these reforms as protecting rights "founded in nature, equity, and religion."[106] Nature, equity, and religion, seen as mutually reinforcing in a British context, were seen as at odds in India. As deliberations about legal reform in India during the early nineteenth century made clear, colonial officials' unwillingness to perceive rationality in Indian religions made it impossible for them to envision a single, unified legal system.

### The Difficulty of Untangling Domestic and Economic Transactions: Foreshadowing Problems to Come

By 1864, the Indian Law Commission had largely established the parameters through which religious personal laws would be assigned to domestic matters. But deliberations over specific legislation in the 1860s and 1870s reveal that the problem of how to differentiate between domestic and economic transactions continued to haunt efforts to delineate the boundaries of religious personal laws.

The drafting of the Indian Majority Act of 1875 is a case in point. The Indian Legislative Council at first assumed that this branch of law could safely be treated under universal, civil codes on the premise that "any civilized state" should possess a uniform age of majority for contractual relations. The Muhammadan Literary Society of Calcutta protested, arguing that under Muslim law the age of majority depended not

---

[105] Mary Poovey, "Covered but Not Bound: Caroline Norton and the 1857 Matrimonial Causes Act," *Feminist Studies* 14 (1988): 467–85.
[106] Von Savigny, *Von Savigny's Treatise on Possession.*

only on age, but also on the development of sexual capacity and the ability to distinguish right from wrong in relation to business transactions. The Legislative Council dismissed the Society's complaints by asserting that the act was for "purely civil purposes and not for anything provided by the sanction of religious authority."[107] The same problem resurfaced again in 1878 when the legislature was considering laws governing relations between master and servant. Early on in its deliberations, some colonial officials suggested that aspects of these laws might come under the jurisdiction of personal laws, with different provisions for Muslim, Hindu, Buddhist, and other employers. The proposal, which the legal expert James Fitzjames Stephen described as "absurd," was eventually dropped.[108]

The legal status of inheritance proved the most controversial issue, exposing the inherent instability of the boundaries between economic and domestic life. During the preparation of the Indian Succession Act, several members of the colonial administration advocated making some of its provisions universally applicable. Home Secretary E.C. Bayly argued for standard rules for determining the validity of a will, including requirements that it be written and attested. Bayly argued that, because inheritance practices changed over time, they were therefore not governed by unalterable divine laws. He emphasized the relative novelty of will-making among Hindus, crediting its adoption to the influence of English law. Bayly also argued that contributions to religious endowments should be limited, complaining that, "A Native testator, in the absence of anything like what is technically called the rule against perpetuities, may lock up his estate for an indefinite time, and thus obstruct the circulation of property, check the improvement of land, and withdraw capital from its natural employment in commerce."[109] Bayly thus framed the question of inheritance in economic terms, emphasizing its relation to commerce, property rights, and investment – areas where the colonial state was extending its power to regulate Indian social interactions.

Prominent Indians, including the well-known Muslim leader Sayyid Ahmad Khan, countered by protesting against the universal provisions included in the draft act. Khan's influential tract on the causes of the Indian Rebellion made him a favorite consultant on native opinion

[107] Indian Majority Act, 1875, National Archives of India [hereafter NAI], Legislative Department Proceedings A, March 1875, nos. 26–49, 1–2, 18.
[108] Codification of Indian Substantive Law, NAI, Home Judicial Proceedings A, January 1878, nos. 1–3. Justice Stephen, Memorandum on Codification in India, NAI, Legislative Department Proceedings A, August 1879, nos. 217–20, 15.
[109] E.C. Bayley to the Government of India, August 22, 1865, India Legislative Consultations, August 1865, no. 41, IOR/P/208/11, 924–5.

within government circles. He cautioned the government that, "Unlike other business, engagements, and contracts, Wills are inseparable from religions, customs and observances, and hence their validity in our Courts is dependent on the Futwa."[110] Yet while Khan argued against extending the Indian Succession Act to Muslims and Hindus, he later advocated for new legislation to change the way in which Muslim inheritance was regulated. He thus was not necessarily opposed to altering Muslim inheritance, but rather was fiercely committed to ensuring that it remained securely within the domain of religious laws, over which Indians themselves were granted greater control.[111]

Colonial officials interpreted such protests as proof that Indian religious principles were irreconcilable with modern economic rationality. For example, W.C. Plowden, the Secretary to the Board of Revenue in the North-West Provinces, insisted that religious endowments could not be governed according to "received principles of political economy." Instead he insisted that, "Religious or superstitious prejudices are, of all others, the most difficult to deal with ... [being] governed by a power stronger than that of reason." He therefore concluded that, "where such prejudices are found to exist throughout a nation, they cannot be prudently disregarded."[112]

The very ambiguity surrounding the borders between domestic and economic transactions created the need to clarify and reiterate the distinctive qualities of religion. As the category of religious personal law became further entrenched in colonial law, the range of different parties with stakes in its administration introduced new voices into these discussions, from colonial officials, to elite Indians like Sayyid Ahmad Khan, to more ordinary litigants. While each of these groups had an interest in defining the boundaries surrounding personal law, and thus the category of religion itself, they often disagreed as to where these parameters should be set. Even when they converged, as when Khan and Plowden agreed that they encompassed inheritance, the reasoning used to reach that conclusion could still diverge. Khan was interested in marking off inheritance as a zone in which elite Indians like himself should be consulted, a process that did not exclude the possibility of revising laws in tandem with changing economic conditions. In contrast, Plowden viewed religious inheritance laws, which he saw as

---

[110] "Proposed Extension of a Portion of the Indian Succession Act to Hindoos, Mahomedans, and Buddhists," Home Department, Legislative Proceedings, April 1866, no. 6, IOR/P/436/53,127.

[111] Kozlowski, *Muslim Endowments*, 157–62.

[112] "Proposed Extension of a Portion of the Indian Succession Act," 118.

fundamentally irrational, as at odds with modern political economy. The difficulty of fully untangling domestic from economic transactions therefore contributed to ongoing debates about the jurisdictional boundaries separating personal laws from secular laws. This underlying instability in turn transformed legal arenas into key sites for contesting the meaning of religion.

## Conclusion

By the last quarter of the nineteenth century, the basic structures of secular legal governance in India were in place. Between the 1820s and 1860s, a new category of religious personal law gradually solidified, first through theoretical discussion of *lex loci* and then through more concrete reforms undertaken after the Rebellion of 1857. Because early Company officials had referenced Muslim law in a broad range of areas, including in cases involving non-Muslims, colonial officials had to justify its demotion to domestic matters. During debates about *lex loci*, British officials marginalized Muslim law by emphasizing its specifically religious character, distinguishing it from the supposedly more rational, and therefore universal, principles embodied in English law. Their subsequent decision to limit religious laws to marriage, inheritance, and ritual matters created a new association between religion, irrational sentiment, and the family. On the flipside, the exclusion of religious laws from the new commercial codes created a newly distinct sphere of economic activity, which colonial lawmakers imagined as rational, universal, and therefore secular in nature.

As debates over laws governing the age of majority, relations between master and servant, and inheritance demonstrate, distinguishing between domestic and economic transactions proved difficult in practice. When litigants showed up in court, the ambiguities surrounding the division between domestic and economic matters continually raised questions about the relationship between religious and secular laws, infusing secular legal governance with deep currents of instability.

# 2    Personal Law and the Problem of Marital Property

A mere three years after the Indian Law Commission clarified that religious personal laws would be limited to familial and ritual concerns, a case came before the Judicial Committee of the Privy Council that illustrated the difficulty in applying this formula. Deliberating in its London chambers on Downing Street, the Privy Council served as the highest court of appeal for over a quarter of the world's population, including India and Britain's other colonial territories.[1] In 1867 the Privy Council, ensconced in its metropolitan perch, found itself poring over the marital and financial difficulties of a rich Muslim couple, Shumsoonnissa and Buzloor Ruheem, who were unhappily quarreling thousands of miles away in Bengal.

In 1856 Shumsoonnissa had left her husband because she suspected that her spouse, a deeply indebted landowner, was furtively stealing the considerable fortune she had inherited. Under Muslim law, this property remained separate and under her control – giving Muslim wives greater economic independence than their British counterparts, who until the passage of the Married Women's Property Act in 1882 were largely barred from owning their own property. In adjudicating the dispute between Shumsoonnissa and her husband, the Privy Council had to delineate what aspects of the quarrel were domestic, and therefore governed by Muslim law, and what aspects were economic, and therefore subject to non-sectarian bodies of civil law. They concluded that the question of whether Shumsoonnissa should be "restored" to her husband's home was clearly a domestic matter, and thus governed by Muslim law. But what of her disputed financial dealings with her husband? The financial ties linking husbands and wives, as well as the

---

[1] P. A. Howell, *The Judicial Committee of the Privy Council 1833–1876* (Cambridge: Cambridge University Press, 1979), 168. An Indian member was appointed to the Privy Council starting in 1909, and Indian lawyers started pleading cases before the Privy Council in the 1920s. Sharafi, *Law and Identity in Colonial South Asia*, 53–6.

broader question of women's property rights, raised perplexing questions about where the domestic ended and the economic began.

The Privy Council eventually answered this question by dividing Shumsoonnissa's case into two, labeling the dispute over the couple's living arrangements the "restitution" suit and the dispute over their finances the "property" suit. By applying Muslim law to the former but not the latter, the Privy Council reinforced the formula that the Indian Law Commission set out in 1864. But Shumsoonnissa's case, by illustrating the extent to which marital disputes were also often contests over property, foreshadowed the ongoing difficulties that Indian courts would experience in delineating a bounded sphere of religious personal laws.

Far from settling the issue in 1864, the Indian Law Commission, by invoking an inherently unstable boundary between domestic and economic transactions, ensured that the divide between religious and secular law continued to be the subject of ongoing debate. Shumsoonnissa's case, and the case law that cited it as a precedent, show how the courts cyclically called these boundaries into question and reiteratively reinforced them. By tracing discussions of the case and related legal debates across different levels of the colonial judiciary and across state and non-state arenas of legal adjudication, the chapter shows how the structures of secular legal governance relied on dynamic, rather than static, processes of boundary enforcement. These contests involved multiple actors, from litigants to Muslim legal scholars, making secular legal governance a multi-directional and flexible, as opposed to a top-down and rigid, power structure. This dynamism infused secular legal governance with a degree of unpredictability, as the involvement of new parties, including Indian members of the colonial judiciary, could call into question such core assumptions as the irrationality of Indian religious traditions. But by opening up continual opportunities for the legal system to refine and adapt to new pressures, the dynamic qualities of secular legal governance also contributed to its wily persistence.

### The Feuding Couple

Shumsoonnissa's case provides a powerful lens to study these wider dynamics because the divided logic of the Privy Council's decision mirrored the binary logic that defined secular legal governance more broadly. During the time that the Indian Law Commission was debating the merits of declaring a *lex loci* for British India, the couple was recently married: a second marriage for the widow Shumsoonnissa, who had two sons and three daughters; a second as well for Moonshee

Buzloor Ruheem, a *zamindar* with an existing wife.[2] In 1847, the same year that the couple married, Shumsoonnissa secured a considerable inheritance from her deceased father after ten years of litigation. After another protracted legal battle with her brother-in-law, "a large accession of fortune" arrived from her deceased sister in 1853.[3] The financial situation of the wealthy heiress contrasted sharply with that of her new husband. Referring euphemistically to a man who maintained the trappings of a wealthy household through mounting debt, Buzloor Ruheem was, in the words of the Privy Council, "like many landed proprietors, an embarrassed man."[4] Adding further stress to his fragile financial situation, Buzloor Ruheem divorced his first wife Luteefutoonnissa in 1850 – purportedly a condition of his marriage to Shumsoonnissa. Although he claimed that the divorce was by mutual consent, Luteefutoonnissa sued for compensation. In April 1854 the *zila* court, the lowest-level trial court, awarded Buzloor Ruheem's first wife Rs. 26,000, a decision that the Calcutta Sudder Diwani Adawlat, the provincial appellate court, and then the Privy Council upheld.[5]

When Buzloor Ruheem went on an extended trip to Singapore in late 1854 or early 1855, due to what he described as "a pain in my loins," Shumsoonnissa began to suspect that her husband was stealing her

[2] The case was the amalgamation of four separate cases on appeal from the lower courts. The first case, *Moonshee Buzloor Ruheem v. Shumsoonnissa Begum*, was for the restitution of conjugal rights. The second two cases, filed under the same name, involved the dispute over Shumsoonnissa's property. The fourth case, *Judoonath Bose v. Shumsoonnissa Begum*, involved land that had been sold to a third party. The records for all four cases can be found in the Privy Council Records, Printed Cases in Indian & Colonial Appeals Heard in 1867, vol. 2. When I consulted these records, they were housed in the Privy Council's offices on Downing Street. These offices have since moved, and the records are currently being transferred to the National Archives at Kew. Copies of portions of these records, which are cited elsewhere in the book, can also be found in the British Library, Social Sciences Collection and the Lincoln's Inn Library. The published decision can be found under *Moonshee Buzloor Ruheem v. Shumsoonnissa Begum; and Judoonath Bose v. Shumsoonnissa Begum*, in D. Sutherland, *Judgments of the Privy Council on Appeals from India* (Calcutta: Thacker, Spink, and Co., 1880), 3: 59–76. Citations from the judgment will be indicated with the abbreviation [JPC] and citations from the records will be cited [PCOR]. The three cases under the same name will be differentiated as [Restitution], [Property 1], and [Property 2].
[3] *Moonshee Buzloor Ruheem v. Shumsoonnissa Begum* [JPC], 61.
[4] Ibid., 64.
[5] The case involved the payment of *mahr*, a topic discussed in more depth later in the chapter. *Moonshee Buzul-ul-Raheem v. Luteefut-oon-nissa*, PCOR, Printed Cases in Indian & Colonial Appeals Heard in 1861, vol. 1; and *Moonshee Buzul-ul-Raheem v. Luteefut-oon-Nissa*, in Edmund F. Moore, *Reports of Cases Heard and Determined by the Judicial Committee, and The Lords of Her Majesty's Most Honourable Privy Council, on Appeal from the Supreme and Sudder Dewanny Courts in the East Indies*, 8: 379–99.

fortune.[6] She claimed that she had signed over to him government securities worth Rs. 234,800 so he could collect the interest payments on the securities on her behalf. She maintained that the exchange had been in name only, with her retaining actual ownership; he insisted that he had bought them from her. When Buzloor Ruheem returned, the couple quarreled. With the help of her son-in-law and the local magistrate, Shumsoonnissa fled in December 1855. In April of the following year she sued for recovery of her property; on the same day, her husband lodged a civil case against her for restitution of conjugal rights, a category of legal remedy in which the court ordered a spouse to resume cohabiting with his or her partner. The couple battled out their differences over a decade of legal wrangling.

The first legal officers to issue opinions in Shumsoonnissa's case were the Muslim law assistants who advised the colonial courts on interpreting Muslim law before the position was abolished in 1864. The declining influence of these figures is already apparent in Shumsoonnissa's case since the courts that heard the case largely ignored the Muslim law assistants' opinions. The opinions, however, provide insight into how questions of cohabitation were handled by personnel with Islamic legal training, which contrasted with the approach taken by the colonial judges, both Indian and British. The first law assistant advised that if a husband was abusing his wife, then "it is incumbent upon the Cazee to reprove, and compel, and order the husband to give the wife such a place of residence where there is security and safety for her, and to refrain him from committing tyranny."[7] On the grounds that the first *fatwa* was not sufficiently clear, the *zila* court consulted a second law assistant, who issued a conflicting opinion. He stated, "the Judge of the time being will make over his wife to the husband after an inhibition against his being tyrannical and oppressive."[8] All three of the courts that heard the case paid scant attention to the ways in which the Muslim law assistants, albeit to varying degrees, attempted to ensure the safety of the wife. In doing so they effectively obscured the provisions within Islamic legal traditions that, while upholding patriarchal authority, nonetheless attempted to prevent its abuse.

An Indian judge named Tarucknath Sein issued the decision in the local *zila* court. The judge acknowledged the general need to consult Muslim law in cases involving marital relations. Yet he concluded

---

[6] Record of Proceedings, *Moonshee Buzloor Ruheem* v. *Shumsoonnissa Begum* [Restitution, PCOR], 2.

[7] Ibid., 32.

[8] Ibid., 14.

that sending Shumsoonnissa back to her husband, which he believed was mandated by Muslim law, would endanger her life – an interpretation that overlooked the concern expressed for her safety in the law assistants' opinions. Based on his narrow reading of Muslim law, Sein argued that it should not be followed. In its place he invoked the idea of a broad sacred duty to preserve the life of every human being. Sein explained:

The wife is the object of husband's affection, so the husband ought to treat her always with kindness and affection ... That a mode of conduct otherwise than this is against the will of God, the Author of All, is not to be questioned, because God the Most High, has created women and made them subject to men on this condition, that men should endeavour to minister to the comfort and happiness of their respective wives and protect them. The Court should be particularly careful in rendering assistance to the husband who acts otherwise.[9]

Extending the universalizing logic of invoking a non-sectarian God, Sein also argued that the duty to preserve life was "above every other duty, and to perform it the Court is bound before the Father of the World by his order. Therefore that faith and that order can never be violated in any way."[10]

Sein's appeal to a universal conception of shared religious values is particularly striking when read against contemporary developments in colonial law. During the same period, the Indian Law Commission was moving in the opposite direction by limiting Indian religious laws to particular communities. While a universal Christian logic was still imaginable in mid-century Britain, colonial administrators increasingly cast Indian religions as fundamentally irrational. This logic was particularly important in eliminating the application of Muslim law to non-Muslims in criminal and commercial cases, on the grounds that it was only relevant to individuals who believed in its particular tenets. While Sein was also arguing to override Muslim law, he strikingly did not recommend a secular alternative in its place. He instead envisioned a universal religious ethic that could animate laws applied to different Indians, regardless of sectarian affiliation. Sein's decision, which was delivered at the lowest levels of the colonial judiciary, had little influence as a precedent. It nonetheless shows how in the everyday workings of the colonial judiciary, the gradual increase in the number of Indian judges introduced new perspectives into debates about secular legal governance, including a resistance to treating Indian religions as irrational.

[9] Ibid., 61.
[10] Ibid., 62.

These dimensions of Sein's opinions were quickly cast aside by the British judges who heard the case on appeal in the Calcutta High Court. They drew a strong distinction between rational justice and religious law, which they argued gave a Muslim wife no possible relief from the tyranny of her husband. Entirely bypassing the subtler dimensions of the Muslim law assistants' opinions, the court argued that, "under the Mahomedan law, no wife can separate herself from her husband under any circumstances whatsoever." The court therefore concluded that Muslim law was "repugnant to natural justice." Under these circumstances, the judges argued for suspending Muslim law on the grounds that, "The Mahomedan law giving no relief to the woman, be the conduct of the husband ever so bad; it is a case to be disposed of by equity, and good conscience."[11]

In the final appeal the Privy Council departed from the reasoning expressed by both lower courts, instead emphasizing the need to respect Indian religious traditions. Unlike Sein, who overrode Muslim law in the name of a "higher faith," and the Calcutta High Court, which did so by appealing to rational justice, the Privy Council insisted that because the case involved domestic relations, it had to be decided according to Muslim law. They declared: "nothing [is] more likely to give just alarm to the Mahomedan community than to learn by a judicial decision, that their law, the application of which has been thus secured to them, is to be overridden upon a question which so materially concerns their domestic relations."[12]

The Privy Council's overt appeal to the authority of religious law, however, masked the very marginal extent to which it actually engaged with Islamic legal texts and the liberality with which it introduced principles drawn from English jurisprudence. They did not refer to the Muslim law assistants' opinions. They briefly referenced the *Hidaya*, an Arabic legal treatise first translated in 1791, but noted that it merely stated that a disobedient wife or one that traveled without her husband's permission forfeited her right to maintenance. Instead the Privy Council insisted that the right to restitution of conjugal rights was "implied" in these texts as a necessary offshoot of the more general Oriental "principle of keeping a man's harem in seclusion and under his control."[13]

To actually flesh out this supposedly Muslim principle, however, the Privy Council interpreted the Muslim marriage contract in light of principles drawn from canon and English law. They acknowledged that not all of the rights and duties of marriage should or could be enforced by

[11] Ibid., 67.
[12] *Moonshee Buzloor Ruheem* v. *Shumsoonnissa Begum* [JPC], 74.
[13] Ibid., 72.

courts. Referencing canon law, the Privy Council noted, "The canonists lay down many things concerning the relative duties of man and wife which the Courts Christian, at least of our country, feel compelled to leave as duties of imperfect obligation." Their decision insisted, however, on the "broad duty of cohabitation." It quoted Lord Stowell's statement that the courts "are content to take the wife to the husband's door and to leave her there."[14]

If the Privy Council had consulted works on Islamic jurisprudence, they might have found support for the idea that a Muslim wife was obligated to make herself sexually available to her husband. Jurists generally also believed that a wife had a duty to live with her husband, in exchange for which her husband was obliged to maintain her, including providing food, clothing, and servants according to her status.[15] When a woman left her husband's home, her husband was no longer obligated to provide maintenance support. Muslim states, however, generally did not punish a wife for refusing to live with her husband.[16] In contrast, the Privy Council prescribed a larger role for the state in forcing a woman to perform her marital obligations. When the Privy Council heard *Moonshee Buzloor Ruheem* v. *Shumsoonnissa Begum*, the appropriate method of enforcing a court order for restitution of conjugal rights remained ill-defined. While noting that the language of some previous judgments had implied that the "wife was to be given bodily into her husband's hands," the Privy Council expressed doubts about whether under the new Code of Civil Procedure this would be a valid action. They indicated that suits of this nature were likely "enforceable only by imprisonment, or attachment of

---

[14] Ibid., 71.

[15] While the different schools of Islamic law generally agreed that a wife's right to maintenance depended on making herself sexually available to her husband, they differed on what constituted a failure to perform this duty. Hanafi texts, unlike most Maliki and Shafi'i interpretations, treated cohabitation as so critical to sexual availability that as long as a wife lived in her husband's home, even if she refused to have sex with him, she retained her right to maintenance. Kecia Ali, *Marriage and Slavery in Early Islam* (Cambridge: Harvard University Press, 2010), 75–83.

[16] Judith E. Tucker, *In the House of the Law: Gender and Islamic Law in Ottoman Syria and Palestine* (Berkeley: University of California Press, 1998), 63; Kenneth M. Cuno, "Disobedient Wives and Neglectful Husbands: Marital Relations and the First Phase of Family Law Reform in Egypt," in *Family, Gender, and Law in a Globalizing Middle East and South Asia*, ed. Kenneth M. Cuno and Manisha Desai (Syracuse: Syracuse University Press, 2009), 11. Unfortunately, similar accounts for pre-colonial India are much less developed. For the limited scholarship on marriage disputes in Mughal India, see Farhat Hasan, *State and Locality in Mughal India: Power Relations in Western India, c. 1572–1730* (Cambridge: Cambridge University Press, 2004), 71–90; Shireen Moosvi, "Travails of a Mercantile Community: Aspects of Social Life at the Port of Surat (Earlier Half of the 17th Century)," *Proceedings Indian History Congress* 52 (February 1991): 400–9.

property, or both."[17] Restitution of conjugal rights was therefore only nominally governed by religious law; in practice the Privy Council drew heavily on English legal precedents and colonial civil procedure to define and enforce these obligations. Once the Privy Council had set a precedent upholding the restitution of conjugal rights as mandated under Muslim law, however, it became enshrined in colonial law as a husband's sacred right.

In subsequent decades an Indian husband's right to sue for restitution of conjugal rights came to embody the colonial state's commitment to upholding Indian patriarchy, both Muslim and Hindu. In one of the most highly publicized trials in nineteenth-century India, Justice Pinhey of the Bombay High Court called this logic into question when, in 1885, he refused to order the Hindu woman Rukhmabai to cohabit with her husband. Pinhey argued that he found no foundation for restitution of conjugal rights in Hindu law. He instead argued that the provision was an antiquated import from English law, which Britain itself had recently nullified with the passage of the Matrimonial Causes Act of 1884, which abolished the use of penal sanctions in similar cases. The Indian press, however, cast the decision as an assault on the sanctity of Hindu marriage, and by extension on Hindu culture more generally.[18] The appellate court overturned Pinhey's decision in 1887, citing Shumsoonnissa's case as well as a case involving a Parsi couple as precedents.[19] The decision conveniently overlooked the ways in which the parallel enforcement of conjugal rights in Hindu, Parsi, and Muslim marriages revealed their colonial, as opposed to, religious origins. The case law concerning conjugal rights thus illustrated the ability of rhetorical appeals to religious personal laws to mask how a distinctly colonial imagining of Indian patriarchy operated as a hidden common denominator across supposedly distinct bodies of religious law.[20]

---

[17] *Moonshee Buzloor Ruheem* v. *Shumsoonnissa Begum* [JPC], 72. The procedures governing suits for restitution of conjugal rights were clarified with the passage of the Limitation Act (XV of 1877) and the revised Code of Civil Procedure (XIV of 1882). These included provisions for seizure of property and a six-month term in a civil jail for failure to resume cohabitation. In contrast, in Britain, the Matrimonial Causes Act of 1884 abolished imprisonment and seizure of property as punishments for women who refused to follow a court's order for restitution of conjugal rights. Dagmar Engels, "The Limits of Gender Ideology: Bengali Women, the Colonial State, and the Private Sphere, 1890–1930," *Women's Studies International Forum* 12, no. 4 (1989): 428.

[18] There is a considerable literature on the Rukhmabai case. See for example Sudhir Chandra, *Enslaved Daughters: Colonialism, Law and Women's Rights* (Delhi: Oxford University Press, 1998).

[19] *Dadaji Bhikaji* v. *Rukhmabai* [1886] ILR 10 Bombay 301.

[20] For other accounts emphasizing the underlying similarities between British interpretations of different bodies of religious personal law, see Mitra Sharafi, "The Marital Patchwork of Colonial South Asia: Forum Shopping from Britain to Baroda," *Law and*

Turning to the second half of the case, the Privy Council took a markedly different approach in the property suit by overtly overriding the
dictates of Muslim law. The decision overturned the contracts between
Shumsoonnissa and her husband, which had transferred her property over to him. Shumsoonnissa argued that the transfer of the property was merely a convenience, based on her and her husband's mutual
understanding that he would collect the interest payments on her behalf.
The Privy Council, however, ruled the transfer void on different grounds.
They argued that Shumsoonnissa was vulnerable to economic exploitation because of her gender and the fact that she observed *pardah*, a term
literally meaning covered but generically used in South Asia for a woman
of any religion who observed some form of seclusion. The Privy Council
argued that in their dealings with such women contracting parties bore
an extra burden of proving that the woman had knowingly and willingly
consented to the contract. The Privy Council did not feel that Buzloor
Ruheem had met this extra burden of proof and therefore ruled the
transfer of property to him void. This was Shumsoonnissa's desired
outcome: her property was returned to her. The reasoning behind the
decision, however, cast her as economically incapacitated – an evalu-
ation distinctly at odds with the considerable skill with which she, or her
agents, navigated the legal system.

In reaching its decision the Privy Council followed a growing body
of law that treated *pardah nashins* (women observing *pardah*) as inherently vulnerable to exploitation and therefore lacking the full capacity to
engage as independent, mature economic agents.[21] Expounding on this
logic, the Calcutta High Court ruled in 1867 that Hindu women who
observed *pardah* should be extended the economic protections normally
accorded to "the weak, ignorant, and infirm."[22] Since most of the early
cases involving *pardah nashins* concerned Hindu women, however, the
Privy Council faced the unsettled question of a Muslim woman's legal
capacity – a potentially more vexed question. They acknowledged that in

*History Review* 28, no. 4 (2010): 994; Rebecca Grapevine, "Family Matters: Citizenship
and Marriage in India, 1939–1972," (Ph.D. diss., University of Michigan, 2015).

[21] The Code of Civil Procedure (1882) defined *pardah nashins* as "women, who according
to the customs and manners of the country ought not to be compelled to appear in
public." Sir Dinshah Fardunji Mulla, *The Code of Civil Procedure: Being Act XIV of
1882, Incorporating Amending Enactments with Explanatory Notes and Amendments*,
2nd edn (Bombay: N.M. Tripathi, 1907), S. 404, S. 640. See also J.N. Mukerjee and
N.N. Mukerjee, *The Law Relating to Pardanashins in British India (Civil & Criminal)*
(Calcutta: R. Cambray, 1906), 1–11.

[22] William Rattigan, "The Parda Nashin Woman and Her Protection by British Courts of
Justice," *Journal of the Society of Comparative Legislation* 3, no. 2, New Series (January
1901): 259–60.

some areas "the Mahomedan law is more favourable than the Hindoo law to women and their rights, and does not insist so strongly on their necessary dependence upon, and subjection to, the stronger sex." In fact the Lords recognized that "in all that concerns her power over her property, the former is by law more independent than an Englishwoman of her husband."[23]

The Privy Council thus recognized that Muslim women retained property after marriage, but they nonetheless resisted the idea that Muslim women possessed rights that British women would only gain with the passage of the Married Women's Property Acts during the 1870s and 1880s.[24] To solve this dilemma, they therefore argued that whatever property rights Muslim women enjoyed in theory, in practice their actual capacity to manage this property was still inferior to that of a mature male. Explaining that "the Mussulman woman of rank, like the Hindoo, is shut up in the zenana," the Privy Council reasoned by extension that she must be prey to economic exploitation. The Privy Council therefore concluded, "it would be unsafe to draw from the letter of a law, which, with the religion on which it is chiefly founded, is spread over a large portion of the globe, any inference as to the capacity for business of a woman of a particular race or country."[25] The Privy Council concluded that they were justified in suspending the formal requirements of Muslim law with respect to the property transfer between Shumsoonnissa and Buzloor Ruheem to accommodate Indian women's cultural, as opposed to religious, disabilities. As a result, while in Islamic legal traditions seclusion was not associated with commercial or proprietary incapacity, the Privy Council re-imagined *pardah* as a state of economic vulnerability, to which both Muslim and Hindu women were subjected.

While the Privy Council cast its decision in the property suit as one that extended special legal protections to Indian women, in the long term the ruling tended to weaken, rather than strengthen, women's financial position. By instituting an assumption of undue influence and contractual incompetence, colonial courts undermined women's ability to buy, sell, or gift their property. Cornelia Sorabji, who was the first woman of any race to train in law at Oxford and to be admitted to the British bar, criticized the impact of such legal protections on women observing

[23] *Moonshee Buzloor Ruheem* v. *Shumsoonnissa Begum* [JPC], 62.
[24] Lee Holcombe, *Wives and Property: Reform of the Married Women's Property Law in Nineteenth-Century England* (Toronto: University of Toronto Press, 1983).
[25] *Moonshee Buzloor Ruheem* v. *Shumsoonnissa Begum* [JPC], 62. In a separate but related dispute, the Privy Council did uphold the contracts between Shumsoonnissa and a third party, Judoonath Bose.

*pardah.*[26] Highlighting the considerable difficulty that such women faced in securing their legal rights, she argued: "Indeed, the position of the woman is almost worse than it was before the law took her under its protection." Given the risk that a contract might be overturned on the grounds that a woman was not acting as a free agent, Sorabji noted, "the outside world is chary of dealing with *purdahnishins,* and insists on particularly good terms if it does so deal." The practical impact of this attitude was that "a *purdahnishin* estate seldom fetches its true price in the market."[27] Sorabji's observations show how colonial judges, in the name of protecting Indian women from their own patriarchal culture, furthered new forms of gender inequality that marginalized Indian women's position within financial markets.

Read together, the two halves of the Privy Council decision exemplify the legal acrobatics that the colonial courts used to buttress the unstable boundaries dividing domestic and economic transactions. Emerging out of the marital disputes of a single couple, the case brought to the fore the entanglements between domestic and economic concerns that made the binary logic of secular legal governance challenging to translate into practice. By dividing the case in two, however, the decision reasserted the domestic/economic binary and grafted it onto the diverging logic of upholding and suspending Muslim law.

The seeming tidiness of this approach, however, was undermined by the undercurrents of similarity that united the two parts of the decision, including the Orientalized vision of Indian patriarchy that undergirded both. Viewed from Shumsoonnissa's perspective, the divided decision must have seemed a perverse legal fiction that masked the united impact the two rulings had on her life. While the Privy Council offered her protection from her husband's financial thievery in the property suit, they threatened her with the prospect of returning to this same thief's home in the restitution suit. Even the Privy Council seemed to appreciate the precarity of this logic and ultimately remanded the case to the lower courts to decide whether Buzloor Ruheem posed a physical threat to her. Meanwhile the Privy Council recommended that the couple enlist the help of friends and family to reconcile outside of court.[28] At this point, however, the legal record dries up, providing no clues as to whether the feuding couple continued their struggles inside or outside the courts.

---

[26] Suparna Gooptu, *Cornelia Sorabji: India's Pioneer Woman Lawyer* (New Delhi: Oxford University Press, 2006).
[27] Cornelia Sorabji, "Safeguards for Purdahnishins," *Imperial and Asiatic Quarterly Review and Oriental and Colonial Record,* Third Series 15, no. 29–30 (April 1903): 75–6.
[28] *Moonshee Buzloor Ruheem v. Shumsoonnissa Begum* [JPC], 75.

The larger impact of the Privy Council's decision is easier to trace. Both halves of the decision contributed to a growing body of case law that subtly reshaped Indian patriarchy in ways that cast it as a more primitive version of the forms of gender inequality practiced in Britain. In the restitution suit the Privy Council transplanted to India the legal supports that helped buttress British husbands' domestic control over their wives. In the property suit the Privy Council enacted a legal presumption of women's inferior economic capacity. Both these conditions were much more clearly grounded in English law and practice than in precedents drawn from Muslim law, or close study of Indian custom. Both were also areas of the law that Britain itself actively reformed in the 1870s and 1880s to provide greater domestic and economic independence for British women – reforms that were not replicated in India. From the standpoint of understanding the impact of colonial law on Indian women, the two parts of the decision therefore largely complimented each other.

Despite this fundamental unity, however, the binary logic of secular legal governance proved remarkably powerful, reemerging in the way the judgment was treated in colonial legal reference works, which shaped future judges' and lawyers' understanding of the case law. The two halves of the decision were treated in separate literatures, with the restitution suit cited in textbooks on Muslim law and the property suit cited in separate texts on laws governing women who observed *pardah*, which were applied regardless of a woman's religious affiliation.[29] For example, *The Law Relating to Pardanashins in British India (Civil and Criminal)*, published by two Indian lawyers in 1906, referenced the property-suit portion of Shumsoonnissa's case over a dozen times without ever mentioning that the case also entailed a suit for restitution of conjugal rights.[30] By teasing apart the two halves of the case, the reference literature masked the cumulative impact that Shumsoonnissa's case had in strengthening male dominance and female subordination in both the domestic and economic spheres.

The complex plays of logic which characterize the judicial reasoning surrounding Shumsoonnissa's case – the unity of the couple, the division of the decision, its reunifying assumptions about Indian patriarchy,

---

[29] For examples of texts citing the restitution suit (but not the property suit), see Sir Dinshah Fardunji Mulla, *Principles of Mahomedan Law*, 2nd edn (Bombay: Thacker & Company, 1907), 119–20; Nawab A.F.M. Abdur Rahman, *Institutes of Mussalman Law: A Treatise on Personal Law According to the Hanafite School, with References to Original Arabic Sources and Decided Cases from 1795 to 1906* (Calcutta: Thacker, Spink & Company, 1907), 119.

[30] Mukerjee and Mukerjee, *The Law Relating to Pardanashins*, 2, 4, 5, 7, 19–20, 40, 44, 46–8, 60, 76, 78, 80, 91, 123, 126–7.

and its redividing in the legal literature – mirror the larger dynamics that animated secular legal governance. The instability of the domestic/economic divide continually resurfaced in legal practice, leading courts to struggle to define the jurisdictional boundaries that separated religious personal laws from secular bodies of civil and criminal law. Shumsoonnissa's case illustrates how such moments of instability spurred courts to rearticulate these boundaries, issuing legal opinions that cyclically repeated the formula that the Indian Law Commission set out in 1864. Inbuilt ambiguities and contradictions within the binary logics of secular legal governance therefore led the judiciary to repeatedly reassert, and more deeply entrench, these oppositions. The case thus provides a powerful example of what I referred to in the introduction as the "rubber-band" state, whose internal flexibility was a source of cumulative power. As the following discussion will explore, however, these same instabilities also left critical areas of the law unsettled. These unsettled areas made secular legal governance the subject of continual contestation and debate, working against its solidification into a rigid, unchanging body of law.

## *Mahr* and Conflicts in Colonial Case Law

The tendency of the unstable domestic/economic divide to create persistent areas of dispute can be seen in the ways that questions about unpaid *mahr* perplexed judges in subsequent cases involving Muslim marriages and restitution of conjugal rights. *Mahr* was an obligatory payment made by a Muslim husband to his wife, which was written into their marriage contract and generally partially paid at the time of marriage, with remaining funds to be paid in the event of divorce or widowhood. In Shumsoonnissa's case the issue of *mahr* came up in relation to the fees that the civil court charged in the restitution suit. In civil suits, courts assessed fees according to the value of the property being disputed. In this restitution suit, the "property" in dispute was the person of Shumsoonnissa. Undeterred, the court valued her person according to the *mahr* specified in their marriage contract. Shumsoonnissa's legal counsel protested this decision, insisting, "The disputed property of this suit is neither money borrowed nor landed property. It is a human being."[31] As counsel's comments vividly illustrate, when confronted with the financial components of marriage, colonial courts often felt

---

[31] Record of Proceedings, *Moonshee Buzloor Ruheem* v. *Shumsoonnissa Begum* [Restitution, PCOR], 11.

compelled to equate the person of the wife with a form of property – an analogy that troubled courts, but which they struggled to resolve.

These issues proved particularly vexing when courts were forced to rule on whether a husband's failure to pay his wife the portion of her *mahr* due at the time of marriage freed her from her conjugal responsibilities. Unpaid *mahr* was common in India, where Muslim families routinely specified a high sum in the marriage contract, an act taken as a sign of the couple's elite status, but tacitly agreed to accept a smaller sum in practice. This custom opened up opportunities for Muslim wives to use unpaid *mahr* as a defense against suits for restitution of conjugal rights instituted by their husbands. Several courts felt compelled to endorse this logic in the 1870s and early 1880s, even as judges expressed discomfort with its wider implications for gender relations. Thus, in one such case, a British judge declared, "It might be supposed reasonable that before a woman could put forward her claim to the dower at all she ought in the first place to put herself in the right position for asking it by doing her duty as a wife by her husband." Yet, typifying the colonial construction of Muslim law as essentially irrational, he concluded that, "this reasonable and natural state of things does not appear to find a place in Muhammadan law."[32]

In 1886 the Allahabad High Court attempted to halt this potentially troubling trend by arguing in a similar case, *Abdul Kadir* v. *Salima*, that the financial and conjugal dimensions of a couple's marriage contract operated independently from each other. The author of the decision, Syed Mahmood, was the first Indian Muslim to serve as a high-court justice, a position he gained after earning a BA at the University of Cambridge and completing his legal training at Lincoln's Inn in London.[33] (Syed Mahmood was also the son of the reformer and educationalist, Sayyid Ahmad Khan, mentioned in the previous chapter.) Syed Mahmood was part of a new generation of Muslim judges who, in the latter decades of the nineteenth century, blended knowledge of colonial law with Islamic scholarship. Unlike the Privy Council, whose pronouncements relied on vague statements about a husband's control over his *zenana*, Syed Mahmood grounded his analysis of restitution of conjugal rights in detailed references to Islamic legal texts. Complaining about the poor quality of the available English translations, he provided

[32] *Eidan* v. *Mazhar Husain* [1877] ILR 1 Allahabad 483, quoted at 486. See also *Sheikh Abdool Shukkoar* v. *Mussumat Raheem-oon-nissa and Mussumat Sagni Beebee* [1874] North-West Provinces High Court Report 6 94; *Wilayat Husain* v. *Allah Rakhi* [1880] ILR 2 Allahabad 83.

[33] Alan M. Guenther, "Syed Mahmood and the Transformation of Muslim Law in British India" (Ph.D., McGill University, 2005), 58.

his own translations of key passages and included the original Arabic in the footnotes.

Syed Mahmood noted that the relationship between payment of the *mahr* and a husband's conjugal rights was a point of contention among jurists from the Hanafi school, one of the four principal schools of Islamic jurisprudence and the one most commonly followed in the Indian subcontinent. Referring to the *Hidaya*, Mahmood explained that Abu Hanifa, the leading jurist of the Hanafi school, had said that a wife had a right to "deny herself to her husband until she receive the dower, and she may prevent him from taking her away [for purposes of travel]." Abu Hanifa's disciples, Abu Yusuf and Imam Muhammad, however, specified that the wife did not have this right after the consummation of the marriage, even if the *mahr* was unpaid.[34] Attempting to find a solution to the dispute between the founding jurists, Syed Mahmood argued, "I take it as a general rule of interpreting that law, that whenever there is a difference of opinion, the opinion of the two will prevail against the opinion of the third."[35]

While situating the case firmly within the domain of religious personal law, Syed Mahmood ultimately turned to an analogy with commercial law and the Indian Contract Act to clinch his argument. He concluded that treating the failure to pay *mahr* as freeing a woman from the obligation to live with her husband distorted the Muslim marriage contract. He insisted: "the right of dower does not precede the right of cohabitation which the contract of marriage necessarily involves, but that the two rights come into existence simultaneously and by reason of the same incident of law."[36] To clarify his point, he compared the relationship between *mahr* and conjugal rights to a seller's lien on goods while the sale price remained unpaid. On this basis Syed Mahmood concluded that, under the Indian Contract Act of 1872, a "lien essentially presumes the right of ownership in the vendee, and terminates as soon as delivery has taken place."[37] Likewise, after the consummation of a marriage, a woman could not withhold herself from her husband on the basis of the unpaid *mahr*. Erroneously linking conjugal rights to payment of the *mahr* could, in Mahmood's opinion, cast a shadow of illegitimacy across all relations between husband and wife before the payment of the dower. Raising the threat of bastard children, Mahmood insisted that this false logic

---

[34] *Abdul Kadir v. Salima and Another* [1886] ILR 8 Allahabad 142, 159. The discussion referred only to the portion of the *mahr* paid by the husband to his wife at the time of their marriage.

[35] Ibid., 166.

[36] Ibid., 164.

[37] Ibid., 166.

risked implying that "the issue of such cohabitation would be illegitimate."[38] Thus Syed Mahmood, like the Privy Council, insisted that conjugal rights should be governed according to Muslim law. At the same time, he relied heavily on colonial precedents and legislation to determine how the marriage contract should be enforced.

In subsequent years courts in different regions of India followed Mahmood's decision in similar cases, but the relationship between *mahr* and conjugal rights remained an area of legal dispute. A few years after Mahmood authored his decision, a lower-level court in Rai Bareilly issued a conflicting judgment in the case *Musammat Rasulan and Zahooran v. Mirza Naim-Ullah Beg*. The presiding judge, Moulvi Samee-Ullah Khan Bahadur, privately published his decision as a short pamphlet with English and Urdu text and lengthy Arabic translations. Objecting to Syed Mahmood's description of Muslim marriage as a civil contract, Samee-Ullah Khan insisted that "marriage is a religious rite, although it is in its form a secular transaction."[39] He took particular issue with Mahmood's definition of *mahr* "as a token of respect for its object (the woman)." He argued that this definition was based on a mistranslation of the word *mahal* in the relevant passage from the *Hidaya*. Rejecting the esteemed judge's more abstract rendering of the phrase, Samee-Ullah insisted, "the word '*mahal*' does not stand for a woman but refers to her private parts."[40] He therefore argued that a husband should only be able to sue for restitution of conjugal rights after he had paid his wife her *mahr*.

Samee-Ullah's pamphlet lay at the cross section of growing bodies of both state-sponsored and independent publications on colonial law, in which various groups contested the correct interpretation of Islamic legal principles. The pamphlet's bilingual format demonstrated how the rapidly expanding Indian public sphere blurred the boundaries between legal adjudication inside and outside the courts. Although not an official publication, his pamphlet resembled the law reports that the colonial government began to publish for all of the high courts after 1875. As an Urdu text, however, it also contributed to a growing vernacular literature on Islamic law that, unlike Arabic, Persian, or English works, was accessible to a wider Indian reading public. As a lower-court judge, Moulvi Samee-Ullah Khan's decision did not set an official precedent.

---

[38] Ibid., 171.
[39] Moulvi Samee-Ullah Khan Bahadur, *Judgment Containing an Exposition of the Muhammadan Matrimonial Law* (Allahabad: Indian Press, 1891), 35.
[40] Ibid., 18.

Yet in subsequent years colonial courts favorably cited his pamphlet as a dissenting opinion to Syed Mahmood's decision.[41]

Two important colonial textbooks on Muslim law, Syed Ameer Ali's *Mahommedan Law* (1892) and Roland K. Wilson's *A Digest of Anglo-Muhammadan Law* (1895) also referenced the pamphlet, ensuring the wide circulation of Samee-Ullah's argument. Syed Ameer Ali, also a high-court justice, criticized Mahmood's analogy between unpaid *mahr* and a lien on sold goods. He rejected Mahmood's argument that, in cases of disagreements between Abu Hanifa and his disciples, the opinion of the majority should be followed. Ameer Ali castigated the Allahabad bench for furthering "a general rule of interpretation, for which there seems to be no authority whatever."[42] Wilson, in his *Digest of Anglo-Muhammadan Law*, also criticized the analogy to commercial law. He objected that "a Muhammadan marriage is not a contract for the delivery of the woman like a bale of goods to the husband as absolute owner." Instead, he argued, if the *mahr* was at all comparable to a sale, it was more analogous to a delivery by installments because it was a contract "for *repeated* acts of submission to the sexual desires of the husband." Wilson therefore argued, "the delivery of one installment would *not* extinguish the vendor's lien in respect of the remainder."[43]

During the second and third decades of the twentieth century, opposition to Mahmood's logic mounted. The Judicial Commissioner of Oudh, head of the highest court of appeal for that province, issued a rebuttal of Mahmood's logic in a case decided in 1912. Based on an alternative reading of the Arabic passages from the *Hidaya* which Mahmood cited, the Oudh court allowed non-payment of *mahr* to be used as a defense against a suit for restitution of conjugal rights.[44] In 1933 Mahmood's own bench, the Allahabad High Court, also revisited the issue. The chief justice, Sir Shah Sulaiman, acknowledged the considerable criticism that had been lodged against Mahmood's opinion. Yet Sulaiman was wary of directly challenging Mahmood's precedent, emphasizing the importance of "the well-recognised principle of stare decisis." He, however, found a way to circumvent the precedent by arguing that the court could make

---

[41] See for example *Anis Begam* v. *Malik Muhammad Istafa Wali Khan* [1933] AIR Allahabad 634, 638.

[42] Syed Ameer Ali, *Mahommedan Law, Compiled from Authorities in the Original Arabic*, 2nd edn (Calcutta: Thacker, Spink, 1892), 499.

[43] Roland Knyvet Wilson, *A Digest of Anglo-Muhammadan Law: Setting Forth in the Form of a Code, with Full References to Modern and Ancient Authorities, the Special Rules Now Applicable to Muhammadans as Such by the Civil Courts of British India* (London: W. Thacker, 1895), 45.

[44] *Wajid Ali Khan* v. *Sakhawat Ali Khan* [1912] Oudh Cases 15 127.

a decree for restitution of conjugal rights contingent on the husband first paying any *mahr* due to his wife.[45] With this legal sleight of hand, Sulaiman demonstrated how the courts, while outwardly favoring stability, found backdoor routes for introducing legal change – powering an important evolution in the interpretation of religious laws.

The persistent debates surrounding cases involving *mahr* and restitution of conjugal rights show how currents of change flowed beneath the rhetoric of stasis that the courts often embraced when discussing Muslim law. These dynamics of contestation and change often centered on legal issues that fell on the unsteady fault line dividing domestic, personal laws from economic, civil laws, as courts struggled to navigate ambiguous analogies and competing sources of law. As growing numbers of Indian members of the colonial judiciary joined these debates, they injected new perspectives and forms of expertise, unsettling precedents that had been set by British judges. Together these dynamics ensured that religious personal law, far from becoming an ossified body of unchanging doctrines, remained the subject of ongoing debate. As the following section shows, in the late nineteenth and early twentieth centuries these debates often circulated beyond the courts, bringing state-sponsored legal forums into conversation with non-state spaces of legal adjudication.

### *Fatwas* on Marriage: Debates beyond the Colonial Courts

When the Privy Council suggested to Shumsoonnissa and Buzloor Ruheem that they should settle their difficulties outside court, or when Samee-Ullah privately published his judicial decision, colonial courts hinted at the wider worlds in which legal disputes unfolded. The following section turns to these wider worlds to trace how interactions between state courts and non-state forums of legal adjudication interfaced with each other, often in ways that infused further ambiguity into contested areas of Muslim law. This discussion draws inspiration from ethnographic research on contemporary India which has provided rich accounts of how legal disputes move between state-sponsored courts; organized non-state forums, including village councils and religious courts; and informal networks for dispute resolution, such as extended families. Rather than operating as hermetically sealed arenas, these different sites and structures of authority overlap and interpenetrate

---

[45] *Anis Begam* v. *Malik Muhammad Istafa Wali Khan*, 638–9. In Pakistan the courts overruled Syed Mahmood's decision in *Rahim Jan* v. *Muhammad* [1955] PLD 2 Lahore 122.

each other. Litigants sometimes use the threat of a court case to harass an opposing party into reaching a settlement outside of court, which might ultimately be mediated through village elders or family members. Parties might also address different dimensions of the same dispute through multiple channels: for example, a couple might seek a ruling from a religious court to acquire moral sanction for their divorce, while simultaneously pursuing a case in the state courts to settle the financial dimensions of their separation.[46]

Unfortunately for the historian, informal forms of dispute resolution are difficult to trace in written historical records. Unlike the anthropologist who can interview his or her subjects, historians must often be satisfied with the hints of these alternative processes that lurk at the margins of state-produced judicial documents. Some non-state legal institutions, however, began keeping regularized records during the colonial period that provide important insight into legal developments beyond the colonial courts. One of the most important of these was the new *madrasa* or school at Deoband, which was established in 1866.[47] In addition to their educational functions, the scholars at Deoband encouraged Muslims to seek their help in settling disputes outside of the colonial courts. To streamline the process of offering legal guidance, Deoband opened a new *dar-ul-ifta*, or *fatwa*-issuing department, in 1893.[48]

In issuing its own *fatwas*, Deoband continued a practice with deep roots in Islamic traditions of learning. As early as the tenth century CE, Islamic institutions issued *fatwa*-writing manuals and manuscript compilations. Historically *fatwa* literature was extremely wide-ranging, addressing questions of law, ethics, and philosophy. The genre, however, was united by its use of the question-answer format.[49] A *fatwa*, unlike a court ruling issued by a *qazi*, was also non-binding, and therefore often translated into English as an "opinion." The queries that served as the

---

[46] This account of contemporary legal pluralism draws on the ethnographic work of a number of scholars, including Perveez Mody, "Love and the Law: Love-Marriage in Delhi," *Modern Asian Studies* 36, no. 1 (2002): 223–56; Gopika Solanki, *Adjudication in Religious Family Laws: Cultural Accommodation, Legal Pluralism, and Gender Equality in India* (Cambridge: Cambridge University Press, 2011); Katherine Lemons, "At the Margins of Law: Adjudicating Muslim Families in Contemporary Delhi" (Ph.D., University of California, 2010).

[47] Barbara Metcalf, who has written the seminal study of Deoband, lists the founding date as 1867, but Deoband's own website describes the first foundation stone for the school as being laid in 1866. Metcalf, *Islamic Revival*, 88. "A Brief Introduction," accessed May 3, 2017, www.darululoom-deoband.com/english/.

[48] Metcalf, *Islamic Revival*, 146–7.

[49] On the significance of the question-answer format, see Muhammad Khalid Masud, "The Significance of Istiftā' in the Fatwā Discourse," *Islamic Studies* 48, no. 3 (Autumn 2009): 341–66.

starting point for most *fatwas* could come from a variety of different sources. A *qazi* might ask a *mufti* for a *fatwa* for guidance on an unknown point of law, a practice mirrored to some degree in the advisory function that Muslim law officers played in colonial courts until 1864. Individual litigants might also approach a *mufti* for a *fatwa*, which they could use to support their case in court, or, if the *fatwa* was not to their liking, they might serially approach different *muftis* looking for a more favorable interpretation. An individual could also seek out a *fatwa* for ethical advice on matters such as ritual observance, which might not relate to a matter cognizable in court. Finally *muftis*, even without being approached with an outside query, could independently author *fatwas* to provide interpretations of disputed matters, legal or otherwise, which they thought required further elaboration.[50]

While drawing on this tradition, the new *dar-ul-ifta* at Deoband was also shaped by the shifting contexts of colonial rule. This balance between continuity and change is apparent in the fourteen-volume *fatwa* collection that Deoband published out of the early records of its *dar-ul-ifta*. The *fatwas* were credited to the *dar-ul-ifta*'s first head, Aziz-ul-Rahman Usmani, who ran the department from its founding until his death in 1928. The scale of operations at the *dar-ul-ifta* was staggering; Deoband estimated that under Usmani's leadership the *dar-ul-ifta* issued over 100,000 *fatwas*, although only a small fraction of these are reproduced in the collection itself. This scale of production reflected the geographical spread of Deoband's influence, which spanned the entire subcontinent and was facilitated by its active use of the colonial postal service to communicate with its followers.

Deoband's influence also reflected its embrace of new forms of bureaucracy. In her work on Deoband, Barbara Metcalf has emphasized how the *madrasa* relied on new organizational forms that mirrored British institutions, including the creation of a separate campus independent from an established mosque, the professionalization of its staff, the fixing of curricula, and the administration of yearly examinations.[51] Similar dynamics animated the *dar-ul-ifta*. The creation of a separate department, with an appointed head, was an innovation that Deoband embraced to deal with an ever-mounting number of queries. The *dar-ul-ifta* also instituted more systematic record-keeping in 1911, and the

---

[50] For an overview of the history of the *fatwa* genre, see the introduction to the volume Muhammad Khalid Masud, Brinkley Messick, and David S. Powers, eds., *Islamic Legal Interpretation: Muftis and Their Fatwas* (Cambridge: Harvard University Press, 1996), 3–32.

[51] Metcalf, *Islamic Revival*, 93.

first *fatwas* in the published collection date to this period.[52] These trends
culminated in the publication, after independence, of the *Fatawa Dar-
ul-Ulum Deoband* (The Fatwas of the College at Deoband), in volumes
organized by topic.[53] With their detailed tables of contents, the volumes
presented the output of the *dar-ul-ifta* as a streamlined and accessible source for determining Deoband's official position on a range of
disputed legal questions – making it a viable alternative to compilations
of colonial case law and textbooks on Muslim law written by British and
British-trained Indian lawyers and judges. Unlike compilations of colonial cases, however, the *fatwa* collection did not include dates for individual opinions, endowing them with a sense of timeless authority.

In addition to the increasing scale and bureaucratization of the *fatwa*-
writing process, the contents of the volume reflected the close association of religion with domestic and ritual matters – a colonial innovation
to which the *ulama* largely, but not entirely, acquiesced. Thus, in the
fourteen-volume *fatwa* collection, volumes one to six deal with ritual
matters; volumes seven to eleven deal with marriage, divorce, and parentage; volume twelve deals with questions of faith (*iman*); volume thir-
teen addresses partnerships and religious endowments; and volume
fourteen addresses ritual spaces and includes shorter sections on business
transactions, interest, gambling, and insurance.[54] The predominance of
ritual and domestic matters among the published *fatwas* suggested that
the *ulama* began to see these areas as their core sphere of influence. They
nonetheless had to compete with the colonial courts for jurisdiction
when adjudicating disputes involving marriage, divorce, and inheritance.

While the *ulama* presented their own legal services as an alternative
to the colonial courts, in practice Indian Muslims often engaged both

---

[52] Usmani, *Fatawa*, 1: 49.
[53] Usmani's published *fatwa* collection was compiled from the records of the *dar-ul-ifta*
at Deoband, and the first twelve volumes were published between 1962 and 1972.
Muhammad Qasim Zaman reports that, since 2009, Deoband has begun reissuing additional volumes of Usmani's *fatwas*. *Modern Islamic Thought in a Radical Age: Religious
Authority and Internal Criticism* (Cambridge: Cambridge University Press, 2012),
179. For references to other important collections of colonial-era *fatwas*, see Barbara
D. Metcalf, "Two Fatwas on Hajj in British India," in *Islamic Legal Interpretation: Muftis
and Their Fatwas*, ed. Muhammad Khalid Masud, Brinkley Morris Messick, and David
Stephan Powers (Cambridge: Harvard University Press, 1996), 191.
[54] Because the publication of Usmani's *fatwas* has been curated, and Deoband continues to
issue new volumes, it is difficult to ascertain the precise relationship between his output
and the topical distribution of the collection. Other collections of *fatwas* from the early
twentieth century, however, show a similar focus on questions related to ritual and the
family. Muhammad Khalid Masud, "Apostasy and Judicial Separation in British India,"
in *Islamic Legal Interpretation: Muftis and Their Fatwas*, ed. Muhammad Khalid Masud,
Brinkley Morris Messick, and David Stephan Powers (Cambridge: Harvard University
Press, 1996), 198; Metcalf, *Islamic Revival*, 147–8.

simultaneously. References to proceedings in courts regularly appear within the published *fatwas*. For example a *fatwa*, which the *dar-ul-ifta* received from a Muslim scholar, mentioned court proceedings in the context of questions related to *iddat*, the period a Muslim woman must wait after divorce (or the death of her husband) before contracting a new marriage. Unlike most of the *fatwas* in the Deoband collection, the published query included a litany of precise dates, which were necessary for determining whether the marriage had occurred during or after the *iddat*, but which also signaled the more temporally fixed proceedings of the colonial courts:

Question 525: A woman testified in court on November 16, 1916, that her husband was impotent, her father-in-law was sleeping with her, and she had become pregnant. This woman's husband in another case on July 30, 1917, testified in a second court that after his wife's statement in court on November 16, 1916, he had declared her *haram* [forbidden] to him. Subsequently on April 15, 1917, he also gave a written divorce. And according to the wife, during the time of her pregnancy, he also swore in front of three or four men that she was *haram* to him. Taking this all into consideration, I married this woman to another man on April 16, 1917, at her and her father's request. Under these circumstances, when did the divorce of this woman go into effect and did this marriage occur within the period of *iddat* or not?

Answer: If the husband's intention in making the statement on November 16, 1916, declaring that his wife was *haram* to him was to divorce her, then the divorce was effective from that date. *Iddat* also commenced from that date. And because the woman was pregnant at the time, her *iddat* was complete after she gave birth. Occurring after the birth, the second marriage on April 16, 1917, was *sahih* [correct]. And if the intention of the husband in making the statement above was not divorce, then the divorce went into effect on the date of the written divorce on April 15, 1917. In that case, the second marriage occurred within the *iddat* period and was *batil* [null and void].[55]

In the *fatwa* the references to proceedings in courts were mentioned as a way of dating various aspects of the marriage and divorce. Otherwise the proceedings in the secular courts were treated as irrelevant, and the nature and outcome of the court case itself was left unspecified. By excluding this information, the *fatwa* asserted a moral monopoly over deciding the legitimacy of a Muslim marriage. In other *fatwas* Usmani made the point even more explicit by emphasizing that a divorce decree issued by a state court was not necessarily morally valid if it was issued under circumstances that the *ulama* did not view as sanctioned under the *sharia*. Thus when the *dar-ul-ifta* received a query about whether a woman could remarry after receiving a divorce from the courts but

---

[55] Usmani, *Fatawa*, 9: 282–3.

without the consent of her husband, Usmani emphatically replied that she could not. In doing so he made it clear that the practical jurisdiction that secular courts exercised over Muslim marriage and divorce did not endow their decisions with moral sanction, which the *ulama* alone could provide.[56]

The potential for divergences between *fatwas* and the rulings of the colonial courts is particularly apparent in the opinions that Usmani issued on women's right to live separately from their husbands. Unlike Syed Mahmood, when Usmani received a request for a *fatwa* concerning a woman whose husband failed to pay her *mahr*, he did not hesitate to draw a direct link between the husband's unfulfilled financial duties and his wife's conjugal obligations. He declared that the financially delinquent husband sacrificed his right to sexual intercourse with his wife.[57] In response to a similar query, Usmani advised that, as long as her *mahr* remained unpaid, a woman was allowed to leave her husband's home and stay with her parents without being considered a *nashiza*, or disobedient wife.[58]

In other *fatwas* Usmani also advised women that they could refuse to live with their husbands in response to a range of different forms of abuse, whether involving physical or sexual mistreatment.[59] Thus even as colonial courts were more rigorously enforcing a husband's conjugal rights over his wife, the *ulama* were urging women to withhold themselves physically and sexually as a strategy for dealing with errant or abusive husbands. The *ulama*'s greater willingness to check the power of abusive husbands reflected Muslim scholars' different investment in upholding Muslim men's authority over their wives. Colonial commentators often cast Indian men's power over their female dependents as inherently excessive, as part of a larger framework in which the low status of Indian women was taken as evidence of India's less advanced civilizational status in comparison to Britain. The *ulama*, however, were more concerned with portraying Muslim patriarchy as essentially benevolent. They therefore attempted to check abuses of patriarchal dominance. Doing so allowed the *ulama* to defend Islamic marriage, when practiced correctly, as a just mode of balancing of men and women's different social roles.

These divergences reflected larger divisions between how the *ulama* treated the ethical compulsions of marriage and the mechanisms available through the colonial courts for enforcing marital rights and duties.

[56] Ibid., 7: 373.
[57] Ibid., 8: 179.
[58] Ibid., 8: 190.
[59] Ibid., 10: 156, 163.

Islamic jurists have traditionally viewed law and ethics as overlapping but distinct fields, with certain forms of ethical behavior recommended by jurists, who nonetheless recognize that their decisions cannot, and should not, be legally enforced.[60] This gap, however, widened in colonial India, as many Muslims engaged with the courts for pragmatic reasons, since they alone could enforce decrees. They did not necessarily mean that they viewed the courts' interpretations of Muslim law as religiously sanctioned. The influence of the *ulama*, in contrast, rested entirely on their moral authority, since they were largely cut off from state-sanctioned mechanisms of enforcement.

The problems opened up by this widening gap between ethics and law is clear in a query that the *dar-ul-ifta* received from a father who was desperately trying to save his daughter from an abusive marriage. The daughter had run away to her parents' home, and her husband had gone as far as calling her his mother, a transgression of familial relations so severe that it called their marriage into question. The case came before the courts, which asked the family to provide a *fatwa* to support their position. (Interestingly, the existence of this *fatwa* provides evidence that the courts sometimes unofficially consulted Muslim scholars even after the abolition of the office of the *qazi* in 1864.[61]) In response, Usmani issued the following *fatwa*:

Question 80: I married my daughter to a man who has caused her great trouble. She has been continually tolerating these troubles for twelve years. Becoming unnerved, she came to my house, and one time told me that her husband had said to her that you are like a mother to me, and I am your eldest son. Now it has come before the courts. The court has asked for a *fatwa* according to the *sharia*; otherwise it will have to force the woman to return to her husband. Therefore please give us an order according to the *sharia*, so that we can present the *fatwa* in court, and the girl might be released from this torment.

Answer: Calling (one's wife) mother does not produce a divorce. However, when a husband and wife are not in agreement, and the husband is causing his wife all sorts of trouble, the wife should not be sent back to him. Rather the husband should be compelled to give his wife a divorce or to maintain her and deliver all of her *huquq-i-zaujiyyat* [marital rights].[62]

Usmani's *fatwa* was emphatic that the woman had a right to remain at her father's house, but he left the question of divorce ambiguous, implying that the family should pressure the husband to agree to a divorce. For

---

[60] Baber Johansen, *Contingency in a Sacred Law: Legal and Ethical Norms in the Muslim Fiqh* (Leiden: Brill, 1999), 69–70.
[61] For additional examples of the courts asking *ulama* for *fatwas*, see Masud, "Apostasy and Judicial Separation in British India," 197.
[62] Usmani, *Fatawa*, 9: 64.

Usmani, the husband had an ethical duty to either treat his wife better or release her, but he felt unable to endorse a divorce, without the husband's consent, as legal.

The ambiguity in the *fatwa* was the result of the limited conditions under which the Hanafi school of Islamic jurisprudence, which Usmani followed, allowed for a divorce without the consent of the husband – conditions which became even more difficult in colonial India. While a Muslim husband could unilaterally pronounce a divorce by *talaq*, his wife's ability to initiate divorce was more limited. Unless she could convince her husband to agree, or her marriage contract specified conditions under which she had a right to divorce, a Muslim wife had few options. In extreme circumstances, Muslim jurists allowed for divorce by judicial decree, known as *faskh* or *tafriq*, which eliminated the need for a husband to consent.[63] Hanafi jurists traditionally only granted women a divorce by *tafriq* when their husbands were impotent. In contrast, jurists from other schools of Islamic jurisprudence gave this right to women in a broader range of circumstances, including a husband's failure to provide financial maintenance, insanity, leprosy, or extended absence.[64] Even when Hanafi jurists did allow women to initiate a divorce, they required that an official *qazi* issue the *tafriq*.

After the abolition of state-appointed Muslim law officers in 1864, many *ulama*, including Usmani, were troubled by how this condition could be met.[65] They refused to see members of the secular judiciary, the vast majority of whom were not Muslim, as possessing the required religious authority, but they also hesitated to assume this mantle themselves without the backing of the state. For the *ulama*, the extraordinary act of pronouncing a *tafriq* required the dual backing of religious authority and political sovereignty – a uniquely challenging condition under the conditions of secular legal governance.

While undated, Usmani's diverging position in different *fatwas* related to *tafriq* suggested that his views evolved over time, as he looked for ways to adapt to the particular challenges posed by colonial rule. Departing from the more limited conditions under which the Hanafi school

---

[63] Asaf Ali Asghar Fyzee, *Outlines of Muhammadan Law*, ed. Tahir Mahmood, 5th edn (New Delhi: Oxford University Press, 2008), 119–32.

[64] For a more detailed discussion of different schools' approach to *faskh*, see Fareeha Khan, "Traditionalist Approaches to Shari'ah Reform: Mawlana Ashraf 'Ali Thanawi's Fatwa on Women's Right to Divorce" (Ph.D., University of Michigan, 2008), 90–132.

[65] Usmani, *Fatawa*, 10: 142. On the abolition of the office of the *qazi*, see Yaduvansh, "The Decline of the Role of the Qadis," 155–71. Although subsequent provincial acts and the all-India Kazi Act of 1880 partially restored the office of the *qazi*, their official role was largely restricted to registering marriages. Additional research is needed into the more informal role such officials played in dispute resolution.

permitted *tafriq*, Usmani borrowed from other schools of Islamic jurisprudence to justify *fatwas* that allowed women to secure a divorce in cases
of a husband's extended absence. In doing so, he noted that his approach
of borrowing from other schools, also known as *talfiq*, was not novel, and
that esteemed Hanafi jurists had deployed a similar strategy to expand
the range of *tafriq* in the past.[66] More challenging for Usmani, however,
was how to solve the problem of the absence of a state-appointed *qazi*.
In some *fatwas*, he portrayed this absence as an absolute impediment to
securing a *tafriq*, even in a case of impotence, the one condition under
which the Hanafi school itself recognized this right.[67] In other *fatwas*,
however, he found a work-around by looking to other schools of law. For
example, in another *fatwa* Usmani was approached about the case of a
woman whose husband had been missing for eight years and who had
remarried without an official *tafriq*. When members of the *ulama* came
to know about the marriage, they separated the couple out of fear they
were committing adultery (*zina*) because the woman's prior marriage
had not been properly dissolved. Clearly concerned that this was an
untenable solution, the *ulama* asked whether an *alim* [scholar] could
take the place of the *qazi* and sanction the woman's divorce and remarriage. In response Usmani noted that the Maliki school of law allowed a
woman after her husband had been missing for a minimum of four years
to remarry without requiring an official *tafriq*, although obtaining one
was still recommended. In the absence of a *qazi*, Usmani suggested that
under the circumstances a pious (*dindar*) member of the Muslim community could sanction the divorce and remarriage.[68]

Usmani's efforts to find alternatives to the requirement for a state-
appointed *qazi* echoed broader innovations in how the Indian *ulama*
attempted to bridge the divide between law and ethics in the 1920s and
1930s. In 1921 the scholar Abul Mahasin Muhammad Sajjad founded
a community-based political organization in Bihar, called the Imarat-i-
Sharia, which built up a system of *dar-ul-qaza*, or Islamic courts, that
operated outside the official colonial legal system.[69] The movement

---

[66] Usmani, *Fatawa*, 10: 172–81. Rashid Ahmad Gangohi, one of the founders of Deoband,
issued a similar *fatwa*, explaining that under circumstances of necessity Hanafi jurists
were permitted to adopt rulings from another school. Rashid Ahmad Gangohi,
*Fatawa-yi-Rashidiyah (Kamil)* (Karachi: Muhammad Ali Karkhanah-yi-Islami Kutub,
1987), 471–4. On the practice of adopting opinions from different schools, see J.N.D.
Anderson, "Modern Trends in Islam Legal Reform and Modernisation in the Middle
East," *International and Comparative Law Quarterly* 20 (1971): 13–14.
[67] Usmani, *Fatawa*, 10: 143.
[68] Ibid., 10: 181–2.
[69] Papiya Ghosh, "Muttahidah Qaumiyat in Awalliat Bihar: The Imarat i Shariah, 1921–
1947," *Indian Economic and Social History Review* 34, no. 1 (1997): 1–20.

reflected the *ulama*'s involvement with Gandhian Non-Cooperation, which boycotted state institutions, and the Khilafat Movement, which sought to protect the Ottoman sultan as a figure of global Islamic authority when the European powers threatened to dismantle his empire after World War I. Drawing on these broader ideological trends, the Imarat-i-Sharia's network of *qazis* promoted self-reliance and forged new forms of Muslim sovereignty outside of the state. Embracing this trend, Usmani issued *fatwas* upholding divorce decrees issued by the Imarat-i-Sharia and other community courts.[70]

While some *ulama* focused on non-state institutions, other *ulama* lobbied to reform the ways in which colonial courts handled Muslim divorce cases. This push for reform followed a series of sensational cases in which colonial courts granted divorces to Muslim women who renounced Islam on the grounds that apostasy automatically dissolved a Muslim marriage. The prospect of Muslim women being forced to convert because it was the only legal means of divorce open to them brought long-standing tensions between the legal regulation of Muslim marriage and its ethical status to a breaking point. Spurred by this crisis, one of Usmani's colleagues at Deoband, Ashraf Ali Thanawi, published an influential *fatwa* in 1933 that argued in favor of expanding Muslim women's legal access to divorce.[71] Thanawi's *fatwa* ultimately provided key sanction for legislative change, culminating in the Dissolution of Muslim Marriage Act of 1939. The act empowered colonial courts to grant Muslim women divorces in a range of circumstances, including abandonment and abuse.[72] By making a direct legislative change to Muslim personal law, the act broke with prior patterns of secular legal governance, which had generally avoided direct legislative interventions in religious laws.[73] The act was thus part of a larger dynamic unfolding between the 1920s and 1940s that called into question colonial patterns

---

[70] Usmani, *Fatawa*, 8: 113, 116.

[71] Khan, "Traditionalist Approaches to Shari'ah Reform"; Masud, "Apostasy and Judicial Separation in British India."

[72] Rohit De, "Mumtaz Bibi's Broken Heart: The Many Lives of the Dissolution of Muslim Marriages Act, 1939," *Indian Economic and Social History Review* 46, no. 1 (2009): 105–30.

[73] Other legislative reforms of Muslim personal law include the Wakf Validating Act of 1913 and the Muslim Personal Law (Shariat) Act of 1937, discussed in more depth in Chapter 6. For a general overview of these legal reforms, see Gail Minault, "Women, Legal Reform, and Muslim Identity," *Comparative Studies of South Asia, Africa and the Middle East* 17, no. 2 (September 1997): 1–10. On the Wakf Validating Act, see Kozlowski, *Muslim Endowments*, 179–90. A law passed in 1891 that raised the age of consent to twelve represents an important exception to the general absence of legislative interventions in family law during the second half of the nineteenth century.

of secular legal governance – challenges that will be discussed in more depth in the latter chapters of the book.

## Conclusion

Tracing legal debates on marriage shows how colonial law's normative commitment to stasis and fixity was often belied by its fluidity and dynamism in everyday practice. Unfortunately, scholarship on colonial law has often mistaken colonial norms for actual practice.[74]

In contrast, this chapter shows how, throughout the late nineteenth and early twentieth centuries, interpretations of religious personal law continued to be contested inside and outside of colonial courts. These ongoing contests were linked to core features of colonial law. Most importantly, the inherent instability of the boundary between domestic and economic concerns meant that the administration of religious personal laws was continually animated by jurisdictional struggles between competing sources of law, including codes of civil procedure and contract.

Other features of colonial law tended to exacerbate the potential for diverging interpretations. The existence of regionally independent high-court benches for different areas of India allowed for different precedents to develop in key areas of religious personal law, as occurred when the Oudh bench declared unpaid *mahr* a defense against restitution of conjugal rights. The pan-Indian circulation of legal texts, from compilations of colonial case law to such Urdu publications as Samee-Ullah's pamphlet, ensured that these different interpretations circulated across different regions. The legal landscape of colonial India was thus simultaneously regionally diverse and also increasingly interconnected, providing ample material for debate. Meanwhile the high cost in time and money of using the state courts opened up opportunities for non-state legal forums, such as the *dar-ul-ifta* and Imarat-i-Sharia, to compete with state courts. Together these elements ensured that interpretations of religious personal laws remained far more diverse and contested than previous scholarship has suggested.

This interpretive diversity and the fluidity of interactions between state and non-state legal actors, however, should not be taken as evidence of the weakness of colonial law or the limits of its impact. As Shumsoonnissa's case and the subsequent case law on *mahr* and conjugal rights suggests, contested areas of laws pushed courts to come up with

---

[74] For an account emphasizing the rigidity of colonial law, see Kugle, "Framed, Blamed and Renamed," 257–313. For a broader discussion of these themes in the existing scholarship, see the Introduction.

creative new ways of reasserting the link between domesticity and religious law. While competition between colonial courts and non-state legal actors, such as the *ulama* at Deoband, led to diverging interpretations on particular issues, their more general presentation of Muslim law often converged. Both increasingly emphasized the particular importance of religious laws in adjudicating domestic matters, although they disagreed about who should preside over these deliberations. Both also often cultivated an image of Muslim law as more unified and stable than it actually was in practice. The courts supported this sense of stasis by emphasizing their respect for past precedents, even when, as in the case law governing *mahr* and restitution of conjugal rights, they actually introduced important legal innovations. Similarly, the *ulama* created the impression of immutability with regards to Islamic legal doctrines through practices such as omitting dates from published collections of *fatwas*, giving them a sense of timeless authority. As we shall see in the next chapter, secular legal governance accentuated this internal tension between the normative projection of Muslim law as unified and static and the practical accommodation of diversity and change through its recognition of customary law.

# 3    Taming Custom

The British recognized custom as a source of law from at least the beginning of the nineteenth century. But in the wake of the Rebellion of 1857, which many colonial administrators credited to inadequate accommodations to Indian cultural differences, the British further incorporated customary law into the legal system. During the 1860s, at the same time that it attempted to solidify the domestic parameters of religious personal law, the Indian Law Commission also expanded opportunities for accommodating custom. The presence of Henry Maine, perhaps the most influential legal historicist in Britain, on the Commission from 1862 to 1869 contributed significantly to this trend. In the latter decades of the nineteenth century and in the early twentieth century, colonial judges and administrators routinely cited Maine's *Ancient Law* (1861) and *Village Communities in the East and West* (1871) to selectively privilege customary practices over orthodox Hindu and Muslim law.[1]

This chapter looks at how concessions to custom complicated the application of religious personal law in domestic cases. The expanding role of custom provides a powerful example of how secular legal governance produced, and strategically marshalled, internal sources of ambiguity and contestation. Concessions to custom destabilized the binary logic of secular legal governance in several important ways. Religious personal laws organized Indians into discrete, supposedly internally homogenous communal groups, in particular assuming a stable divide between India's two largest religious groups, Hindus and Muslims. In contrast, as colonial ethnographies and courts documented an increasingly diverse range

---

[1] Clive Dewey and Alan Diamond, "The Influence of Sir Henry Maine on Agrarian Policy in India," in *The Victorian Achievement of Sir Henry Maine: A Centennial Reappraisal* (Cambridge: Cambridge University Press, 1991). Despite his emphasis on cultural difference, Maine actually supported codification in India because he believed that many indigenous social structures had already been irrevocably altered. Karuna Mantena, *Alibis of Empire: Henry Maine and the Ends of Liberal Imperialism* (Princeton: Princeton University Press, 2010), 89–118.

of customary practices among both Hindus and Muslims, the idea of homogenous religious communities came under increasing pressure. Even more troubling to the communal logics of religious personal law, legal texts and judicial decision also recognized the existence of customs which were practiced by both Muslims and Hindus in certain regions, suggesting that geography was at least as important as religion in determining cultural practices.

Customary law also cut across the domestic/economic logic of secular legal governance. In addition to modifying the administration of religious personal laws, concessions to custom were also incorporated into legislation regulating tenants' rights, the sale of agricultural land, and peasant debt.[2] At a theoretical level, customary law thus muddled core divisions, whether between communities or between domestic and economic transactions, that structured secular legal governance. At a practical level, incorporating custom alongside religious personal laws led to constant legal wrangling, as shown by the relatively high rates of litigation in regions of India in which courts made greater accommodations to custom.[3]

So why did the British further complicate the already daunting task of administering different bodies of religious personal laws by adding custom to the mix? Ideologically, the incorporation of custom reflected the ascent of ideas of cultural difference in the late nineteenth century.[4] But just as important, although often less acknowledged by colonial officials themselves, the selective incorporation of custom favored patriarchal control over labor and property. Of course, colonial law did not invent patriarchy; both religious laws and regional customs contained their own male biases. But each also had features that endowed women with limited economic powers. By sometimes favoring religious personal laws and in other cases favoring custom, while liberally reinterpreting both, colonial officials thus constructed a more robustly patriarchal legal regime than would have been possible by drawing on a single source of law. Most critically for Muslim women, the Quran mandated that they receive one half of the share of their male relatives in the division of

[2] Peter Robb, *Ancient Rights and Future Comfort: Bihar, the Bengal Tenancy Act of 1885, and British Rule in India* (Richmond, Surrey: Curzon Press, 1997).
[3] The rate of court cases to population was one to ninety persons in the Punjab, compared to one to 320 in Bengal, one to 390 in Awadh, and one to 403 in the Northwest Provinces. While there are other potential explanations for the higher rate of litigation in the Punjab, including its relative wealth, Ayesha Jalal argues that the province's greater concessions to customary law was the driving factor behind its litigiousness. *Self and Sovereignty: Individual and Community in South Asian Islam since 1850* (New York: Routledge, 2000), 147.
[4] Andrew Sartori, *Bengal in Global Concept History: Culturalism in the Age of Capital* (Chicago: University of Chicago Press, 2008).

the estates of deceased family members, providing women with, at least in theory, a degree of independent property. However, in key agrarian regions, and especially British India's breadbasket, the Punjab, courts voided these Quranic rights on the grounds that customary practices in the region did not recognize female heirs. On the flipside, in some professional groups, particularly among courtesans and female entertainers, customary practice favored female over male heirs. In these cases, however, colonial courts often disqualified customs on the grounds that they were "immoral," and instead divided estates according to religious personal laws.

To make sense of the British approach to custom, we therefore need to analyze it in the wider context of the critical role that family-based agrarian production played in the colonial economy in the latter decades of the nineteenth century. As Indian farmers came under increasing pressure to produce for global commodity markets, with their attendant cycles of profit and loss, they responded to greater economic volatility by increasing the unpaid labor output of women and children.[5] Thus in some regions of British India, women who had once worked for wages – including at tasks for which they were considered particularly well suited, such as rice husking – were forced instead to labor on family farms.[6] Colonial law provided the tailwind behind these shifting patterns of labor deployment. It decreased women's economic independence by giving men greater control over familial property and by restricting women's sexual relations and labor recruitment.

The incorporation of custom, which at first might seem to undermine the coherence of secular legal governance, thus in fact endowed it with critical strategic flexibility – furthering the ability of Britain to extract maximum profit from Indian production.

## Gendering Customary Law: Disinheriting Daughters

A central paradox animated colonial officials' approach to administering customary law in India. They justified incorporating custom into law as a concession to cultural difference. The way they implemented customary law, however, overwhelmingly favored the formation of male-headed households that conformed to Victorian gender norms, meaning

---

[5] Sugata Bose, *Peasant Labour and Colonial Capital: Rural Bengal since 1770* (Cambridge: Cambridge University Press, 1993), 66–111.

[6] Mukul Mukherjee, "Impact of Modernisation on Women's Occupations: A Case Study of the Rice-Husking Industry of Bengal," in *Women in Colonial India: Essays on Survival, Work, and the State*, ed. J. Krishnamurty (Delhi: Oxford University Press, 1989).

that concessions to customs actually homogenized rather than diversified family structures. The roots of this paradox lay in the fact that legal historicists operated from a developmental model that ordered societies along a scale of human progress. While these legal theorists recognized and indeed emphasized differences between societies, they simultaneously assumed that certain core features of human nature were common across different societies. Gender played an essential role in these assumptions. Adherents to the developmental model largely assumed that male economic agency and female subordination were trans-cultural features of human nature. Drawing on these universalizing assumptions, British officials favored patriarchal interpretations of customary law, particularly in the economically crucial region of the Punjab, where colonial courts overwhelmingly excluded women from inheriting familial property.[7]

While scholars like Henry Maine are better known for their arguments about human difference, universalizing undercurrents profoundly shaped historicist thinking. For example, in a lecture that Maine delivered to the graduating class at the University of Calcutta in 1865, he explained, "if indeed history be true, it must teach that which every other science teaches, continuous sequence, inflexible order, and external law."[8] Maine applied these assumptions about sequence and order to his understanding of cultural differences, which he viewed as hierarchal stages in a unified process of human development. Indian customs were of profound interest to Maine precisely because he assumed that they provided a living archive of practices that Europe itself had cast aside in its transition from primitive to modern social forms.[9]

This Eurocentric developmental model of human difference was crucial in shaping Maine's writings on custom and family. In *Ancient Law*, Maine linked the development of Indo-European law to the evolution of the patriarchal family. While Utilitarians such as Bentham had taken the individual as the fundamental building block of human society, Maine

---

[7] David Gilmartin, "Customary Law and Shariat in British Punjab," in *Shariat and Ambiguity in South Asian Islam*, ed. Katherine P. Ewing (Berkeley: University of California Press, 1988), 43–62.

[8] Henry Sumner Maine, "Address to the University of Calcutta," in *Village-Communities in the East and West: Six Lectures Delivered at Oxford, to Which Are Added Other Lectures, Addresses, and Essays*, 3rd edn (London: J. Murray, 1876), 266.

[9] John W. Burrow, "Henry Maine and mid-Victorian Ideas of Progress"; Raymond Cocks, "Maine, Progress and Theory"; and Krishna Kumar, "Maine and the Theory of Progress," in *The Victorian Achievement of Sir Henry Maine: A Centennial Reappraisal*, ed. Alan Diamond (Cambridge: Cambridge University Press, 1991), 53–87. For a longer chronology of the relationship between concepts of culture and civilization, see Andrew Sartori, "The Resonance of 'Culture': Framing a Problem in Global Concept-History," *Comparative Studies in Society and History* 47, no. 4 (October 2005): 676–99.

argued that individuals were only gradually freed from the bonds of kinship groups, a process he described as the movement from status-based to contract-based relations. Maine's model of the family centered on the "despotic pater-familias," who in primitive societies was "absolutely supreme in his household" and whose "dominion extends to life and death, and is as unqualified over his children and their houses as over his slaves."[10] To demonstrate the critical role that the male-headed household played in social development, Maine argued that Indo-European societies generally favored paternal over maternal relations during the transfer of inherited property between generations. Maine's emphasis on patriarchy provided a backdoor route for introducing Victorian norms into models of cultural difference. His primitive family echoed Victorian domestic ideals in which male breadwinners supported, and publically represented, their dependents.[11] Maine believed that the power of the patriarchal family waned as advancing societies emphasized contractual over kinship relations. Yet for some Victorian conservatives, the unchallenged authority of Maine's "despotic pater-familias" held romantic appeal.

Reflecting Maine's popularity among colonial officials in India, works on custom in Punjab reproduced his core assumptions about male dominance over kinship and communal structures. In a massive three-volume work, *Punjab Customary Law*, C.L. Tupper, who served both in the local Punjab administration and in the Government of India, invoked the idealized concept of female subordination that undergirded colonial legal research on custom. In the introduction to the second volume, he replied to a hypothetical question about what standard practice would be in a Punjabi village, undisturbed by outside influence or Muslim law. Tupper explained:

Women would be under a perpetual tutelage, under the guardianship either of their husbands, or, failing these, of the nearest agnates [ancestors through the male line] by blood or marriage. The marriage of women would be universal, for a deeply implanted distrust of female chastity, not improbably in part the

---

[10] Maine, *Village-Communities in the East and West*, 107; Henry Sumner Maine, *Ancient Law: Its Connection with the Early History of Society, and Its Relation to Modern Ideas*, 3rd edn (New York: Henry Holt and Company, 1875), 119. Several prominent contemporary scholars challenged Maine's account of the patriarchal origins of the family, arguing instead for the matriarchal origins of kinship relations. Elizabeth Fee, "The Sexual Politics of Victorian Social Anthropology," *Feminist Studies* 1, no. 3/4 (January 1973): 23–39; Ann Taylor Allen, "Feminism, Social Science, and the Meanings of Modernity: The Debate on the Origin of the Family in Europe and the United States, 1860–1914," *The American Historical Review* 104, no. 4 (October 1999): 1085–113.

[11] Adam Kuper, *The Reinvention of Primitive Society: Transformations of a Myth*, 2nd edn (London: Routledge, 2005).

consequence of that seclusion or subordination of women which facilitated the certainty of male parentage, would forbid celibacy to adult females. By marriage, sisters and daughters would be provided for in another clan; there would be no need to give them part of the village patrimony; and indeed, to do so would be to bring into the community an outsider.[12]

When colonial officials turned from theorizing about custom to documenting actual practice, they reproduced the same homogenizing assumptions as Tupper's hypothetical account. After the passage of the Punjab Laws Act of 1872, which officially privileged customary law in the region, colonial officials fanned out to villages across the Punjab, armed with detailed questionnaires on local customs.[13] These surveys were often biased in favor of finding the paternalistic patterns that officers were primed to expect. For example, an officer was sent out to the Bannu District to determine the "extent of the *Patria Potestas*," or power of the father, in the area. He asked the villagers whether a father was required to pass on his property to his male issue. The officer reported, "The Banuchis at first unanimously declared that he could give away all to whomsoever he chose, such being the Shara [*sharia*] rule." The officer, however, was incredulous about the truth of this statement, which implied that members of the tribe had complete freedom to bequeath their property to whomever they wanted (and possibly even to female relatives). The officer therefore asked for examples of such bequests, which his informants did not provide, leading him to conclude that familial property in fact did inevitably pass to male issue. The officer, with a surprising degree of candor, admitted that "the people were over and over again driven to admit that their first replies were erroneous." He added: "Here and there I shaped public opinion on most questions in the direction which I myself and others of long experiences thought equitable."[14] Thus ethnographic research into custom often produced results that were influenced more by officers' own assumptions about tribal societies, which privileged Victorian notions of patriarchy, than by the often more ambiguous statements they gathered from their informants.

The patriarchal bias of British constructions of customary law remained constant despite significant evolutions in the method of administering customary law between the middle of the nineteenth and middle of the twentieth century in the Punjab. While colonial administrators

---

[12] C.L. Tupper, *Punjab Customary Law*, vol. 2: *Statements of Customary Law in Different Districts* (Calcutta: Superintendent, Government Printing, 1881), 71.
[13] David Gilmartin, *Blood and Water: The Indus River Basin in Modern History* (Berkeley: University of California Press, 2015), 77.
[14] Charles Arthur Roe, *Tribal Law in the Punjab: So Far as It Relates to Right in Ancestral Land* (Lahore: Civil and Military Gazette Press, 1895), 16–17.

produced reams of correspondence debating the relative importance of village versus tribal collectives and the harmful versus beneficial effects of moneylending, their gendered understanding of "traditional" society went largely unchanged.[15] In fact, the assumption that women were excluded from inheriting in rural areas only intensified over the course of the nineteenth century, with officials increasingly finding reasons to disregard exceptions and regional variations.[16]

Male ownership over landed property thus emerged as a key feature of the agrarian economy of the Punjab under British colonial administration. The gendering of the Punjab economy should be read against the wider context of the area's colonial development as a key source of cheap agrarian outputs and military labor. Over the course of the nineteenth century, the Punjab emerged as one of India's most agriculturally productive, and heavily commercialized, regions.[17] Punjab's integration into global markets created greater volatility for farmers. The transition from producing for self-consumption to growing cash crops exposed them to greater seasonal fluctuations in income and the boom-bust cycles of the global economy. Some of the most prosperous regions of the Punjab were therefore often the most heavily indebted, as commercialization yielded both profits and economic shocks. For many peasants, the looming threat of losing one's land to the moneylender became a constant spur to greater productivity.

Despite these dramatic shifts in the agrarian economy, peasant families, rather than wage labor, continued to dominate the workforce, whether as small-scale peasant proprietors or sharecroppers. Peasant families responded to the new economic pressures of commercial production by increasing their own labor input, which often involved upping the hours worked by women and children.[18] Many families also developed alternative income streams by sending male members out to work for wages – a

---

[15] For a detailed account of various debates concerning custom in the Punjab, see Matthew J. Nelson, *In the Shadow of Shari'ah: Islam, Islamic Law, and Democracy in Pakistan* (New York: Columbia University Press, 2011), 15–111.

[16] Ibid., 31–2. On the courts' more general shift away from recognizing new customs in areas where colonial texts or precedents already existed, see Chandra Mallampalli, "Escaping the Grip of Personal Law in Colonial India: Proving Custom, Negotiating Hindu-Ness," *Law and History Review* 28, no. 4 (2010): 1043–65.

[17] For a more in-depth discussion of transformations in the agrarian economy of the Punjab, see Richard Gabriel Fox, *Lions of the Punjab: Culture in the Making* (Berkeley: University of California Press, 1985), 14–78.

[18] The pattern of intensifying labor in response to the commercialization of agriculture, often referred to as involution, was present, in different forms, across much of Asia in the nineteenth century. Clifford Geertz, *Agricultural Involution: The Process of Ecological Change in Indonesia* (Berkeley: University of California Press, 1963); Sugata Bose, *Peasant Labour*, 97–111.

strategy particularly prevalent in the Punjab, where many men joined the Indian Army or traveled abroad as migrant laborers.[19] In this context, families' ability to control women's labor became all the more important, as women were often left behind to tend the family farm.[20] While this may not have been their intent, British colonial administrators' preference for subjecting women to patriarchal patterns of inheritance, which effectively excluded them from independent sources of income and wealth, contributed to gendered patterns of land-ownership by subordinating women to male-headed household units.

Even more than it enabled the male extraction of female labor, strengthening the legal basis of the patriarchal property regime served the colonial administration's ideological commitment to "traditional" society as a bulwark against the destabilizing impacts of economic transformation. From the constant pressure to pay off the moneylender, to men's prolonged absences and exposure to traumatic military experiences, the Punjab's relative prosperity came at considerable costs. As the Punjab became ever more critical to the economy and security of India and the British Empire more generally, colonial officials were anxious to ameliorate these impacts.

Steeped in a wider ideological context that equated traditional society with patriarchy, colonial administrators constructed a regime of customary inheritance that flattened diverse practices into a far more homogenous pattern of male privilege. Cast as a concession to "tradition," strengthening male control over agrarian property in fact aided Britain's larger goal of transforming Punjab into a breadbasket, and garrison, for global empire.

### Delegitimizing Non-normative Families: Culling "Immoral" Customs

If selectively overriding Muslim personal law in favor of customary law facilitated the formation of a patriarchal property regime in the Punjab, the reverse process, in which officials overrode custom in favor of personal law, could also marginalize women's economic rights. Over the course of the latter decades of the nineteenth century, a growing body of

---

[19] By 1914 over three-fifths of the Indian Army came from the Punjab, although the province only represented one-tenth of British India's overall population. Ian Talbot, "The Punjab under Colonialism: Order and Transformation in British India," *Journal of Punjab Studies* 14, no. 1 (2011): 4.

[20] On the relationship between male migrant labor and women and children's agricultural labor, see Gail Omvedt, "Migration in Colonial India: The Articulation of Feudalism and Capitalism by the Colonial State," *Journal of Peasant Studies* 7, no. 2 (1980): 185–212.

case law delegitimized customs that supported alternative, female-headed family units. The Chief Court of the Punjab was faced with deciding one such case in 1883 when the court pondered who should inherit the house of Mussammat Mehrban. The plaintiff, Mussammat Dowla, claimed that Mehrban was her *nauchi*, a Punjabi term for a dancing girl. Her legal counsel argued that this bond "resembles that between a mother and her adopted daughter."[21] On this basis Mussammat Dowla claimed the right to inherit Mehrban's property according to the customs of women of her class, among whom property remained within a prostitute's adopted family. In contrast, a man claiming to be the dead woman's husband argued that he should inherit her property under Muslim law. The wide-ranging provisions for recognizing custom as a source of law in the Punjab seemingly favored Mussammat Dowla. Yet the court ultimately sided with Mehrban's husband on the grounds that customs that bound together families of prostitutes were immoral.

Mussammat Dowla's case provides a potent example of how colonial courts circumscribed the acceptable range of customs by enforcing universalizing norms of gendered morality. The dispute was one of a number of important cases in which female performers, courtesans, and temple dancers asked courts to recognize customary familial and property relationships within their adopted households.[22] While courts occasionally recognized such customs, in Mussammat Dowla's case, the judges recoiled from "sanctioning a custom which enables a whore-mistress, the very *fons et origo mali*, to ask the Courts to aid her in obtaining one class of the profits of her infamous trade."[23] When women attempted to pit custom against religion or visa versa, colonial law introduced its own patriarchal bias, favoring male-dominated structures of ownership on the grounds that they were moral, natural, or rational.

In a particularly striking portion of the decision, Judge Powell acknowledged, "we recognize, especially in the Punjab, a great deal of customary law, that is to say, we adopt unwritten rules regarding inheritance, succession, alienation of property and so forth, because they have attained a prescriptive observance uniformly among large natural classes of the population, such as Jats, Rajputs, Pathans, Biluchis and the like." Powell further elaborated, "On the analogy of the same principle, we recognize customs of trade obtaining among large classes engaged in

---

[21] *Murad Baksh* v. *Mussammat Dowla* [1884] Punjab Record 19 249, quoted at 252.
[22] Kunal M. Parker, "'A Corporation of Superior Prostitutes' Anglo-Indian Legal Conceptions of Temple Dancing Girls, 1800–1914," *Modern Asian Studies* 32, no. 3 (July 1998): 559–633.
[23] *Murad Baksh* v. *Mussammat Dowla*, 261.

different forms of commerce." Powell insisted, however, that such customs had to be rooted in forms of association that were natural, innocent, and rational. As he clarified:

But in all cases in which we recognize the custom, the aggregation of the body
among which that custom prevails, and the circumstances and relations of the
members of that body which the custom acknowledges and regulates, are themselves perfectly lawful and right, because they are either the result of tribal and
national distinctions, the work of nature in fact, or else are the consequences of
an association more or less artificial (at least in its early origin), but for purely
innocent and rational purposes.

In contrast, he argued that Mussammat Dowla asked the court to recognize "an association, the inception and end of which are alike immoral
and often involve actual crime." Powell invoked what he clearly felt were
self-evident, trans-cultural, standards of morality, reason, and nature
to condemn the familial bonds Mussammat Dowla sought to defend.
Evoking the concern of the colonial state with productivity – whether
sexual or economic – he announced that the relation she claimed with
her *nauchi* was of "a debased character and *out of which no legal right can
grow*."[24]

In 1893 the Privy Council upheld the practice of refusing to recognize
so-called immoral custom among Muslim prostitutes in the case *Ghasiti
v. Umrao Jan*. The case involved a complex web of dependence and
entitlement in a family in which aunts were also mothers and business
managers were also husbands. In her will, Mussammat Bando left her
sizable estate to her "darling" adopted daughter Ghasiti, while also specifying amounts from the estate that should be used to maintain a boy
she had raised, her household manager, and her aunt.[25] After Bando's
death, her brothers and sisters by birth, as well as her aunt, sued for control of her estate. In contrast, another of Bando's sisters, who claimed
to be Ghasiti's mother by birth, defended Ghasiti's right to the estate.
Describing how she had given Ghasiti to her sister Bando to be trained
in singing and dancing, Bando's sister argued that Ghasiti now had an
exclusive claim to Bando's estate based on the customs of the Kanchans
caste of prostitutes. Bando's sister also explained that the boy named

---

[24] Ibid., 253–4.
[25] For the published decision see *Ghasiti v. Umrao Jan; Ghasiti v. Jaggu* [1893] ILR 21
Calcutta 149. I consulted the unpublished proceeding for this case in the British
Library's copy of the Privy Council's Official Records [PCOR], which are held in the
Social Sciences Reading Room. In these records the case is referred to as *Mussummat
Ghasiti, Minor, per Guardianship of Mussummat Nanni Jan, and Mussummat Nanni
Jan v. Mussummat Amir Jan and Mussummat Ilahi Jan and Jaggu and Sannu* [UKPC
42, 1893]. The will is printed in PCOR, Record of Proceedings, 43–4.

in Bando's will was the son of Bando's adopted sister. The household manager had apparently shared *dosti* (friendship) with Bando's mother and later married her. Bando's sister insisted that this adopted family, not Bando's blood relations, were entitled to her estate according to the custom of prostitutes of her caste.[26]

While the colonial courts painstakingly weeded through detailed testimony about Bando's household, they ultimately disregarded the claims of her adopted family on the grounds that its very existence furthered an immoral custom. The district judge who initially decided the case portrayed "family brothels" as an inversion of Victorian conceptions of male economic agency and women's domestic dependence. He described the division of labor within these families as one in which the women worked as prostitutes while the men led "a life of ease and idleness." These peculiar gender relations were mirrored in the management of family property. As the judge explained, "All the members of the family in the family brothel succeed jointly. The management and control, however, of the members of the brothel goe by succession or election to the eldest daughter or sister of the deceased woman, as the case may be." The judge therefore concluded that control over the joint family estate vested in the women of the family, while the men were only "entitled to food and raiment from the joint family business." Yet, for the judge, these practices were of no judicial relevance because the court could not uphold "immoral" customs. He asserted: "All these rules or customs of the Kanchans aim at the continuance of prostitution as a family business ... They have a distinctly immoral tendency, and as such cannot be enforced in our Courts."[27] After two appeals, the Privy Council upheld the decision of the district court.

As disputes over prostitutes' estates demonstrate, colonial courts' selective incorporation of custom supported a particular, and divided, conception of the family and economy. Complaining about men who lived off the sexual labor of their female relatives, courts in cases such as *Ghasiti* v. *Umrao Jan* enforced normative definitions of both female sexuality and male economic agency. Their attempts to regulate prostitution through inheritance law marked the boundaries of not just sexual, but also economic, morality. In addition to rejecting prostitutes' inheritance claims, the courts enforced special provisions of the Indian Contract Act that outlawed contracts that furthered so-called immoral purposes. By refusing to enforce lease, sale, or labor agreements made with prostitutes, the courts significantly limited prostitutes' ability to engage

---

[26] PC Record of Proceedings, 46–9.
[27] Ibid., 103–4.

in market transactions.[28] Colonial economy, while supposedly founded on principles of free exchange, nonetheless depended on excluding certain products, and people, from the market.[29] Prostitutes thus occupied a liminal space in colonial law. When faced with their troubling presence, judges repeatedly appealed to supposedly universal standards of morality to exclude them from both the economy and the family, while never outlawing prostitution outright.

### Securing Women's Labor: Demonizing Lower-Class Marriage Customs

Prostitutes were not the only women whose claims to customary rights were rejected on the grounds that they were immoral. Colonial case law governing immoral customs also disallowed marriage practices, such as bride price, that seemed to "marketize" sexual relations by turning women into objects of exchange. Courts also ruled against customs that allowed women to have multiple partners or to easily leave their husbands, on the grounds that they made marriage into a transactional exchange in which women could upgrade male partners when the right opportunity came their way.[30] Courts, colonial ethnographers, and Indian social reformers converged in their attacks on these customs, arguing that they reflected the inferior moral standards prevalent among the lower classes, both Hindu and Muslim.[31] United in their disapproval, the courts and middle-class social reformers worked in tandem to impose normative models of marriage, which they often equated with the supposedly more enduring and "sacramental" forms of marriage common among high-caste Hindus. The courts also drew on a third branch of law, penal sanctions, to enforce conjugal monogamy among lower-class women. As the following section explores, a central paradox animated the courts' multi-pronged attempt to regulate lower-class marriages. While courts joined with middle-class reformers in decrying the economization of marriage among the lower classes, they in effect provided men with new legal tools to control their wives' labor.

---

[28] See Section 23.9 of the Indian Contract Act. M.C. Dutt, *Dutt on Contract: The Indian Contract Act, 1872*, ed. Salil K. Roy Chowdhury and H.K. Saharay, 8th edn (Calcutta: Eastern Law House, 1994), 235–7.

[29] Johan Mathew, *Margins of the Market: Trafficking and Capitalism across the Arabian Sea* (Oakland: University of California Press, 2016).

[30] For further examples, see "Illegal and Immoral Customs," in Sripati Roy, *Customs and Customary Law in British India* (Calcutta: Hare Press, 1911), 556–69.

[31] Sturman, *The Government of Social Life*, 158–72.

As in the field of inheritance, colonial officials' interest in custom fueled a wave of research on regional marriage practices. The findings complicated earlier colonial texts which had treated Hindus and Muslims as separate and opposing groups governed by distinct bodies of textual, religious law. Instead ethnographers began uncovering local customs which were shaped by shared regional norms that cut across Hindus and Muslims. For example, early ethnographers in Bengal noted that both Hindus and Muslims used the term *nikah*, which technically referred to a Muslim marriage contract, to describe less socially prestigious marriages with lower-class women, widows, or second wives.[32] *Qanoon-E-Islam, or The Customs of The Moosulmans of India* (1832), a text compiled as a collaboration between a Muslim physician Jaffur Shurreef and an East India Company army surgeon Gerhard Andreas Herklots, referenced this idiosyncratic use of the term *nikah*. The text explained, "*Neekah* and *Shadee* are often used synonymously; though in Bengal the former is only applied to a secondary kind of marriage, called half marriage. By the ignorant, it is esteemed unlawful and disreputable, equivalent to keeping a mistress. Whereas, in reality, it is the foundation of matrimony."[33]

Such ethnographic accounts of the diversity of Hindu and Muslim custom, and their entanglement with each other in some areas, fueled greater legal recognition of customary practices. In the realm of marriage, however, both colonial officials and Indian writers delegitimized alternative customs by marking them as departures from an increasingly idealized upper-caste, Hindu norm. For example, an official account of the customs of the people of the Bhundara district in the Central Provinces, published in 1867, equally condemned marriage among lower castes and Muslims:

Nowhere is the marriage tie less considered, than among the lower castes here; more especially among the women, who often divorce themselves from their husbands, and select, of their own will, several mates in succession, without any opposition from their lawful lords. All, except the higher classes of Hindoos, – such as Brahmins and Purdesees, – also adopt a ceremony call Pat, in lieu of a formal marriage, for joining a man and woman who agree to live together. This, however, can only take place after the death of the first husband or wife, and is

---

[32] In contrast the term *shadi*, which technically referred to marriage celebrations, was used to denote a more prestigious marriage. Chatterjee, *Gender, Slavery, and Law in Colonial India*, 86–7.

[33] Jaffur Shurreef, *Qanoon-E-Islam, or the Customs of the Moosulmans of India; Comprising a Full and Exact Account of Their Various Rites and Ceremonies, from the Moment of Birth till the Hour of Death*, translated by G.A. Herklots (London: Parbury, Allen, and Co., 1832); S. Vatuk, "Shurreef, Herklots, Crooke, and Qanoon-E-Islam: Constructing an Ethnography of 'The Moosulmans of India,'" *South Asian Research* 19, no. 1 (1999): 5–28.

considered a kind of lawful concubinage. This ceremony much resembles the 'Nikka' marriage, common among Mahomedans.[34]

Commentators increasingly blamed the supposedly loose nature of Muslim and lower-caste marriages on their "contractual" nature, which they contrasted with the supposedly "sacramental" qualities of Hindu (and Christian) marriage practices. An article published in 1888 explained, "The sacramental marriage is a very old Aryan institution ... Among the Hindus even death does not dissolve it." In contrast, the author described marriage among "Semites" as contractual, meaning, "What is made by contract can be unmade by contract; and so marriage by contract is always accompanied by the greatest facilities for divorce – a man can take new wives, and get rid of old ones."[35] Describing Muslim marriage (and often by extension lower-caste Hindu customs) as "contractual" equated them with economic transactions. From here it was only a short step to seeing these marriages as little better than prostitution. Thus, Romesh Dutt, a Bengali civil servant who became well known for his writings on Indian economy, wrote, "In the eye of the law and religion the *Nika* is valid marriage, but in practice it is often nothing more or less than concubinage."[36]

The moral outrage of middle-class Hindus such as Dutt contributed to active social reform movements that attempted to generalize upper-caste, Hindu practices into a normative ideal.[37]

Muslim social reformers embraced similar efforts to reign in customary forms of marriage, particularly practices that were associated with deviant economic transactions or more transient forms of marriage. For example the *ulama* issued *fatwas* condemning payments made to a bride's family (as opposed to *mahr*, which was given to the bride herself).[38] Sunni reformers also criticized certain Shia practices, including *muta* or temporary marriages, for being little better than adultery.[39]

When social reform and legal prohibitions against "immoral" customs proved inadequate to stamp out what colonial authorities deemed deviant sexual behaviors, the courts increasingly supplemented them

---

[34] *Gazetteer of the Central Provinces*, Part 1 (Nagpore: Chief Commissioner's Office Press, 1867), 41–2.

[35] "Christianity and Islam," *The Asiatic Quarterly Review* 6 (October 1888): 306.

[36] Romesh Chunder Dutt, *The Peasantry of Bengal: Being a View of Their Condition under the Hindu, the Mahomedan, and English Rule, and a Consideration of the Means Calculated to Improve Their Future Prospects* (Calcutta: Thacker, Spink & Co., 1874), 65.

[37] Charu Gupta, *Sexuality, Obscenity, Community: Women, Muslims, and the Hindu Public in Colonial India* (Delhi: Permanent Black, 2001), 123–95.

[38] Zaman, *Modern Islamic Thought in a Radical Age*, 179.

[39] Justin Jones, *Shi'a Islam in Colonial India: Religion, Community and Sectarianism* (Cambridge: Cambridge University Press, 2011), 69–70.

with penal sanctions. Criminal laws, unlike religious personal laws, were in theory religiously neutral, applying equally to all Indians.[40] In their implementation, however, colonial officials often administered penal sanctions in ways that reinforced normative assumptions that singled out Muslims and members of the lower classes as sexually deviant. For example, colonial officials described the crime of enticement, one of the most heavily used penal sanctions, as both particularly prevalent among the lower-classes and among Muslims. In Bengal the law against enticement, which had its origins in English legal traditions, was introduced in 1819 to target the recruitment of married women to work as prostitutes.[41] But during the drafting of the new Indian Penal Code, the Indian Law Commission learned that the courts used this law primarily to police infidelity among the lower classes. According to the logic of colonial officials, upper-class Indians rarely took legal action in cases of adultery because they were ashamed of public exposure. Lower-class husbands, however, readily used enticement charges so as to recover a wandering spouse by threatening her illicit lover with imprisonment. The courts therefore recommended that enticement be included in the new Penal Code because it was "well suited to the feelings of the lower classes of the community."[42]

The charge of enticement was particularly common in regions with large agrarian Muslim populations, where authorities saw residents as doubly prone to marital infidelity because of their low socio-economic status and their religion. W.W. Hunter, a member of the Indian Civil Service who was known for his writings on Indian Muslims, explained that in the Bakarganj District, located in the heavily Muslim areas surrounding Dhaka, one of the most common criminal charges was for enticing away a married woman. He explained its prevalence by arguing that "early marriage, domestic quarrels arising out of the peculiar constitution of the Musalman household, pecuniary temptations, strong passion and love of intrigue, combine to make breaches of the marriage law of very common occurrence."[43] In a similar vein, a police report

---

[40] On the differential application of criminal law to Indians and Europeans, see Elizabeth Kolsky, *Colonial Justice in British India* (Cambridge: Cambridge University Press, 2010).

[41] A.D. 1819 Regulation VII, *Papers Relating to East India Affairs: viz. Regulations Passed by the Governments of Bengal, Fort St. George, and Bombay, in the Year 1819* (House of Commons, 1821), 22–4.

[42] Indian Law Commission, "Second Report on the Indian Penal Code," Copies of the Special Report of the Indian Law Commissioners," 75, HCPP, 1847–8 (330) XXVIII.117.

[43] Sir William Wilson Hunter, *A Statistical Account of Bengal* (London: Trübner & Co., 1875), 5: 232. Hunter published his well-known work *The Indian Musalmans: Are They Bound in Conscience to Rebel Against the Queen* in 1871.

complained, "The *nika* system prevailing amongst the Mussulmans is extremely loose in its nature, and by no means sufficient to keep the parties within the limit of their mutual contract. The consequence is that wives invariably run away with their paramours; the disappointed husband comes to the court and complains of the abduction."[44]

Officials also worried that, despite the large numbers of cases involving offences against marriage among Muslims, rates of conviction were low. This was because there were rarely records to prove the initial marriage. In response, Bengal passed the Mohammedan Marriages and Divorce Registration Act in 1876 to combat "loose notions regarding the marriage tie prevalent among the lower orders of Mahomedans," and to encourage Muslims to register their marriages with a new group of officially appointed *qazis*.[45]

By emphasizing the loose and transient nature of Muslim marriages, colonial legal commentary on enticement echoed contemporary discourses that unfavorably compared "contractual" Muslim marriages to their "sacramental" Hindu or Christian counterparts. Yet while seemingly condemning the economic aspects of marital practices, the colonial application of enticement laws in practice perpetuated an essentially economic construction of lower-class marriage. In his original notes on drafting the Indian Penal Code, Macaulay himself argued that lower-class men whose wives eloped, "generally complain, not of the wound given to their affections, not of the stain on their honour, but of the loss of a menial."[46] Macaulay's notes on marriage were reprinted in subsequent editions of the Indian Penal Code, popularizing these sentiments among the judges and lawyers who routinely referenced them.[47]

Taking this reasoning to its logical conclusion, by the late nineteenth century some courts were broadening their interpretation of the crime of enticement to cover the recruitment of women for plantation labor.[48] While overall the Indian agrarian economy relied on small-scale family

---

[44] W.L. Heeley, *Administration Report of the Jails of the Lower Provinces for the Year 1873* (Calcutta: Bengal Secretariat Press, 1874), 72.

[45] Abstract of the Proceedings of the Council of the Lieutenant-Governor of Bengal, January 2, 1875, p. 1, in NAI, Home Judicial Proceedings, B, January 1876, nos. 92–102.

[46] Thomas Macaulay, "Notes on the Indian Penal Code," in *The Works of Lord Macaulay, Complete*, ed. Lady Trevelyan (London: Longmans, Green, and Co., 1866), 7: 541.

[47] See for example W.R. Hamilton, *The Indian Penal Code with Commentary* (Calcutta: Thacker, Spink & Co., 1895), 553; and Ratanlal Ranchhoddass, *A Manual of the Indian Penal Code* (Bombay: Radhabai Atmaran Sagoon Book-seller, 1896), 297.

[48] See for example "Attempted Sale of a Woman," *Madras Mail*, September 11, 1888, 3; and Samita Sen, "Unsettling the Household: Act VI (of 1901) and the Regulation of Women Migrants in Colonial Bengal," in *Peripheral Labour: Studies in the History of Partial Proletarianizationan*, ed. Shahid Amin and Marcel van der Linden (Cambridge: Cambridge University Press, 1997), 145.

farms, in certain sectors, including tea production in Assam, large-scale plantations dominated.[49] Indians, working under contracts of indenture, also increasingly supplied the man- (and woman-) power for plantations across Southeast Asia, South Africa, and the Caribbean. Colonial administrators charged with regulating labor recruitment, both for India and overseas, believed that the presence of women among migrant populations would stabilize potentially disruptive unattached male migrants by encouraging family formation.[50] Regions from which women were recruited, however, including Bengal, saw the plantations' gain as their loss. Local Bengali newspapers were flooded with sensational stories about unscrupulous recruiters kidnapping or luring away vulnerable women. Yet newspaper accounts often also portrayed women migrants as sexually licentious, a charge that implicitly suggested that their decision to migrate was voluntary. The slippage in these accounts between the enticements of paid labor and of alternative sexual partners suggested the authors viewed work outside of the family farm, and sex outside of marriage, as essentially synonymous.[51]

In a rare alignment with the vernacular press, colonial officials were often sympathetic to complaints that labor recruiters were threatening the integrity of the peasant household, both as a conjugal and an economic unit. As a district commissioner explained in an official report about the problem:

I allude to the frequent practice of coolly recruiters inveigling away married women from their husbands and children ... The inducements held out at the time are presents of ornaments and clothes, and the glowing accounts the recruiters give of the ease and luxury the women will enjoy in the tea districts, which contrasted by them with the hard fare and work to be done at home, often succeeds in inducing them to leave their families ... The result of such emigration, there can be very little doubt, is that the women thus leaving their husbands go into keeping with other men, and the act of enlistment, though not illegal at the time, eventually becomes tantamount to inducing a married woman to leave her husband for an immoral purpose, which the recruiter knows full well will be the result, and yet that he can recruit such a woman with perfect impunity.

[49] Piya Chatterjee, *A Time for Tea: Women, Labor, and Post/Colonial Politics on an Indian Plantation* (Durham: Duke University Press, 2001), 80–82.

[50] Madhavi Kale, "Projecting Identities: Empire and Indentured Labor Migration from India to Trinidad and British Guiana, 1836–1885," in *Nation and Migration: The Politics of Space in the South Asian Diaspora*, ed. Peter van Der Veer (Philadelphia: University of Pennsylvania Press, 1995), 80–3; Brij V. Lal, "Kunti's Cry: Indentured Women on Fiji Plantations," *The Indian Economic and Social History Review* 22, no. 1 (1985): 55–71.

[51] The *Report on Native Papers* for Bengal from the late 1880s includes numerous examples of stories about the deceitful recruitment and sexual exploitation of female laborers on Assamese tea plantations.

The district commissioner urged the government to intervene, insisting that "a married woman may be said to have entered into a contract with her husband, which precludes her from engaging in services to another party for a term of years without his consent."[52]

In 1901 the government officially endorsed this logic when it issued new restrictions on the recruitment of women and children as part of the Assam Labour and Emigration Act. The act specified that officers charged with registering emigrants could turn down and detain women who did not have the consent of their male guardian.[53] The act thus added one more tine to secular legal governance's multi-pronged regulation of marriage. While primarily the domain of religious personal laws, marriage law also selectively drew on custom, penal sanctions, and labor laws. Together these various branches of law "domesticated" the household not by eliminating its economic functions, but by endowing the conjugal family with a more monopolistic control over women's sexual and physical labor. Yet by depicting the economic dimensions of marriage as lower-class and Muslim deviations from an idealized upper-caste Hindu norm, colonial law masked its own role in producing the household as a key site for extracting women's labor.

## Conclusion

The selective incorporation of customary law, and the careful ways it was interwoven with religious personal law and criminal law, endowed secular legal governance with strategic flexibility. This flexibility allowed courts to consistently favor practices that buttressed the male-headed household unit. Patriarchal control over labor and property reinforced secular legal governance's domestic/economic binary, not by eliminating women's productive labor, but by removing it from the market and subordinating it to familial modes of extraction. These family units undergirded the colonial strategy of commercializing agrarian production on the cheap. Male-headed households were armed with the legal tools to extract the ever-greater labor needed to meet the demands of imperial markets without having to raise the wages of female family members. Colonial law masked its own role in empowering the economic exploitation of Indian women by cloaking patriarchal bias in the garb of "tradition" – as a concession to India's primitive culture rather than as an engine of colonial profits.

---

[52] Colonel J.R. Pughe, *Report on the Police in the Lower Provinces of the Bengal Presidency for the Year 1872* (Calcutta: Bengal Secretariat Press, 1874), 69–70.
[53] Sen, "Unsettling the Household," 148.

To the historian, the selective braiding of personal and customary laws in the service of patriarchy can seem like an elegantly designed plan, carefully assembled by a brilliant legal architect. In reality, however, these patterns developed in a haphazard fashion. The basic parameters set out by the Indian Law Commission in 1864, which specified that religious personal laws should be applied in cases involving marriage, inheritance, and ritual, did not cover the myriad complexities that the courts encountered in the following decades. Still less did the Commission provide clear instructions for how custom should be incorporated into this formula. Instead courts and provincial legislatures built the larger apparatus of secular legal governance one decision, or law, at a time, often while expressing their own confusions and doubts. Frequently the most powerful impacts of their decisions were unintended. Laws that undermined women's ability to engage in market transactions were, if we take judges and legislatures at their word, often designed to protect women from economic exploitation, whether from their own financial incapacity (as was the case with Shumsoonnissa in the previous chapter) or from unscrupulous labor recruiters (as was the case with women migrating to plantations in this chapter).[54]

Recognizing the haphazard and unintended workings of the law on a case-by-case basis, however, should not be mistaken for lack of systemic impact. Judges and colonial officials, sometimes working alongside middle-class Indian social reformers, engaged in the daily activities of secular legal governance in wider ideological and material contexts. Victorian gender norms gave secular legal governance its structural glue, providing strands of continuity that operated across personal, customary, criminal, and civil law. The law's systemic patriarchal biases channeled colonial economic development into distinctly gendered patterns of exploitation, whether or not this result was intended by British officials. Together these twinned ideological and material contexts assured that the uncoordinated and volatile workings of everyday legal governance cohered into a systemic pattern of women's economic marginalization.

---

[54] For a comparable discussion of the role of "protective" legislation in Victorian Britain, see Sonya O. Rose, "Protective Labor Legislation in Nineteenth-Century Britain: Gender, Class, and the Liberal State," in *Gender and Class in Modern Europe*, ed. Laura L. Frader and Sonya O. Rose (Ithaca: Cornell University Press, 1996), 193–210.

# 4    Ritual and the Authority of Reason

In February 1891 the Privy Council attempted to resolve a legal question that had been plaguing lower courts in British India – what was the role of colonial courts in mediating ritual differences among Muslims? The case, *Fazl Karim v. Maula Baksh*, involved a dispute in a mosque in Tajpore, an agrarian region in the Bihar region of the Bengal Presidency.[1] The *imam* and caregivers of the mosque brought a civil case against twelve members of the congregation for interfering with the *imam* during prayers. The defendants had acted because they objected to changes that the *imam* had recently made, including saying the phrase *amin* in a loud voice and raising his hands to his ears while bowing in the prayer sequence. These ritual differences were linked to the parties' differing views on the binding authority of the Hanafi school of jurisprudence. The *imam* and these members of his congregation disagreed about the respective roles of individual interpretation of religious texts, or *ijtihad*, and the accumulation of an authoritative body of law through *taqlid*, or following an established authority. Individuals who advocated different approaches to *ijtihad* and *taqlid* often embraced diverging ritual practices – disputes that sometimes ended up in colonial courts.

Over the course of the nineteenth century in British India, debates proliferated about the correct forms of Muslim rituals and embodied comportment, from practices associated with worship at Sufi shrines, to styles of clothing and grooming, to the embodied gestures of daily prayers. These disputes led to the proliferation of new sectarian divisions among Sunni Muslims, including the Deobandis, Ahl-i-Hadith, and Barelwis. When debates between these sects landed in court, colonial judges had to decide whether to intervene, that is, to

---

[1] The following account draws on the published decision, *Fazl Karim and another* v. *Maula Baksh and others* [1891] ILR 18 Calcutta 448, and the Privy Council Office Records for the case, *Fuzal Karim and Fuzal Rahim* v. *Haji Mowla Baksh (alias Kinya) Rahim and Fuzlu*. I refer to the printed decision as *Fazl Karim v. Maula Baksh* (ILR) and the Privy Council records as *Fuzal Karim v. Haji Mowla Baksh* (PCOR). For this particular case I used copies of the PCOR held at Lincoln's Inn.

compel ritual conformity directly; or to allow Muslims to enforce conformity themselves, for example by ejecting worshippers in violation of established practices from mosques. In the Tajpore case, which set a precedent which was applicable to future decisions by courts in both British India, and potentially elsewhere in the British Empire, the Privy Council declined to do either.[2] It instead declared that the *imam*, despite his altered ritual practice, had a right to retain his office and could not be ejected by other Muslims at the mosque. The decision solidified the colonial judiciary's hands-off approach to governing ritual differences. In comparison to cases involving marriage and inheritance, the colonial courts were unlikely to intervene in ritual disputes, unless they were reframed as disputes over property or as threats to public order.[3]

In taking this approach to ritual practice, the colonial state ran ahead of its domestic counterpart, effectively turning India into a laboratory for modes of secular governance that Britain itself adopted more gradually. As scholars of religious life in Europe have argued, the Protestant Reformation ignited a long-term trend among Protestant Christians of treating outward ritual practices as less important than inward personal beliefs.[4] This shift, however, unfolded slowly, and in fits and starts. Britons, much like their Indian counterparts, engaged in fierce debates over ritual during the second half of the nineteenth century.[5] In 1874, Parliament attempted to impose a degree of conformity in Anglican worship through the Public Worship Regulation Act, which established a new court charged with enforcing the Church of England's official practice. The court faced heavy public opposition and fueled growing public discomfort with state interventions in religious life, but the act remained

---

[2] Demonostrating its diverse influence on subsequent case law outside India and among other religious groups, *Fazl Karim* v. *Maula Baksh* was later cited in a Ceylonese dispute in a Buddhist temple. *Gooneratne Nayake Thero* v. *Punchi Banda Korala* [1926] The New Law Reports 28 Ceylon 145, cited on 146.

[3] Asad Ahmed, "Adjudicating Muslims: Law, Religion and the State in Colonial India and Post-Colonial Pakistan" (Ph.D., University of Chicago, 2006), 72–5. On the policy implications of colonial nonintervention for questions of caste, see Anupama Rao, *The Caste Question: Dalits and the Politics of Modern India* (Berkeley: University of California Press, 2009), 81–117; Rupa Viswanath, *The Pariah Problem: Caste, Religion, and the Social in Modern India* (New York: Columbia University Press, 2014), 118–43.

[4] Talal Asad, *Genealogies of Religion: Discipline and Reasons of Power in Christianity and Islam* (Baltimore: Johns Hopkins University Press, 1993), 55–82.

[5] Josef L. Altholz, "Warfare of Conscience with Theology," in *Religion in Victorian Britain*, ed. Gerald Parsons, vol. 4: *Interpretations* (Manchester: Manchester University Press, 1988), 150–69; Herbert Schlossberg, *Conflict and Crisis in the Religious Life of Late Victorian England* (New Brunswick: Transaction Publishers, 2009).

officially in force.[6] In comparison, the colonial state took a more radically noninterventionist stance in ritual disputes, a position spurred by colonial officials' own perceived distance from the religious practices of their Indian subjects. Apparently, it was easier to see others' ritual differences as matters of relative insignificance than to practice this same tolerance at home.

Colonial authorities' noninterventionist approach to ritual practice, and its divergence with domestic developments in Britain, points us towards another set of binaries which animated secular legal governance in colonial India: the perceived divide between reason and Indian religions and between state and religious, or in colonial-parlance, "communal" authority. While Chapters 2 and 3 explored the generative instability of the family/economy binary, the next two chapters explore how these additional binaries shaped conflict among Sunni Muslims (this chapter) and between Muslims and Hindus (Chapter 5). As shown in Chapter 1, colonial secular governance, with its links to unitary notions of territorial sovereignty, emphasized the rationality of new colonial codes by opposing them against the perceived irrationality of Indian religious laws. Echoing this assertion of unitary sovereignty, colonial courts claimed a monopoly over the right to back reasoned judgments with sovereign force. Colonial courts took over the power to administer personal laws from Indian religious communities, instead of allowing them to operate their own independent legal institutions, as was the case under the Mughals. In British India religious community therefore became a *category* of governance, through the administration of personal laws, the inclusion of religious affiliation in regular censuses, and, after the introduction of limited representative institutions, through separate elections for religious minorities. Religious community ceased, at least in theory, to operate as a separate *unit* of governance, with its own internal methods of legal regulation and enforcement. In practice, however, the colonial state, which possessed a limited formal police force, often relied on communal collectives to enforce order among their members.[7] Yet the formal legal mechanisms for recognizing communal governance were often oblique, such as

---

[6] James Bentley, *Ritualism and Politics in Victorian Britain: The Attempt to Legislate for Belief* (Oxford: Oxford University Press, 1978); G.I.T. Machin, "The Last Victorian Anti-Ritualist Campaign, 1895–1906," *Victorian Studies* 25, no. 3 (April 1982): 277–302.

[7] On the importance of both formal and informal mechanisms of outsourcing policing to native elites and collectives, see Washbrook, "Law, State and Agrarian Society in Colonial India," 677; Sandria B. Freitag, "Crime in the Social Order of Colonial North India," *Modern Asian Studies* 25, no. 2 (May 1991): 230; K. Sivaramakrishanan, *Modern Forests: Statemaking and Environmental Change in Colonial Eastern India* (Stanford: Stanford University Press, 1999), 37–8.

inflicting collective punishments and fines.[8] Drawing out the tensions between these different approaches, the following chapters show how the colonial state's recognition of religious community as a *category* of governance, coupled with its ambiguous non-recognition/recognition of it as a *unit* of governance, led to proliferating conflict within and between religious groups.

This chapter traces these tensions by showing how the Privy Council's decision not to intervene in disputes over ritual difference elided the reasoned logics of Islamic jurisprudence and blocked Muslims from effectively mediating conflicts. Outwardly the Tajpore decision upheld the principle of religious freedom, or the right of Indian subjects to pray as they liked. Embedded in the logic of the decision, however, was a negative corollary: by constructing ritual as a matter of personal belief (rather than rational group deliberation) the courts prevented Indians from mediating these disputes through legal channels, whether within or beyond the state. The courts' construction of ritual differences therefore ignored its relationship to critical debates in Islamic jurisprudence about *taqlid*, which includes following the authoritative judgments of past jurists on questions of ritual practice. In contrast, the following analysis reconnects colonial case law on ritual to rich fields of vernacular legal literature on *taqlid*. Reading these state and non-state legal archives in tandem reveals the intimate links between proliferating conflicts over ritual and crises of authority that roiled Indian Muslims in the wake of colonial conquest and the spread of print. By delinking ritual from authority, the colonial courts left unaddressed the question of how Indian Muslims would respond to these social upheavals, both as individuals and as social collectives. At the same time, the courts made it more difficult for Muslims to develop new modes of self-governance. As a result, the hidden cost of colonial religious freedom was often exacerbated intra-communal conflict.

## Religious Reform and the Varied Meanings of Reason

Understanding the conflict that unfolded in the Tajpore mosque requires stepping back into the eighteenth and early nineteenth centuries to trace the development of Islamic reform movements that raised profound questions about religious authority. After a sustained period of political expansion and cultural flourishing stretching across the sixteenth and seventeenth centuries, the Mughal Empire entered a period

---

[8] On the role of collective punishment, see Taylor C. Sherman, *State Violence and Punishment in India* (London: Routledge, 2010).

of crisis in the eighteenth century, a pattern echoed across early-modern Islamic empires. The decline of Mughal power was accompanied by the rise of new regional states, a phenomenon that not only fractured political power but also fostered new centers of learning. Islamic reform movements that sought new structures of community filled the resulting power vacuum. This atmosphere of crisis and reform intensified as British power expanded in the subcontinent. Alongside rapid political change, shifting modes of social communication, and especially the spread of print from the 1820s onwards, further unsettled established hierarchies of religious leadership and learning. While formal literacy remained low in colonial India, the proliferation of "literacy awareness," or access to printed material through practices such as reading books aloud, democratized religious knowledge.[9] During the early nineteenth century, Indian Muslims grappled with these crises of authority through debates about the relationship between *taqlid*, methods of interpreting texts, and customary rituals associated with Sufi and Hindu practices.

Debates about the relative role of *taqlid* and *ijtihad* were at the core of these religious reform movements. The two terms are difficult to translate, and different definitions of their meanings often map onto diverging juridical methods. At the most basic level, however, *ijtihad* refers to the effort of forming an independent judgment, often through direct consultation of the Quran and *hadith*. *Taqlid*, in contrast, describes the act of following or submitting to the authority of another person's interpretation, and is often associated with conforming to the decisions of one of the four schools of Sunni jurisprudence.[10] Drawing on terminology that echoes the concepts of European Enlightenment, scholars sometimes describe *ijtihad* as rational interpretation and *taqlid* as blind imitation or faith.[11] Defining the two terms as the presence or absence of reasoning, however, misses key aspects of the nineteenth-century debate. In encouraging Muslims to consult the Quran and *hadith* directly, some reformers who endorsed *ijtihad* were actually suspicious of *aql*, or human reason, which they believed distorted the meaning of a divine text that should

---

[9] The term "literacy aware" is borrowed from C.A. Bayly, *Empire and Information: Intelligence Gathering and Social Communication in India, 1780–1870* (Cambridge: Cambridge University Press, 1996), 39, 154.

[10] Knut S. Vikør, *Between God and the Sultan: A History of Islamic Law* (London: Hurst & Co., 2005), 53, 156–61.

[11] For examples of how definitions of *ijtihad* and *taqlid* juxtapose ideas of rationality and blindness, see Ayesha Jalal, *Partisans of Allah: Jihad in South Asia* (Cambridge: Harvard University Press, 2008), xiii, 13, 41, 75; Filippo Osella and Caroline Osella, eds., *Islamic Reform in South Asia* (Cambridge: Cambridge University Press, 2013), 147–8, 506, 509; and Muqtedar Khan, "What Is Enlightenment? An Islamic Perspective," *Journal of Religion and Society* 16 (2014): 2.

be read literally. In contrast, groups who promoted *taqlid* defended the role that past jurists and scholars played in interpreting divine texts whose meaning was often less than apparent.[12] Analyzing these debates as contests over how different Muslims should interact with texts, rather than between reason and blind faith, focuses attention on the different forms of religious authority and reasoning that would be subsequently obscured by colonial courts' decisions governing ritual.

Nineteenth-century debates about *ijtihad* and *taqlid* often cited the foundational work of Shah Waliullah (1703–62). Waliullah experienced the decline of Mughal power from its center in Delhi, living through a period in which ten different emperors succeeded to the throne and multiple waves of invaders arrived from Persia, Afghanistan, and the Maratha territories. Demonstrating the capacity of crisis to breed intellectual creativity, he composed a vast corpus of scholarship. He initiated his disciples in multiple Sufi *tariqahs* (paths or orders), but also worked to weed out Sufi practices that he believed conflicted with the *sharia*.[13] Although Shah Waliullah extolled the importance of *ijtihad*, he took a moderate approach to *taqlid*, advocating a careful balance between independent reasoning and reliance on the schools of law.[14] He insisted, "the belief that a Mujtahid [a qualified practitioner of *ijtihad*] is not to be found in our times, founded on the former belief, is basing a corrupt belief upon another corrupt belief."[15] Yet Shah Waliullah carefully distinguished between those who engaged in absolute *ijtihad*, exercising complete juristic independence, and affiliated *ijtihad*, or those who exercised *ijtihad* within a school of law.[16] He claimed the latter status for himself. Waliullah understood this to mean following the legal opinions of the jurist founder, Abu Hanifa, when his judgments were unequivocal, but in more ambiguous matters or new legal questions, exercising *ijtihad*, while drawing on Hanafi methods of reasoning and analogy.[17] Waliullah, however, did not recommend this course for every Muslim. If a person had

[12] Francis Robinson, "Strategies of Authority in Muslim South Asia in the Nineteenth and Twentieth Centuries," *Modern Asian Studies* 47, no. 1 (2013): 1–21.
[13] Jalal, *Partisans of Allah*, 40–57; Ahmad Aziz, "Political and Religious Ideas of Shah Wali-Ullah of Delhi," *Muslim World* 52, no. 1 (1962): 22–30; J.M.S. Balijon, *Religion and Thought of Shah Wali Allah Dihlawi, 1703–1762* (Leiden: E.J. Brill, 1986); Saiyid Athar Abbas Rizvi, *Shah Wali-Allah and His Times: A Study of Eighteenth Century Islam, Politics and Society in India* (Canberra, Australia: Ma'rifat, 1980).
[14] Rudolph Peters, "Idjtihad and Taqlid in 18th and 19th Century Islam," *Die Welt Des Islams* 20, no. 3/4 (January 1980): 137, 143.
[15] Muhammad Daud Rahbar, "Shah Waliullah and Ijtihad: A Translation of Selected Passages from His 'Iqd al-Jid fi Ahkam al-Ijtihad Wa-l-Taqlid,'" *The Muslim World* 45, no. 4 (October 1955): 347.
[16] Ibid., 349–50.
[17] Balijon, *Religion and Thought of Shah Wali Allah*, 165–7.

not yet acquired thorough knowledge of the Quran, *hadith*, the decisions of previous jurists, Arabic grammar, and analogical reasoning, Waliullah instructed him to follow the judgments of someone who had these skills.[18]

Shah Waliullah's family dominated the scholarly and religious life of Delhi for several generations. His son Shah Abdul Aziz was a renowned scholar in his own right, respected for his conciliatory style and his strategic approach to negotiating relations with the British, who seized control of Delhi in 1803.[19] In contrast, Shah Ismail, Shah Abdul Aziz's nephew, gained a reputation for provoking controversy. He became the spiritual disciple of Sayyid Ahmad Barelwi, a charismatic but controversial young man. While Sayyid Ahmad studied under Shah Abdul Aziz, he never showed a particular zeal for scholarly endeavors (he was described as "nearly illiterate") and spent a number of years working as a mercenary cavalryman. Sayyid Ahmad nonetheless attracted disciples among Delhi's religious elite, including Shah Ismail, who purportedly ran barefoot next to his palanquin as a show of devotion.[20] While linked with the Waliullah legacy, Sayyid Ahmad and Shah Ismail's style was far more antagonistic and less subtle than earlier critiques of *taqlid*.[21] They relentlessly attacked customary rituals that they believed were not soundly based in the Quran and *hadith*, often enraging other Muslims in the process. For example, local residents in Delhi asked the Mughal emperor to intercede after Shah Ismail created an uproar by converting a group of lower-caste sweepers and bringing them – unbathed – to Delhi's central mosque.[22] By bringing together notions of ritual purity associated with the physical space of the mosque with caste-based understandings of cleanliness and social status, Shah Ismail's action implied a critique of Indian Muslims who had absorbed cultural practices from their Hindu neighbors.

For many observers in Delhi, the spectacle of a half-literate soldier challenging the norms of polite, Muslim society epitomized the spirit of

---

[18] Rahbar, "Iqd," 348–9.

[19] Jalal, *Partisans of Allah*, 67–9; Mushirul Haq, *Shah Abdul Aziz, His Life and Time: A Study of India Muslims' Attitude to the British in the Early 19th Century* (Lahore: Institute of Islamic Culture, 1995), 16–27.

[20] "Notice of the Peculiar Tenets Held by the Followers of Syed Ahmed, Taken Chiefly from the 'Sirat-ul-Mustaqim,' a Principal Treatise of That Sect, Written by Maulvi Mahommed Ismail," *Journal of the Asiatic Society of Bengal* 1, no. 11 (November 1832): 481.

[21] Marc Gaborieau, "A Nineteenth-Century Indian 'Wahhabi' Tract against the Cult of Muslim Saints: al-Balagh al-Mubin," in *Muslim Shrines in India: Their Character, History, and Significance*, ed. Christian W. Troll (Delhi: Oxford University Press, 1989), 207.

[22] "Summary of the News on the Surroundings, Reported on 1 March 1825," in Margrit Pernau and Yunus Jaffrey, eds., *Information and the Public Sphere: Persian Newsletters from Mughal Delhi* (Mumbai: Oxford University Press, 2009), 123–4.

the times, in which foreign and local upstarts were displacing traditional authorities. Opponents of Sayyid Ahmad and Shah Ismail began referring to them as "Wahhabis" to associate them with the controversial, foreign sect of reformers who rose to prominence in the eighteenth century in the Arabian peninsula. The men's followers, however, preferred the label Tariqah-yi-Muhammadi (way of Muhammad).[23] Their radical reputation was secured when Sayyid Ahmad and Shah Ismail raised an armed *jihad* against the Sikh kingdom and were killed in battle in 1831.[24]

Although Sayyid Ahmad communicated through oral preaching rather than written works, his followers, and particularly Shah Ismail, avidly embraced vernacular print. Some of the first texts by Indian Muslims printed in Urdu spread his message.[25] Written in colloquial language, several of these works explicitly addressed women and children, instructing them on the correct method of performing rituals such as washing before prayer. The texts also advised people to read them aloud and included poems that could be committed to memory.[26] Shah Ismail's *Taqwiyat-ul-Iman* is emblematic of the long and multilingual publishing histories of these works. Originally composed in Arabic, the book was first published in Urdu in Calcutta in the 1820s, partially translated into English in the *Journal of the Asiatic Society* in 1852, reprinted multiple times in Urdu, and translated into Bengali in 1881. By some accounts, no less than six million copies of the book have been printed; the work is still in circulation today.[27] In contrast, critics of the Tariqah-yi-Muhammadi were slower to adopt the printed vernacular. By continuing to rely on manuscript texts

[23] Muhammad Siddik Hasan Khan, *An Interpreter of Wahabiism*, trans. and ed. Sayyad Akbar 'Alam (Calcutta, J.W. Thomas, Baptist Mission Press, 1884), 76.

[24] Jalal, *Partisans of Allah*, 58–113.

[25] Robinson, "Technology and Religious Change," 240.

[26] Khurram Ali Bilhauri, *Nasihat-ul-Muslimin* (Reprint Lucknow: Darulisha'at-i-Islamiyah, 1964), 42–3. The introduction to *Nasihat* indicates that it was written in 1238 [1822/1823], but the earliest known edition was printed in Calcutta in 1848. Karamat Ali Jaunpuri, *Miftah-ul-Jannat* (Reprint Lucknow: Nawal Kishor, 1916), 6–8. The first printed edition of *Miftah* was published in Calcutta in 1826/1827. Marc Gaborieau, "Late Persian, Early Urdu: The Case of 'Wahhabi' Literature (1818–1857)," in *Confluence of Cultures: French Contributions to Indo-Persian Studies*, ed. Françoise Nalini Delvoye (New Delhi: Manohar, 1994), 176.

[27] The online catalogue of the British Library's Indian vernacular literature collection lists the following editions: Delhi, 1853; Delhi, 1875; Delhi, 1876; Lucknow, 1876; and Calcutta, 1881 (Bengali). "Holdings of 19th Century Publications at the British Library's Oriental and India Office Collections," accessed February 21, 2011, http://dsal.uchicago.edu/ bibliographic/oioc/oioc.php. For estimates of its total print-run, see M. Ashraf Darr, "Introduction," *Support of the Faith: English Translation of Shah Isma'il Shahid's Taqwiyat ul-Iman*, trans. Mir Shahamat 'Ali, ed. M. Ashraf Darr (Lahore: Sh. Muhammad Shraf, 1974), xiii.

and Persian, the language of scholarly learning in much of north India, they limited their communication to a more narrow, educated elite.[28]

In addition to embracing the vernacular medium, Shah Ismail voiced a democratizing message that common Muslims should trust their own interpretation of the Prophet's commands over those of elite mediators, whether Sufi *pirs* (spiritual guides) or *ulama*. In *Taqwiyat-ul-Iman* he explained:

At present people in religious matters follow many ways. Some grasp onto the customs of their forebears; many look to the stories of holy men; some rely on the authority of the sayings invented by the *maulavis*, from the ingenuity of their own minds; others allow their own *aql* [reasoning] to interfere. But better than all these ways is to take as principles the word of God and his Prophet and to rely on their authority alone and not to allow one's own *aql* to interfere ... The prevailing opinion among the common people is that, "It is difficult to comprehend the words of Allah and the Prophet ..." This is a great error, because Allah said that the contents of the Holy Quran are very clear and plain.[29]

By suggesting that common Muslims did not need the guidance of learned scholars or religious leaders, Shah Ismail advanced a far more radical critique of *taqlid* than did Shah Waliullah. Arguing that the meaning of divine texts was self-evident, Shah Ismail, unlike his eighteenth-century forebear, de-emphasized the importance of contextual knowledge and interpretive skill for the ability to engage in *ijtihad*. Instead Shah Ismail argued for a literalist approach to texts, which eliminated the risk that the imposition of interpretive interventions, rooted in human reasoning (*aql*), would distort the true meaning of the Quran and *hadith*.

By advancing *ijtihad* at the expense of *taqlid*, Shah Ismail was thus not arguing in favor of freeing human reason from the confines of blind faith; instead he insisted on an unmediated reliance on divine texts, uninfluenced by individual opinion or accumulated expertise. His approach therefore troubles an easy association of *ijtihad* with reason or *taqlid* with

---

[28] A large number of the early refutations of the *Tariqah-yi-Muhammadi* were in manuscript form. Some of these manuscripts have subsequently been printed. See, for example, the refutation written in Persian by Fazl-i-Haq Khairabadi in 1825. *Tahqiq-ul-Fatwa fi Ibtal-ul-Tughwa. Urdu and Persian*, ed. and trans. Muhammad Abdul Hakim Sharf Qadiri (Lahore: Maktabah-yi-Qadiriyah, 1979), 54, 64. For additional citations of manuscripts written against the *Tariqah-yi-Muhammadi*, see Gaborieau, "Late Persian, Early Urdu," 179–80. In terms of printed books, Gaborieau cites a refutation of *Taqwiyat-ul-Iman* from the 1820s, but the earliest texts I have consulted date to the 1840s. See for example Maulana Khalil-ul-Rahman-ul-Yusafi, *Risala-yi-Fatiha dar Radd-i-Wahabiyah* (Bombay, 1261 [1845]). The real surge in Urdu printed materials criticizing the reformist doctrines, however, occurred in the 1860s.
[29] Shah Muhammad Ismail Shahid, *Taqwiyat-ul-Iman* (Reprint Lucknow: Nami Press, 1967), 20.

its rejection. At the heart of his message was a particular understanding of the relationship between divine texts and meaning, an emphasis that gained salience as rapidly shifting modes of production and circulation made religious texts more widely accessible.

The Tariqah-yi-Muhammadi coupled their emphasis on direct consultation of divine texts with an aggressive campaign against *shirk* (polytheism) and *bidat* (heretical innovations), attacking practices they claimed that Indian Sunnis had adopted from Hindus or Shias. Attempting to point out the tension in the Tariqah-yi-Muhammadi's position on *bidat*, one of their critics wrote with biting humor:

Earlier I wrote a pamphlet in Persian introducing the origins of this sect and the number of *ulama* in this group. However, due to the ignorance of these gentlemen and their contempt for knowledge and scholars, they dismiss anything reasoned or written, and are content with Hindi …

Listen – even Hindi is *bidat* if one calls *bidat* whatever the Prophet did not do or did not say. By this reasoning, all mosques would be *bidat*, and the Quran and *hadith* and books [of religious interpretation] would also be *bidat* because there were not mosques with three towers and two *minars* in the time of the Prophet, and he did not mention their construction. Also, according to Bukhari, the five-hundred-and-forty chapter divisions in the Quran were added by the *ulama* four hundred or so years later. Likewise, Mishkat Sharif, Gulistan, and Bostan were composed after the life of the Prophet. But in reply they will answer – whatever we want, that becomes *sunnat*; and whatever we do not want, that is *bidat*.[30]

Noting the irony that those preaching against *bidat* eagerly embraced the use of vernacular Hindi, the author highlighted the organic ties between tradition and innovation.[31] While Indian *ulama* commonly differentiated between *bidat-i-hasanah* and *bidat-i-sayyia*, or good and bad innovations, the Tariqah-yi-Muhammadi argued more generally against *bidat*, insisting that the Prophet's own life was the best guide for pious Muslims. The

---

[30]  "Radd-i-Wahhabiyah," Urdu MS IO 4297 (i), IOLR, British Library, London, f. 121. The manuscript is unsigned and undated but appears to be in the same hand as several other manuscripts written by Muhammad Karim Allah (d. 1874). The India Office Library and Records include several handwritten tracts by Muhammad Karim Allah criticizing the Wahhabis and defending practices such as saying prayers for the souls of the dead, illuminating mosques, and reading poetry in the *khutbah*. India Office Library, *Catalogue of the Urdu Manuscripts in the India Office Library: Supplementary to James Fuller Blumhardt's Catalogue of 1926*, comp. Salim al-Din Quraishi and Ursula Sims-Williams (London: India Office Library and Records, 1978), 5–13. "Radd-i-Wahhabiya" includes references to events that occurred during the 1820s and 1830s, although it could have been written somewhat later (f. 154). The *Mishkat Sharif* is a collection of *hadith* composed in the twelfth century AD. *Bostan* and *Gulistan* are classic works of Persian literature composed by Saadi in the thirteenth century AD.

[31]  The language the writer referred to as Hindi was written in the Persian script, which today would be labeled Urdu, but the divide between Hindi and Urdu was far more fluid in the early nineteenth century.

famous educationist and reformer Sayyid Ahmad Khan (not to be confused with Sayyid Ahmad Barelwi) insisted that debates about *bidat* were in part a disagreement over semantics. Influenced by the Tariqah-yi-Muhammadi during his youth, Sayyid Ahmad Khan argued that the sect accepted new practices that, while not in formal existence during the time of the Prophet, bore resemblance to the *sunnat* (teachings and practices) of the Prophet. Yet in his early writings even Sayyid Ahmad Khan, who was later renowned for his progressive interpretation of Islamic theology, condemned those who used their own *aql* to decide whether a particular practice was good or bad instead of relying strictly on the *sunnat*. As a later, vocal advocate for *aql*, Sayyid Ahmad Khan's evolving thinking reflected the malleability of reason and authority, open to different constructions rooted in diverging understandings of the relationship between divine texts and human interpretation.[32]

## Governing Religious Reason: Debating *Taqlid*

After the death of Sayyid Ahmad Barelwi and Shah Ismail in 1831, their followers continued to provoke debate, albeit tempered by the absence of the sensational personalities of their leaders. In the wake of the Rebellion of 1857, the British became wary of radical reformers, who they believed helped instigate opposition to colonial rule. In the 1860s and 1870s, a series of suspected "Wahhabi" conspirators were put on trial for sedition, bringing questions of religious reform into colonial legal orbits.[33] With little immediate hope of restoring Muslim sovereignty, Indian Muslims focused on rethinking questions of religious authority in the changed context of colonial sovereignty. These debates increasingly focused on the four schools of Sunni jurisprudence and whether *taqlid* within a single school was obligatory, differences that were often reflected in opposing styles of prayer and other embodied practices. While earlier debates about *taqlid* pivoted around modes of textual interpretation and custom, the focus on schools of law and prayer rituals raised new questions about how interpretations became binding on communities.

Several distinct reform movements evolved from these debates, which divided Sunnis into opposing sectarian affiliations. Some of the most radical reformers came to be known as Muslim modernists. The

---

[32] Sayyid Ahmad Khan, "Rah-yi-Sunnat aur Radd-i-Bidat [The Way of the Prophet and the Rejection of Innovation]," in *Maqalat i-Sar Sayyid*, 2nd edn, ed. Muhammad Ismail (Lahore: Majlis-i-Taraqqi Adab, 1990), 5: 397–413.

[33] For a more detailed discussion of these trials, see Julia Stephens, "The Phantom Wahhabi: Liberalism and the Muslim Fanatic in Mid-Victorian India," *Modern Asian Studies* 47, no. 1 (2013): 22–52.

movement's leading voice, Sayyid Ahmad Khan, harnessed *ijtihad* to calls for cultural accommodations to colonial rule, including an embrace of English education and social intercourse with the British, including adopting aspects of Western dress and eating with non-Muslims.[34] In a review of his earlier writings on *bidat*, he explained these recommendations by clarifying that he now believed that prohibitions on *bidat* applied only to matters of *din* (faith), not *dunyawi* (worldly) affairs. The British treated the accommodationist Sayyid Ahmad Khan as a political spokesperson for Muslim interests, but most Indian Muslims rejected his religious interpretations.[35] Instead, followers of Sayyid Ahmad Barelwi and Shah Ismail extended the project of purifying Islam in other directions. In 1864 Sayyid Nazir Husain coined the name Ahl-i-Hadith, which was soon adopted by others who emphasized direct consultation of the Quran and *hadith* and downplayed the authority of the schools of Islamic jurisprudence. A Muslim's embrace of Ahl-i-Hadith doctrines was often signaled through shifts in his daily prayers and changes to grooming, such as cutting his beard to match the style that certain *hadith* indicated was preferred by the Prophet. While relatively few in number, the Ahl-i-Hadith exerted outsized influence through their polemical writings, their transnational connections, and the visibility of their alterations to ritual and embodied comportment.[36]

In contrast to either of these movements, the majority of *ulama* reasserted their position of leadership by defending *taqlid* and educating other Muslims about the correct performance of rituals according to Hanafi practices. Having ceded political authority to the British, the *ulama* were determined to safeguard their position as religious leaders against attacks from both modernists and the Ahl-i-Hadith.[37] The *madrasa* at Deoband, and its affiliated network of schools and scholars, often known as Deobandis, was at the forefront of these efforts. Meanwhile, a second group of scholars, known as Barelwis after the hometown of their founder Ahmad Riza Khan (1856–1921), defended customary forms of Sufi worship and gained renown for their expertise in the legal sciences

---

[34] Sayyid Ahmad Khan, *Review on Dr. Hunter's Indian Musalmans: Are They Bound in Conscience to Rebel against the Queen?* (Benares: Medical Hall Press, 1872), 37.

[35] David Lelyveld, *Aligarh's First Generation: Muslim Solidarity in British India* (1978; Reprint New Delhi: Oxford University Press, 1996), 130–4. On criticism of Sayyid Ahmad's views, see Metcalf, *Islamic Revival*, 144–6.

[36] Metcalf, *Islamic Revival*, 264–96; Daniel W. Brown, *Rethinking Tradition in Modern Islamic Thought* (Cambridge: Cambridge University Press, 1996), 27–30; Seema Alavi, *Muslim Cosmopolitanism in the Age of Empire* (Cambridge: Harvard University Press, 2015), 267–330.

[37] Muhammad Qasim Zaman, *The Ulama in Contemporary Islam: Custodians of Change* (Princeton: Princeton University Press, 2002), 24.

of *fiqh*.[38] The Barelwis fiercely supported *taqlid* of the Hanafi school, but considered Ahmad Riza Khan a *mujaddid*, or an individual charged with renewing the faith, and sometimes even invoked him as a *mujtahid*, or a person authorized to practice *ijtihad*.[39] Rather than exclusively endorsing either *ijtihad* or *taqlid*, these various groups debated the correct balance between them.

All of these groups issued a flurry of printed materials to define and promote their differing positions. In the aftermath of the Rebellion, the British – anxious to catch any early signs of political dissent – developed elaborate mechanisms for surveilling vernacular literature.[40] Because of the perceived association between certain strands of radical religious reform and political sedition, the British kept an especially close watch on publications arguing for and against so-called "Wahhabi" doctrines, which often included materials debating *ijtihad* and *taqlid*. Between 1868 and 1878 fifty-eight such titles were either entered in the government-issued quarterly catalogues of books for Punjab, North-Western Provinces, Oudh, and Bengal or incorporated into the India Office's collection of vernacular tracts.[41] While this sample is by no means complete or randomly selected, the list of titles nevertheless gives a general overview of the geographical and linguistic patterns in the publication of reformists tracts. The majority of the books were published in Delhi and Lahore, but volumes also appeared from printing presses in such smaller towns as Bareilly, Cawnpore, and Sitapur.[42] Reflecting the growing primacy of vernacular publishing, of fifty-eight titles, forty-one were written

---

[38] Metcalf, *Islamic Revival*, 304.
[39] Usha Sanyal, *Devotional Islam and Politics in British India: Ahmad Riza Khan Barelwi and His Movement, 1870–1920* (Delhi: Oxford University Press, 1996), 177–9.
[40] C.A. Bayly, *Empire and Information: Intelligence Gathering and Social Communication in India, 1780–1870* (Cambridge: Cambridge University Press, 1996), 338–43; Robert Darnton, "Literary Surveillance in the British Raj: The Contradictions of Liberal Imperialism," *Book History* 4 (January 2001): 133–76.
[41] This sample combines information from the Digital South Asia Library's online catalogue for the British Library's Oriental and India Office Collections holdings of nineteenth-century publications, (http://dsal.uchicago.edu/bibliographic/oioc/oioc. php), which includes many, although not all, of the BL's vernacular holdings. It also draws on the British Library's copies of the Quarterly Catalogue of Books for Bengal (shelfmark SV 412/8 and BL ORW.1896.b.149/3), North-Western Provinces (SV 412/ 38), Punjab (SV 412/44), and Oudh (SV 412/42). For Bengal, NWP, and Punjab, the British Library's holdings of the catalogue are nearly complete, but many volumes of the Oudh catalogues are missing. The catalogues explicitly labeled thirty-seven of the books as opposing the Wahhabi viewpoint and seventeen as supporting the Wahhabis. Four of the books are not labeled as pro- or anti-Wahhabi, but listed as linked with the Wahhabi controversy.
[42] The geographical distribution of books was: Bengal (1); Agra (4); Aligarh (1); Allahabad (1); Amritsar (1); Bareilly (1); Bombay (1); Calcutta (3); Cawnpore (1); Delhi (21); Lahore (15); Lucknow (4); Ludhiana (3); and Sitapur (1).

in Urdu, with a couple each in Bengali and Punjabi.[43] In comparison, only nine books were in Persian and only two were written solely in Arabic, although many included Arabic quotations. The broad shift towards printing in the vernacular suggests that earlier trends towards democratizing religious knowledge had not only deepened, but also spread across all the major reformists sects.

The publication of Nazir Husain's Ahl-i-Hadith tract, *Meyar-ul-Haqq*, and the subsequent burst of books and pamphlets either attacking or defending its arguments, provides a glimpse into this much wider body of literature. Nazir Husain (1805–1902) was born in Bihar and met Sayyid Ahmad Barelwi and Shah Ismail as a young man. Deeply inspired by the two men, he moved to Delhi and eventually started his own *madrasa*, where he trained a large number of students in the study of *hadith*. During the late 1860s he was detained but later released in connection with the Wahhabi trials. In a telling reflection of the government's vacillation between suppressing and co-opting religious leaders, the viceroy bestowed on Husain the title of *shams-ul-ulama* (the sun of scholars) in 1897, an award for exceptional scholarship in Oriental languages.[44] Although Nazir Husain spent most of his time teaching and issuing *fatwas*, his *Meyar-ul-Haqq* (The Measure of Truth, [1865 or 1866]) provoked a firestorm of pamphlet warfare.[45]

Nazir Husain claimed that *Meyar* was a reply to *Tanvir-ul-Haqq* (Illumination of Truth), a work criticizing the writings of Shah Ismail.[46]

---

[43] The linguistic distribution of the books was: Urdu (38); Arabic and Urdu (3); Persian (6); Arabic and Persian (3); Bengali (2); Punjabi (2); and Arabic (2). Books listed as written in Arabic and Urdu or Arabic and Persian generally included extended Arabic quotations, often with Urdu or Persian translations, and thus have been counted as Urdu and Persian publications.

[44] Abu Yahya Imam Khan, *Tarajim-i-ulama-yi-hadith-i-Hind* (1938; Reprint Lahore: Markazi Jamiyyat-i-Talabahyi Ahl-i-Hadith, 1971). The title of *shams-ul-ulama* was created in 1887 as part of the Jubilee celebrations marking the fiftieth anniversary of Queen Victoria's accession to the throne. The title was given to Muslim (and some Parsi) scholars, while Hindu scholars were given the Sanskrit title *mahamahopadhyaya* (most mighty teacher). Harriot Georgina Blackwood, Marchioness of Dufferin and Ava, *Our Viceregal Life in India: Selections from My Journal, 1884–1882*, vol. 2 (London: John Murray, 1889), 116.

[45] Sayyid Nazir Husain, *Meyar-ul-Haqq* (Reprint Lahore: Maktabah Naziriyah, [1965]). I have been unable to determine the exact publication date, but *Meyar* was most likely published around 1865 or 1866. One reply to *Meyar* published in 1873 indicated that *Meyar* was written seven or eight years earlier. Sayyid Ahmad Hasan, *Talkhis-ul-Anzar fi ma Buniya Ilah-yi-ul-Intisar* (Delhi: Faruqi Press, 1290H [1873]), 9.

[46] Husain, *Meyar*, 9–11. The authorship of *Tanvir* remains a matter of dispute. The Delhi scholar Muhammad Qutbuddin Khan claimed it as his work in *Taufir-ul-Haqq* ([Lahore]: Ganesh Press, 1869), but Nazir Husain insisted that he had only translated the Persian work of Husain's own student Sheikh Muhammad Shah. Muhammad Jaiballah, introduction to *Madar-ul-Haqq fi Radd Meyar-ul-Haqq ma Rasa'il ... [The*

Nazir Husain's writing style epitomized the personal attacks that were routinely part of the cut and thrust of scholarly debates; he accused the author of *Tanvir* of vanity (*zom*), stupidity (*kaj-fahmi*), and ignorance (*na-waqifiyat*).[47] Nazir Husain offered elaborate critiques of various arguments in favor of *taqlid* of a single school of law. He focused in particular on the Quranic verse (chapter 21, verse 7), "Ask of the people of *zikr*, if you do not know," which had commonly been interpreted by Hanafi *ulama* as supporting *taqlid*. Insisting on a literal reading of the verse, he argued that the phrase "people of *zikr*," roughly translated as "the people of remembrance or telling," could not be constricted to a particular group of people. He further disputed the idea that the Sunni *ulama* had reached a consensus (*ijma*), based on the verse, that made it obligatory to follow the four schools of law.[48] He also rejected the logic that scholars were obligated to follow a single school of law from among the four, comparing the claim to saying that "one was even because four was even."[49]

Turning to the second half of the verse, "if you do not know," Nazir Husain argued that it only sanctioned an individual consulting another person when he lacked knowledge himself. Otherwise, Nazir Husain insisted that whenever possible individuals should act according to their own understanding of the Quran and *hadith*. He did not reject *taqlid* altogether, instead condemning those who followed the rulings of a school of law in opposition to their own understanding of divine texts. He divided *taqlid* into four categories, which ranged from *wajib* (obligatory) to *shirk* (polytheism). In essence, Nazir Husain considered it permissible, and even in some cases necessary, to follow a school of law so long as it conformed to an individual's own understanding of the Quran and *hadith*. However, he castigated those who dismissed the rulings of other schools and called the belief that one must exclusively follow a single school a heretic innovation, or *bidat*. He condemned in the strongest terms those who steadfastly clung to the rulings of their own school of law even when they came to know of *hadith* supporting an opposing practice.[50]

By arguing that individual interpretation should outweigh established doctrine when the two came into conflict, Nazir Husain's framing of *taqlid* significantly undermined the authority of the schools of law. He

Axis of Truth in Refutation of Meyar-ul-Haq with the Pamphlets ...], by Muhammad Shah (1869; Reprint Lahore: Jamiyyat Ahl-i- Sunnat, 1991), 22–4.
[47] Husain, *Meyar*, 12.
[48] Ibid., 37–59.
[49] Ibid., 43.
[50] Ibid., 75–7.

understood individual interpretation to require literacy, but not exceptional learning. He insisted that the Quran and *hadith* could be understood with the aid of an Arabic dictionary. Nazir Husain also rejected
a refrain commonly heard at the time, that contemporary Muslims'
ability to comprehend the Quran and *hadith* had decreased because of
the amount of time that had lapsed since the Prophet's era. He insisted,
"On the contrary, today we have obtained superior understanding than
before because in the initial period *hadith* were taught by word of mouth,
the books had not been compiled, grammar was not systematized,
and the biographies of the reporters of *hadith* were not in existence."[51]
Thus, although *Meyar* did not issue a blanket condemnation of *taqlid*,
it circumscribed its permissible use and shifted the weight of authority
from established precedent to individual interpretation.

The initial responses to Nazir Husain's book were scholarly both
in form and content. Maulvi Irshad Husain (1832–93), a member of
the Mujaddidi Sufi order who had trained in Lucknow and Delhi and
became a leading scholar of *fiqh* at the Rampur court, penned one of the
most substantial replies.[52] His *Intisar-ul-Haqq* (The Victory of Truth), a
book of over 400 pages, was printed in Bareilly in 1873. It accompanied
long passages from *Meyar-ul-Haqq* with blow-by-blow refutations,
allowing the reader to compare the two texts even if he or she did not
have access to a copy of *Meyar*. Irshad Husain acknowledged that the
obligation to follow one of the schools of law could not be derived directly from the Quran or *hadith*. He argued that the institution of *taqlid*
instead emerged as the product of the gradual decline of the unity and
purity of the Islamic community, necessitating a more ordered approach
to deriving legal rulings. As he explained:

[Initially] There was no need to require the fixed following of particular *mujtahids*
because the people among the followers of the Prophet, due to their closeness to
his time and the generation after him, were generally scrupulous and pious. In
fact it would have been harmful. During the time of the four Imams the schools
of law were compiled and the followers of the schools of each of the Imams
collected the important *hadith*. People also began to follow their own individual
desires. For this reason, it became necessary to follow a particular established
*mujtahid*, without which it would have been very difficult for the public to perform God's commands.[53]

[51] Ibid., 70, 74.
[52] Ahmad Ali Khan Shauq, *Tazkirah-yi-Kamilan-i-Rampur* (1929; Reprint Patna: Khuda
Baksh Oriental Public Library, 1986), 30–3.
[53] Muhammad Irshad Husain, *Intisar-ul-Haqq* (1873; Reprint Rampur, 1318H [1900/
1901]), 153.

Elaborating on how changing conditions could create new legal obligations, Irshad Husain explained that the *sharia* contained both direct injunctions that held true at all times as well as legal obligations that emerged from particular contexts. Explaining this distinction, he continued: "It is true that in origin and in essence there is no requirement to follow a particular *mujtahid* ... However, taking into account additional conditions that came forward it is obligatory to follow an established Imam."[54] *Intisar* thus insisted that the Quran and *hadith* had to be read in the context of changing historical circumstances, which could give rise to new legal obligations, including following a school of law.

Echoing the back-and-forth of the public debates that were a vital feature of religious exchange in India, four supporters of Nazir Husain quickly penned replies to Irshad Husain's work. These short pamphlets shifted the tone of the debate from scholarly disputation to polemic. The first, *Barahin-i-Isna-Ashar* [Twelve Arguments], was apparently published only one day after *Intisar*.[55] The second, a twelve-page pamphlet by Ahmad Hasan, claimed to contain a complete summary and refutation of all 400 pages of *Intisar*. Adopting a sarcastic tone, Ahmad Hasan declared: "My intention in the forthcoming work is mostly to please the compiler of *Intisar*. Yet, praise be to God, the compiler has composed his work in a style that almost cuts itself off. Thus taking the compiler's writings from beginning to end, his lengthy dialogue of nonsense can be answered in a very short essay."[56] The substance of Ahmad Hasan's remarks criticized Irshad Husain for misleading people through his skillful use of logic.[57] As Ahmad Hasan declared:

The above-mentioned writer is famous for his expertise in the sciences of reason (*ulum-i-aqliyah*), and in his conceit he has perfected the construction of every type of confusing artifice by means of reason. However, having opposed the writings of great scholars with explanations based on reason, he has produced explanations that neither benefit himself, nor harm his opponents.[58]

Reflecting the Ahl-i-Hadith's deep suspicion of *aql*, Ahmad Hasan was unwilling to even engage with Irshad Husain's argument that the Quran and *hadith* had to be interpreted in the context of changing circumstances.

[54] Ibid., 155.
[55] Jaiballah, introduction to *Madar-ul-Haqq*, 48; Sayyid Amir Husain, *Barahin-i-Isna Ashar* (Delhi: Faruqi Press, 1874).
[56] Hasan, *Talkhis*, 2.
[57] Ibid., 8.
[58] Ibid., 2.

The gradual degeneration of the debate over *Meyar* into personal
attacks reflected both the importance of defending scholarly reputations
and the ways in which debates about *taqlid* brought together highly
nuanced arguments with exchanges directed at broader audiences.
During the debate over *Meyar*, several scholars composed both scholarly works and short pamphlets aimed at wider audiences. The *ulama*
were aware that most Muslims would not read scholarly tomes, and their
fear that their opponents might gain popular support spurred them to
develop more accessible styles of writing. Highly skilled in the art of
oral debate on religious topics, Muslim scholars attempted to translate
these skills onto the written page, mixing visual displays of their learning
in Arabic with witty cuts at their opponents in vernacular Urdu. For
example, in 1869, Muhammad Shah composed *Madar-ul-Haqq* (The
Axis of Truth), a nearly 500-page tome largely consisting of Arabic text
with Urdu translations below each line.[59] In the introduction to a second
work titled *Urvat-ul-Vusqa* (The Firmest Bond), he explained that several *ulama* had asked him to write a work that would bring the benefit
of *Madar* to the general public. Yet although *Urvat-ul-Vusqa* was one-
tenth the length of *Madar* and opened with a lively introduction in colloquial Urdu, it also primarily consisted of Arabic quotations. Either the
distinguished scholar could not bring himself to pander to the masses, or
he felt that the best way to convince the common man of the difficulty
of interpreting religious texts independently was to awe them with the
learned feats of the *ulama*.[60]

The *ulama*'s concern with addressing a broader audience reflected
the close relationship between debates about methods of interpretation
and different ritual forms. In addition to alterations in the performance
of daily prayer, the Ahl-i-Hadith challenged the authority of *taqlid* by
adopting different standards of purity for water used for ritual washing
and alternative styles of dress, such as wearing their trousers above the
ankle. The authors of pamphlets often explained that they had been
motivated to write because of public confrontations over these differences
in ritual and comportment; they attempted to counsel common Muslims
on correct bodily practice. In one such pamphlet responding to *Meyar*,
Sayyiduddin Khan, the son of a student of Shah Abdul Aziz, used a
question-and-answer format that both echoed the *fatwa* form and allowed
him to explain abstract arguments through specific examples. The text

---

[59] Muhammad Shah, *Madar-ul-Haqq fi Radd Meyar-ul-Haqq ma Rasa'il Urvat-ul-Vusqa
va Etiraz-i-Ahl-ul-Sunnat Ala Masa'il Ahl-ul-Bidaat* (1869; Reprint Lahore: Jamiyyat
Ahl-i-Sunnat, 1991).

[60] Muhammad Shah, *Urvat-ul-Vusqa* ([n.d.], Reprint in *Madar-ul-Haqq*).

opened with a description of *maulvis* from Delhi arriving in mosques in villages and small towns and washing before prayers with water from a well in which a dog had fallen and died.[61] When asked why they did not remove the dead carcass, these *maulvis* allegedly quoted from "some newly minted *maulvi* of *hadith* from Delhi and *Meyar* and some Urdu pamphlets which have been published and circulated, and which look like *sanads* or legal decrees."[62] Instructing his readers not to be taken in when people quoted *hadith* in support of their position, Sayyiduddin explained: "The truth of the matter is that every sort of tradition exists in books of exegesis, *hadith*, theology, and Quranic studies."[63]

Cautioning against what he described as the newfangled practice of choosing between the schools of law, Sayyiduddin Khan provided the following question and response:

**Question 3.** Is *taqlid-i-mutlaq* [free or independent *taqlid*] without restriction to a single school obligatory, or is it obligatory to follow one of the established Imams? ... if the legal judgments derived through *ijtihad* are matters of speculation anyway, then why is it necessary according to *sharia* to maintain *taqlid-i-shakhsi* [following a single Imam] – how can a speculative matter become legally absolute?

**Answer.** This is a strange belief that *taqlid-i-mutlaq* is obligatory but following one of the established Imams is *bidat* and *shirk*. This is a strange joke: if *taqlid* of the established Imams, which was settled about two hundred years [after the life of Muhammad] is *bidat*, how can *taqlid-i-mutlaq* be lawful? Those who say such a thing are clearly people who are not aware of the four principles of the Sunnis, and who do not believe that the *ijma* [consensus] of the Sunni *ulama* and *qiyas* [analogy] can serve as legal proofs. They believe that only two principles, the holy Quran and *hadith*, can serve as legal proofs. In this condition many things forbidden by the *sharia* cannot be adduced from only the Quran and *hadith*, for example *bhang* [cannabis] and other drugs, etc. People holding such beliefs cannot prove the prohibition of *bidat* only from the Quran and *hadith*.[64]

Although presented in an accessible manner, the text addressed the key question embodied in debates about *taqlid* – the relationship between human reason and religious authority. The Ahl-i-Hadith attempted to link individual believers as closely as possible to direct sources of divine authority, minimizing the intervention of human agents. In this

---

[61] This example appears repeatedly in the pamphlet literature on disputes between the Ahl-i-Hadith and the Hanafis and was rooted in debates about several conflicting *hadith* concerning the conditions under which water can be contaminated and thus rendered unfit for ablutions. For another discussion of the topic, see Muhammad Ismail Gangohi, *Javab-i-Ishtiha-yi-Ghair Muqallidin* (Ludhiana: Rahmani Press, 1294 H. [1877]), 8.

[62] Sayyiduddin Khan, *Tanqid fi Bayan-ul-Taqlid* (Delhi: Akmal-ul-Matabe, 1869), 11–12.

[63] Ibid., 21.

[64] Ibid., 27–8.

framework religious authority rested with God alone, and no human interpreter could intervene between God and individual Muslims. In contrast defenders of *taqlid* portrayed the expertise of Muslim scholars and jurists as essential to the project of deriving religious guidance from the Quran and *hadith*. They emphasized that, over time, the accumulated reason of the Muslim community offered a better guide to correct practice than the wisdom of any single Muslim interpreting the Quran and *hadith* on his or her own. They thus underlined the human dimension of religious authority, arguing that expert interpretations of divine texts could give rise to obligations that were not necessarily apparent in the text themselves. In this framework *taqlid* served as a method of backing rational interpretations of divine texts, themselves the products of individual human effort, with the authority of law.

In making a case for backing religious reasoning with law, defenders of *taqlid* strayed into the crosshairs of colonial law (most likely unintentionally, given the *ulama*'s broad embrace of political quietism during the decades after 1857). If *taqlid* was at times mandatory, who would enforce it, how, and in what areas? With the state judiciary claiming a monopoly on the right to back rational judgment with force, these questions inevitably drew colonial courts into debates about the respective roles of *ijtihad* and *taqlid*.

### Colonial Law and *Taqlid*

The dispute in Tajpore with which I opened this chapter provides a particularly vivid illustration of how debates about *taqlid* and *ijtihad* translated into a conflict over ritual space that could end up in a colonial court. In his testimony, the sixty-year-old *imam* of the mosque explained that he had changed the way he conducted prayers after a conversation with his brother-in-law. He indicated that he now obeyed all four founding jurists of the principal schools of law. He explained that, although Hanafis did not raise their hands during prayer or say *amin* aloud, followers of the other three schools did, so he followed their practice. He emphasized that he followed the legal interpretations of past jurists, but only "when they are in accord with the Koran and the Hadith (tradition)."[65] In court, the *imam*'s opponents claimed that this meant he had become a Wahhabi. In explaining this position, one of the *imam*'s unhappy congregants, a tailor by profession, argued, "Pronouncing the word 'amen' and raising the hands are not proper in our creed, but these are proper according to

---

[65] Record of Proceedings, *Fuzal Karim v. Haji Mowla Baksh* (PCOR), 436.

the creed of the Safis [sic, Shafi, one of the four schools of law]."[66] While the tailor was by no means a religious expert, he was nonetheless clearly aware of debates about the obligation to follow a single school of law.

The testimony from the court case provides key clues as to how debates about Islamic jurisprudence spilled out of the elite realms of scholarly debate into wider social circles and, eventually, the courts. In their testimony, both the *imam* and the tailor indicated that their beliefs were formed through conversations with other Muslims. While the *imam* mentioned his brother-in-law, the tailor cited a *maulvi* from Peshawar who had passed through Tajpore and informed the residents, "we who belonged to the Hanifi [sic] sect could not acceptably say prayers behind that man."[67] Other parties in the case cited books as the source of their beliefs. An employee in the local Collectorate Office, who helped lead the parties opposing the *imam*, noted that he had read *Intisar-ul-Haqq*, the prominent defense of *taqlid* discussed above.[68] The Tajpore residents' familiarity with these texts illustrates how the interface between textual and oral forms of social communication bridged the gap between elite scholarship and quotidian spaces of religious worship.

While linked to questions of interpretation, the conflict between the *imam* and his congregants played out as physical confrontations. The *imam*'s opponents challenged his authority physically – they refused to imitate the gestures he made during prayer and stood on the raised platform normally reserved for the *imam*.[69] While they clearly disagreed with him about questions of interpretation, the congregants ultimately emphasized their objection to the physical changes that the *imam* initiated. When questioned, the tailor assured the court, "Even now I would say prayers under the leadership of Mowla Buksh if he only gave up uttering 'amen' loudly and raising his hands to his ears."[70] His statement suggests that confrontations over ritual practice, while linked to debates about methods of interpretation, gained added significance because of the power of public, physical performance.[71] The prayer ritual was a particularly democratic form of participating in religious debate

[66] Ibid., 452.
[67] Ibid.
[68] "Deposition of Kader Buksh, Depositions of the Defendants' Witnesses, Remand File of the First Court," *Fuzl Karim v. Haji Mowla Baksh* [PCOR], 454.
[69] Ibid., 435–6.
[70] Ibid.
[71] On prayer as a site of embodiment, see Saba Mahmood, "Rehearsed Spontaneity and the Conventionality of Ritual: Disciplines of Salat," *American Ethnologist* 28, no. 4 (November 2001): 827–53; Gregory Starrett, "The Hexis of Interpretation: Islam and the Body in the Egyptian Popular School," *American Ethnologist* 22, no. 4 (November 1995): 953–69.

that could potentially involve every Muslim, regardless of position or level of education. Confrontations over ritual practice therefore opened up debates about structures of authority within the Muslim community, and forced various parties, including ultimately the colonial state, to define who had the right to control Muslim public spaces.

The community in Tajpore was by no means the first to bring its disputes over ritual practice into the secular courts. The Allahabad High Court issued decisions in the 1880s in three virtually identical cases involving disputes over the volume and gestures used during specific moments in the daily prayer sequence. In the disputes members of the Ahl-i-Hadith, and similar sects, embraced variations which were associated with different schools of Islamic jurisprudence, an embodied statement of their rejection of *taqlid* within the Hanafi school.[72] Syed Mahmood, the Allahabad High Court judge and son of Sayyid Ahmad Khan (and also the author of the *mahr* decision from Chapter 2) played a key role in shaping the Allahabad court's approach to these cases. In the first case, the Allahabad court held that the defendant could be held criminally liable if he intentionally disturbed the peace by using a style of prayer that departed from standard practice in a Hanafi mosque. Mahmood, however, dissented, arguing that such cases involved a "religious usage or institution" and therefore should be adjudicated with reference to Muslim law. Insisting that all four schools of law were equally orthodox, he argued that the "differences of opinion that exist between them are pure matters of detail." Followers of three of the four schools pronounced *amin* aloud; in addition, according to Mahmood, the Hanafi text outlining the strongest argument against pronouncing *amin* merely stated that it was not recommended. Mahmood concluded that holding a person saying *amin* aloud responsible for an ensuing disturbance "would place the minority at the mercy of the majority." Mahmood also argued that a particular group of Muslims, such as Hanafis, could not reserve a mosque for their own exclusive use because "when a mosque is built and consecrated by public worship, it ceases to be the property of the builder and vests in God."[73] In two subsequent civil cases Mahmood's colleagues were partially swayed by his logic. The judgments cited with approval his

---

[72] For a more detailed discussion of the Allahabad cases, see Asad Ahmed, "Adjudicating Muslims," 94–110; Guenther, "Syed Mahmood and the Transformation of Muslim Law in British India," 191–7.

[73] *Queen-Empress* v. *Ramzan and others* [1885] ILR 7 Allahabad 461, quoted at 472–7. The court's treatment of mosques as "divine property" differed significantly from cases that allowed upper-caste Hindus to exclude lower castes from temples. The rationale for this exclusion, however, was framed in terms of property rights rather than as a question of ritual. Rao, *The Caste Question*, 81–117.

argument that the ritual differences in question were legally permissible under Muslim law; therefore, groups such as the Ahl-i-Hadith could not be excluded from public mosques. The court, however, left open the possibility that a defendant might be held criminally liable if ritual differences led to a disturbance of the peace.[74]

Mahmood's analysis of diversity within the Islamic legal tradition departed dramatically from the writings of *ulama* who defended *taqlid*.[75] Given his father's key role in debates about *ijtihad* and *taqlid*, Mahmood was clearly aware of arguments in favor of *taqlid*. He, however, ignored the rationale behind *taqlid* in his opinions. By implying that the coexistence of multiple valid opinions in different schools of law meant that no single opinion could be legally binding, Mahmood obscured the role that *taqlid* within the schools of law traditionally played in Islamic jurisprudence. Muslim jurists generally acknowledged the legitimacy of rulings from other schools of law, but still in most cases followed the rulings of their own school. Scholars of Islamic law have emphasized that this simultaneous recognition of interpretative diversity between the schools of law and effective control within each school ensured that the juridical tradition could promote both continuity and change.[76] As Mohammad Fadel explains, this balancing act is common to many systems of law, which share "the desire for regular and predictable legal outcomes."[77] By ignoring the binding authority of *taqlid* within each school of law, Mahmood therefore effectively obscured the legal logic animating the argument in favor of ritual conformity.

When the Tajpore case came before the Privy Council on appeal, the Lords looked to Mahmood's decisions in Allahabad to justify their construction of Islamic ritual as a zone of individual preference. The author of the Privy Council decision, however, also brought his own personal perspective to the case. Arthur Hobhouse served in India as the law member of the viceroy's council from 1872 to 1877 before returning to Britain and joining the Judicial Committee of the Privy Council in 1881. While on the Privy Council, he authored several controversial decisions on religious questions, including ruling in favor of the independence of the Church of South Africa from the Anglican Church and the legality

---

[74] *Jangu and others* v. *Ahmad-Ullah and others* [1889] ILR 13 Allahabad 419. *Ata-Ullah* v. *Azim-Ullah* [1889] ILR 12 Allahabad 494.

[75] Guenther, "Syed Mahmood and the Transformation of Muslim Law in British India," 58.

[76] Wael B. Hallaq, *Authority, Continuity and Change in Islamic Law* (Cambridge: Cambridge University Press, 2001).

[77] Mohammad Fadel, "The Social Logic of Taqlid and the Rise of the Mukhatasar," *Islamic Law and Society* 3, no. 2 (January 1996): 197.

of Hindu adoption.[78] Hobhouse's willingness to unsettle religious authorities in the colonies was likely shaped by his involvement with secularist movements in Britain. His nephew and biographer described Hobhouse as a "Rationalist." In the last few years of his life, Hobhouse corresponded with George Holyoake, who coined the term "secularism" in 1851, and Hobhouse donated funds to Holyoake's Rationalist Press Association.[79] Victorian secularism has been described as "neutral on the matter of religion, not hostile to it."[80] Yet Hobhouse shared with the self-declared secularists a suspicious attitude towards religious beliefs, particularly when they were backed by force. As Hobhouse wrote, "the religious man, believing that he is obeying the positive commands of a Deity ... often has been led into extravagancies of conceit, pride, folly, and cruelty, which bring mankind into degradation and misery."[81] Hobhouse rarely drew direct connections between his personal views on religion and his work for the Privy Council. A personal letter he wrote to his wife in 1889, however, while reviewing another case involving trusteeship of a Hindu idol, suggests that his views on ritual in Britain shaped his understanding of Indian cases. As Hobhouse noted: "I have been wondering whether our quarrels over candles and wine and water, and the raising of hands, seems to our Rajpoot neighbours as unreal and frivolous as their quarrels about the relative dignity of paintings, sticks, and stones seem to us."[82]

Given Hobhouse's background, it is not surprising that he was unsympathetic to the argument for imposing ritual conformity in India. What is striking about his decision, however, is the extent to which he completely erased the argument in favor of *taqlid*, failing even to introduce the term when he discussed whether a member of a particular school of jurisprudence could adopt the practices of another school. Hobhouse argued, with respect to the opponents of the *imam*: "The evidence is an absolute blank. No book, no opinion, no practice of any community of worshippers is cited." (This statement, however, was belied by the fact that the Calcutta High Court had found grounds for the opposite position, declaring, "the Imam or matwali should have performed his

[78] C.E.A. Bedwell, "Hobhouse, Arthur, Baron Hobhouse (1819–1904)," rev. H.C.G. Matthew, *Oxford Dictionary of National Biography* (Oxford: Oxford University Press, 2004), accessed May 24, 2017, www.oxforddnb.com/view/article/33902.
[79] Ibid., 247, 250–7.
[80] Royle, "Secularists and Rationalists, 1800–1940," 412.
[81] Ibid., 248–9.
[82] Leonard Trelawney Hobhouse and John Lawrence Hammond, *Lord Hobhouse: A Memoir* (London: Edward Arnold, 1905), 211.

duties in the customary manner."[83]) Hobhouse instead emphasized the supposed triviality of the differences in ritual practice. He argued:

it cannot be that an *Imam* should be so bound by his own or his predecessor's previous practice in worship that he cannot make the slightest variation from it in gesture, intonation, or otherwise, without committing an offence. Even a code of ritual can hardly be so minute as absolutely to exclude all individual peculiarity or discretion.[84]

Clearly they were not minute matters, either to the *imams* or to his opponents, who engaged in a lengthy and expensive legal battle to defend and oppose their respective rituals, but Hobhouse was unwilling or unable to grasp the rational basis for the dispute.

In siding with the *imam*, Hobhouse thus not only ruled against *taqlid*, he refused to even acknowledge the possibility of an argument in its favor. His blindness to the possibility of an opposing argument is particularly striking given that Britain had, in the not-so-distant past, subjected Anglican ritual to the courts – a matter obliquely referenced in the letter quoted above. Hobhouse's own radical politics likely played a role in his one-sided view of the case, but his decision also fits comfortably into larger patterns in the colonial regulation of religion. While the Indian Law Commission set aside both family and ritual as areas in which the colonial courts would apply religious laws, in practice the courts treated these two areas quite differently. The courts took an active role in regulating marriage, inheritance, and charitable endowments, very likely because of their entanglement with questions of property. Emphasizing *taqlid* made sense for the courts in these areas because the doctrine allowed them to exert their own authority in the name of maintaining Muslim tradition.

The courts took a far more hands-off approach to regulating ritual, which in many cases did not impinge directly on questions of property. But in marking off ritual as a zone of individual discretion (or peculiarity, in Hobhouse's words), the Privy Council did not just leave Indians to settle these matters for themselves. The Privy Council was neither willing to regulate ritual difference itself, nor willing to delegate the legal authority to do so to others. Thus in the final paragraph of his decision, Hobhouse revised a lower-court ruling that gave the *imam* the authority to turn out his opponents from the mosque. Instead, he implied that the *imam* had to wait for them to cause a disturbance to public order, at which point he could then ask the colonial courts to intervene. In so doing, Hobhouse reasserted the colonial court's monopoly on backing

---

[83] *Fazl Karim* v. *Maula Baksh* [ILR], 457.
[84] Ibid., 458.

reasoning with force, insisting that the colonial state alone enjoyed this sovereign power. And by simultaneously suggesting that violence alone would provoke state intervention, the courts effectively courted crisis, ensuring that ritual differences would remain a source of conflict.

The problems with this approach were foreshadowed by a stray comment from the judge in the one of the Allahabad mosque cases. The judge noted at the end of his decision, "although I have expressed my view of the law, I think it better that persons who differ in matters of ritual should have separate mosques, but this is not the question we have got to decide."[85] Edge's comment implied that he hoped that the Muslim community would find a mechanism of internal self-regulation to prevent future disputes. Yet the judge ignored the fact that the courts reduced the chances for this sort of solution by legally protecting the rights of individual Muslims to embrace divergent rituals while simultaneously barring mosques from enforcing conformity or expelling innovators.

Thus the colonial state's policy of "noninterference" in ritual was far less neutral than it might first appear. It effectively encouraged the formation of break-away sects while limiting Muslims' ability to manage the resulting social fallout. Muslims themselves were often aware of these dynamics, even if the courts were not. In a 1914 pamphlet, members of the Ahl-i-Hadith described recent legal decisions as *Fatuhat-i-Ahl-i-Hadith* (Victories of the Ahl-i-Hadith) – a clear indication that they were emboldened by the courts to continue with their disruptive tactics of ritual nonconformity.[86]

## Conclusion

Britain frequently cited noninterference in Indian religious rituals as one of the great boons of colonial rule – one of the essential freedoms that Britain guaranteed to its Indian subjects. Britain's own foot-dragging in implementing a similar policy at home, however, hints at the potentially deleterious effects of radical nonintervention. The escalation of intra-communal conflicts between Muslims over ritual differences corroborates these suspicions. The outcome of this policy of nonintervention, however, was not preordained, and the preceding analysis should not be interpreted as an argument against religious freedom. Instead, nonintervention was particularly fraught as implemented in colonial India because it pivoted around key contradictions. By upholding *taqlid* in domestic cases, the

[85] *Ata-Ullah* v. *Azim-Ullah*, 502.
[86] *Fatuhat-i-Ahl-i-Hadith* (Amritsar: Roz Bazar Steam Press, 1914).

colonial courts fostered the view that Muslim law was a uniform and unchanging code, even if this idea was often belied in practice. As British colonial rule continued into the twentieth century, many Muslim leaders increasingly echoed this view of the *sharia*, obscuring the ways in which Islamic jurists had diverged on important questions in the past.[87] This emphasis on a singular, unified Islam made Muslims less tolerant of internal differences, including in the realm of ritual. Yet, by refusing to recognize the logic of *taqlid* in ritual cases, the colonial courts encouraged the very diverging interpretations and practices that they discouraged in their own administration of personal law in domestic cases. The result placed the idea of a single, unified *sharia* in volatile conflict with the practical reality of an increasingly fractured Muslim community.

Similarly, by encouraging the spread of print, the British added fuel to democratizing trends in Indian society that date at least to the collapse and reorganization of social hierarchies in the wake of the declining power of the Mughal Empire. Yet the British provided minimal political outlets for these democratizing social trends, effectively preventing Indians from developing new forms of governance that matched their changing social contexts.

The fallout from colonial nonintervention in ritual thus suggests that the recurring, structural contradictions of secular legal governance affected Indian Muslims in concrete, deleterious ways. While the preceding analysis has focused on how these dynamics heightened intracommunal conflicts, the next chapter examines how these contradictions played out in interactions between different religious communities.

---

[87] On the increasing alignment between colonial constructions of Muslim law and Muslims' own imaginary, see Kugle, "Framed, Blamed and Renamed," 302–19; Kozlowski, *Muslim Endowments and Society in British India*, 186.

# 5    Pathologizing Muslim Sentiment

In 1924 the Hindu publisher Mahashay Rajpal printed a satire on the Prophet's domestic life titled *Rangila Rasul*. Translated literally into English, the book's title referred to the "colorful Prophet," but in Urdu and Hindi, it strongly insinuated sexual dalliance. The Punjab government brought charges against Rajpal under Section 153A of the Indian Penal Code, which criminalized "attempts to promote feelings of enmity or hatred between different classes." When the Lahore High Court acquitted Rajpal in May 1927 on the grounds of insufficient evidence that the pamphlet promoted feelings of enmity between Muslims and Hindus, Lahore broke out in riots. The fallout from the case fueled support for a new clause in the Indian Penal Code, Section 295A, which more directly criminalized insults to religion.[1]

Both Section 153A and the even more robust Section 295A were part of a colonial legal arsenal that policed expressions of religious enmity, particularly when they pitted different religious communities against each other. Although Thomas Macaulay drafted the Indian Penal Code in the 1830s, it was not enacted until 1860, concurrently with the Indian Law Commission's deliberation on religious personal law. The Commission's approaches to criminal and personal law were united by a common emphasis on juxtaposing Indian religion with rational thought. Macaulay justified the inclusion of Chapter XV, "Of Offences Relating to Religion," to which Section 295A was later added, for instance, on the basis of Indians' emotional volatility and sensitivity to religious insult.[2] By portraying Indians as having excessive religious sentiment,

---

[1] For another account of these events, see Gene R. Thursby, *Hindu-Muslim Relations in British India: A Study of Controversy, Conflict, and Communal Movements in Northern India 1923–1928* (Leiden: Brill, 1975), 40–71. See also Neeti Nair, "Beyond the 'Communal' 1920s: The Problem of Intention, Legislative Pragmatism, and the Making of Section 295A of the Indian Penal Code," *Indian Economic and Social History Review* 50, no. 3 (July 2013): 317–40.

[2] Asad Ali Ahmed, "Specters of Macaulay: Blasphemy, the Indian Penal Code, and Pakistan's Postcolonial Predicament," in *Censorship in South Asia: Cultural Regulation from*

legal reformers like Macaulay emphasized that only colonial institutions could act as rational, neutral mediators between Indian religious communities which, if left to their own devices, would be constantly in conflict. Instead of maintaining the peace, however, colonial law produced the very volatility that it purported to regulate. Legal provisions such as Section 153A, which made evidence of enmity a precondition for censorship, perversely encouraged more violent or emotive reactions to religious offense to secure outside legal intervention.[3] The British rhetoric of guaranteeing intercommunal peace was thus belied by a historical record of heightened religious conflict, as documented in a broad range of scholarship.[4]

This chapter shifts forward to the 1920s to explore how these established patterns of British secular legal governance were reworked as Indians came to play a larger role in politics, foreshadowing postcolonial transitions to come.[5] In 1909 and 1919 the British introduced limited electoral participation under the Government of India Acts in the hope of staving off anti-colonial protests. As a result the Indian Legislative Assembly, which passed Section 295A in 1927, included both British and Indian members. The Indian members were selected through separate electorates, with voting organized along communal lines and a certain number of seats reserved for Muslims. Intercommunal tensions were, in other words, built into the very logic of Indian elections and would continue to haunt the expansion of democratic participation in the lead-up to independence. Certainly, anti-colonial politics at times inspired intercommunal collaborations, particularly when Gandhi's Non-Cooperation Movement forged alliances with the Khilafat Movement in the 1920s.[6] But these moments of unity were consistently interspersed

---

*Sedition to Seduction*, ed. Raminder Kaur and William Mazzarella (Bloomington: Indiana University Press, 2009), 179–81.

[3] Ibid., 177.

[4] See for example Sandria B. Freitag, *Collective Action and Community: Public Arenas and the Emergence of Communalism in North India* (Berkeley: University of California Press, 1989); Gyanendra Pandey, *The Construction of Communalism in Colonial North India* (Delhi: Oxford University Press, 1990).

[5] This chapter builds on recent trends that extend the chronology of decolonization, starting before actual independence in 1947 and continuing as an unfinished project to date. For a compelling articulation of this argument, see Partha Chatterjee, *A Princely Impostor?: The Kumar of Bhawal and the Secret History of Indian Nationalism* (Delhi: Permanent Black, 2002), 376–7.

[6] Gail Minault, *The Khilafat Movement: Religious Symbolism and Political Mobilization in India* (New York: Columbia University Press, 1982); Shahid Amin, "Gandhi as Mahatma: Gorakhpur District, Eastern UP, 1921," in *Selected Subaltern Studies*, ed. Ranajit Guha and Gayatri Chakravorty Spivak (New York: Oxford University Press, 1988), 288–348.

with flare-ups of intercommunal violence. This period also saw the institutional rise of Hindu majoritarian politics, including the founding of the Rashtriya Swayamsevak Sangh (RSS), the parent organization to the contemporary Bharatiya Janata Party (BJP), the dominant force behind Hindu Right politics in postcolonial India.

In this context, Hindu majoritarian discourses recast Muslim sentiments as not just irrational, but as pathological symptoms of their fanaticism. This chapter traces this transition through the legal debates surrounding the pamphlet *Rangila Rasul*. It recovers the complex range of sentiments that Muslims expressed in response to the controversy, which included injury, vulnerability, anger, and love, focusing on how expressions of emotion were inextricably interwoven with arguments about law and politics. (I intentionally use the term "sentiment" rather than "emotion" to underline the cultivated nature of these expressions.[7]) As the controversy developed, segments of the press and Hindu politicians increasingly demonized these sentiments as the product of religious fanaticism. Some of these same figures called on Indians to embrace secularism, a term not widely in use among Indians until the 1920s. By "secularism," however, these Hindu politicians often meant politics cleansed not of religion in general, but of so-called Muslim fanaticism. By viewing their own religious sentiments as fully compatible with secular democracy while casting suspicion on those of Muslims, Hindu politicians thus infused burgeoning discourses of postcolonial secularism with majoritarian bias.[8]

### Nationalism, Communalism, and Sexual Politics

Intercommunal tensions increased after Gandhi called off the Non-Cooperation Movement in 1922, fueling anxiety about the role that religious sentiments should play in India's expanding democratic politics. During the remainder of the 1920s – a period some historians refer to as the "communal 1920s" – competing religious sects engaged in vicious

---

[7] Muslim sentiments in the nineteenth century were deeply shaped by larger historical contexts, ranging from religious reform movements to Victorian ideals of comportment. Margrit Penau, "Teaching Emotions: The Encounter between Victorian Values and Indo-Persian Concepts of Civility in Nineteenth-Century Delhi," in *Knowledge Production, Pedagogy, and Institutions in Colonial India*, ed. Indra Sengupta, Daud Ali, and Javed Majeed (New York: Palgrave Macmillan, 2011), 227–47.

[8] On rhetoric emphasizing the compatibility of Hinduism, but not Islam, with secular nationalism, see William Gould, *Hindu Nationalism and the Language of Politics in Late Colonial India* (Cambridge: Cambridge University Press, 2004), esp. 153.

campaigns of print warfare, and daily newspaper headlines reported on successive waves of religious riots.[9] Indians began to refer to communalism, or allegiance to religious community, as a threat to secular nationalism, suggesting that religious identity was a barrier to national integration. While the term at least in theory referred to any effort to put the interests of a particular religious community before those of the nation as a whole, communalism, as historian Ayesha Jalal has argued, was disproportionately used by the Hindu majority to discredit Muslim assertions of religious identity.[10]

In this tense environment, literary attacks on religious sentiments became rancorous. Frequently, they attacked the sexual morality of members of another religion or their founding religious personalities. A sampling from the Punjab press demonstrates how imagery linking communal attacks to sexual politics proliferated during this time. Employing a common form of satire that assumed the voice of the other community, the *Guru Ghantal,* a Hindu paper in Lahore, published a conversation between a Muslim *khangi,* an Urdu term for a kept woman, and a Hindu Jat. In the fictional conversation the Muslim prostitute appeared to use her sexual charms to lead the Jat away from the folds of Hindu faith:

KHANGI. – O Jat, embrace our religion.
JAT. – O wretch! What hast though to get from these matters?
KHANGI. – No Sir, it is the order of our Pir of Delhi that we should bring
    our friends within (the fold of) our religion by blandishments, coquetry,
    (displays of) development of breasts and pit in the chin, redness of lips, glow
    of cheeks, net of locks and dagger of eyebrows.[11]

Muslim papers engaged in the same dangerous game as their Hindu competitors.[12] Two days after the *Guru Ghantal* published the conversation between the Muslim *khangi* and the Jat, the *Lahaul* printed an article that claimed to be an open letter to "all *dhoti*-wearers of India." The letter outlined a plan to build an *ashram* of beautiful Hindu girls who would attract converts to Hinduism. The girls "should consider it their duty to propagate religion by every means, should be fond of remaining

---

[9] For an alternative view of the period, see Nair, "Beyond the 'Communal' 1920s."
[10] Ayesha Jalal, "Exploding Communalism: The Politics of Muslim Identity in South Asia," in *Nationalism, Democracy, and Development: State and Politics in India,* ed. Sugata Bose and Ayesha Jalal (Delhi: Oxford University Press, 1997), 89.
[11] *Guru Ghantal,* June 2, 1924, "Supplement to the Note on the Punjab Press No. 31, for the week ending the 2nd August 1924," 1.
[12] *Lahaul,* June 12, 1924, "Supplement to the Note on the Punjab Press No. 21, dated the 5th July," 1.

unveiled, should hate *purdah* and regard ogling as a means of attaining salvation."[13]

Such accounts were meant to amuse readers by portraying women from other religious communities as sexual predators.[14] Yet competitive campaigns to recruit religious converts produced real fear about individuals being induced to convert through romantic attachments. Hindu activists promoted conversion or reconversion of individuals of different religions, and waged campaigns known as *shuddhi* (purity) and *sangathan* (organization). In response, Muslims engaged in *tanzim* (organization) and *tabligh* (propagation). By translating numbers of religious adherents into political power, the new electoral system motivated leaders to increase the census count for their own religious community.[15] The 1920s saw a flurry of reports about intercommunal abduction, enticement, and elopement, alleging that Muslims and Hindus were using sexual attachments to increase their community's numbers.[16]

*Rangila Rasul* adopted this formula of attacking the Muslim community's domestic honor through a ribald satire of the Prophet's multiple marriages. Rajpal's book assumed a superficial tone of historical objectivity, or even studied admiration, for Muhammad's romantic accomplishments. Beneath this veneer, however, the pamphlet was a steady stream of caustic cuts at the Prophet's legacy:

> In this situation, if I call this Rangila Rasul *bibiyon-wala* [man of wives], then won't it be fitting? Say *bibiyon-wala* and you will have found Muhammad, will have found Muhammad's *ruh* [spirit].
> Krishna is the one of the flute; Ram is the one of the bow; Guru Gobind Singh is the one of the *kalgi* [plume of the Sikh turban]; Dayanand is the one of the Vedas. And thus Muhammad is the one of the wives. Each prophet has his *shan* [quality]. Muhammad's *shan* is his wives.[17]

The book suggested that Muhammad's wife Khadija was more suited in age to be his mother and that his wife Ayesha could be his daughter. It

---

[13] *Lahaul*, June 4, 1924, reprinted in "Supplement to the Note on the Punjab Press No. 25, dated the 21st June 1924," 3.

[14] On the intertwining of communal and sexual politics more generally, see Charu Gupta, *Sexuality, Obscenity, Community: Women, Muslims, and the Hindu Public in Colonial India* (Delhi: Permanent Black, 2001).

[15] Bernard Cohn, "The Census, Social Structure, and Objectification in South Asia," in *An Anthropologist among the Historians and Other Essays* (New Delhi: Oxford University Press, 1987), 224–54.

[16] Chatterjee, *A Princely Impostor?*, 376–7.

[17] *Rangila Rasul*, Banaras, n.d., 38–9. The version of the pamphlet from which the selection is quoted is a later reprint published in Banaras in the Hindi script, which is preserved in the National Archives of India (NAI), Home/Political/File 132/II/1927.

therefore extended a specific attack on Muhammad into more general insinuations about the perverse sexuality of the Muslim community.[18]

Attacks on another religious figure's sexual morality – particularly sexual morality in relationship to marriage – were not coincidental. Like patterns of secular legal governance more generally, authors of communalist attacks linked religious identity to control over women. Pamphlets like *Rangila Rasul*, by accusing revered (male) religious figures of excessive lust, also braided notions of irrationality into discourses on religious identity. By implying that Muslim or Hindu men could not control their sexual appetites, these pamphlets called into question their ability to engage in self-governance, both as individuals and as communities – echoing discourses that justified colonial rule on the grounds of Indians' excessive emotionality. As Indians began to assert their right to govern themselves, disputes over the domestic lives of revered religious persons thus turned into battle grounds for larger debates about the role that different religious communities would play in postcolonial politics.

## Muslims "Gone Mad": *Rangila Rasul* on Trial

Against this wider backdrop, government authorities initiated proceedings against Rajpal in July 1924, charging him with promoting feelings of enmity between different classes. While the case attracted intermittent attention from the press during extended legal proceedings, controversy erupted after Justice Dilip Singh acquitted Rajpal on May 4, 1927. Adding to the charged atmosphere, Singh announced the decision the day after intense riots broke out in Lahore over an alleged assault by a Muslim boy on a Sikh girl, violence that left twenty-seven dead.[19] While the riots were not sparked by the decision itself, the overlap in timing linked the two in the minds of British officials, including the Governor of Punjab, who warned that additional religious unrest might break out if the law was not revised.[20] Further complicating matters, within months the Allahabad and Lahore High Courts issued decisions censoring other offensive religious pamphlets, suggesting that the courts themselves were conflicted over the meaning of the law. In response during the summer of 1927, Muslims in the Punjab organized a series of mass meetings at

---

[18] The magistrate's decision included a detailed summary of the contents of the book. For a copy of the decision, see NAI, Home/Political/1927/File 132/I, 31–6. Page numbers are given according to the overall count in the file, not the pagination of individual documents.

[19] "No More Trouble at Lahore," *TOI*, May 16, 1927, 12; John W. Cell, *Hailey: A Study in British Imperialism, 1872–1969* (Cambridge: Cambridge University Press, 1992), 144.

[20] Cell, *Hailey*, 145.

mosques to demand that the government revise the penal code to ensure that similar materials would not be published in the future.[21] They also organized a High Court Day on July 22 to demand the removal of Justice Singh.[22] While these protests passed without major violence, the mainstream press and Hindu leaders began to cite Muslim responses to Rajpal's acquittal as evidence that they had "gone mad" – effectively equating their political activism with fanaticism.

During Rajpal's trial the ambiguous boundary between legitimate religious criticism and deliberate efforts to provoke enmity led different courts to reach conflicting decisions. The trial before the magistrate dragged on for over two years. Rajpal's lawyers defended the pamphlet as a legitimate tool for education and conversion by calling witnesses to testify that the allegations about Muhammad's life were "historically true."[23] While neither of the lower courts found this argument compelling, Justice Singh was more convinced. He insisted that the law was meant to protect living members of a religious community and therefore could not prevent "all adverse discussions of the life and character of a deceased religious leader." While acknowledging that the pamphlet could "only arouse the contempt of all decent persons," he refused to find "that it would necessarily promote feelings of enmity and hatred between different classes."[24]

During the months following, newspapers juxtaposed the decision in Rajpal's case against two similar cases before the Allahabad and Lahore High Courts that censored similar books insulting the Prophet. The case before the High Court in Allahabad involved a book titled *Vichitra Jiwan* (Strange Life), published in Agra in 1923. Justice Lindsay of the Allahabad court argued that he was not able "to appreciate the distinction between an attack upon a system of religion in the abstract and one upon the people who believe in it." He concluded, "it is contrary to all reason to imagine that liberty to criticize includes a licence to resort to the vile and abusive language which characterizes the book now before me."[25] Later in the summer of 1927, the Lahore High Court cited the

---

[21] For details of these meetings, see NAI, Home/Political/1927/File 132/I, 1–9.

[22] Thursby, *Hindu-Muslim Relations in British India*, 66.

[23] Letter from His Excellency Sir Malcolm Hailey, June 23, 1927, NIA, Home/Political/1927/File 132/I, 1.

[24] *Raj Paul* v. *Emperor* [1927] All India Reporter [hereafter AIR] 14 Lahore 590, quoted at 592.

[25] *Emperor* v. *Kali Charan Sharma* [1927] ILR 49 Allahabad 856, quoted at 862–3. The legal dispute over *Vichitra Jiwan* involved two cases; one was about the government seizure of the book and the other the actual prosecution of its author under Section 153A. The first case came before the Allahabad High Court in February 1927, several months before Justice Singh's decision in the *Rangila Rasul* case. For the second decision see *Kali Charan Sharma* v. *Emperor* [1927] Criminal Law Journal of India 28 785.

Allahabad decision with approval in convicting the author and publisher of an article titled "Sair-i-Dozakh" (Trip to Hell). Together, these two decisions cast doubt on Justice Singh's decision in the Rajpal case.[26]

Although these conflicting decisions left ample room to criticize the existing penal code as ambiguous and in need of clarification, the mainstream press and Hindu commentators instead increasingly caricatured Muslims' demands for legal reform as the product of religious fanaticism. They repeated variations on the theme that Indian Muslims had been driven mad by irrational religious sentiments. In a letter he sent to his son Jawaharlal, the future prime minister of India, Motilal Nehru declared: "The Mussalmans of India have gone mad."[27] The Hindu Mahasabha, a radical organization promoting a narrowly Hindu nationalist agenda, passed a resolution announcing that the Muslim protest against Justice Singh's decision had "exceeded the bounds of reason and propriety."[28] The *Civil and Military Gazette* of Lahore printed letters decrying the "senseless agitation."[29] The newspaper *Haryana Tilak*, in an article entitled "Mazhabi Diwanapan ki Zahiniyat" (The Mindset of Religious Madness) warned: "If this state of religious fanaticism continues in the same fashion among our Muslim brothers then the chains of slavery of this unfortunate country will never loosen."[30]

These accounts of Muslim rage vacillated between portraying all Muslims as fanatics and pitting "reasonable" Muslims against those who inappropriately played up religious injury for political gain. A cartoon from the newspaper *Milap* of Lahore (Figure 2), for example, drew a sharp visual contrast between the *kuch samajhdar musalman* (the somewhat-reasonable Muslim), outfitted in waistcoat and bowtie, and the *mazhabi diwana* (religious crazy or fanatic), bearded and jumping up and down in a fit of passion. In the cartoon, the "religious fanatic" declared, "If we commence civil disobedience, then the government will have to bow before us." The "somewhat reasonable Muslim" replied: "Stop it. I've heard enough. Don't be a braggart. You save your own head by asking for forgiveness and want to establish your leadership by fooling and ensnaring others."[31] The caricature in *Milap* worked as a veiled threat: Muslims would only be included in a "rational" discourse

---

[26] *Devi Sharan Sharma* v. *Emperor* [1927] AIR 14 Lahore 594.
[27] Motilal to Jawaharlal, July 7, 1927, in *Selected Works of Motilal Nehru*, ed. Ravinder Kumar and H.D. Sharma, vol. 5 (New Delhi, 1982), 260.
[28] Extract from Resolutions Passed by the Working Committee of the Hindu Mahasabha Held at Banaras on the August 3, 1927, NAI, Home/Political/1928/File 217, 16.
[29] "A Senseless Agitation," *Civil and Military Gazette*, July 15, 1927, 3.
[30] "Mazhabi Diwanapan ki Zahiniyat," *Haryana Tilak*, October 10, 1927, 5.
[31] *Milap*, July 17, 1927, 5.

Figure 2. In the cartoon the "religious fanatic" declares: "If we commence civil disobedience, then the government will have to bow before us." The "somewhat-reasonable Muslim" replies: "Stop it. I've heard enough. Don't be a braggart. You save your own head by asking for forgiveness and want to establish your leadership by fooling and ensnaring others." *Milap*, July 17, 1927, 5.

Image courtesy of the Centre of South Asian Studies, Cambridge University.

of nationalist politics if they agreed to sideline "communal" demands for legal protection from religious injury.

Though the resonance is surely unintentional, scholars' subsequent accounts of the *Rangila Rasul* controversy have similarly emphasized the role of Muslim emotion. In some of the most interesting and most cited scholarly work on the issue, historian David Gilmartin has argued that emotive appeals to Muslims' feelings of devotion to the Prophet powered new forms of urban politics.[32] The emphasis on emotion in his and similar

---

[32] David Gilmartin, "Partition, Pakistan, and South Asian History: In Search of a Narrative," *The Journal of Asian Studies* 57, no. 4 (November 1998): 1076–8; David

accounts echoes a broader interdisciplinary surge of interest in affect.[33] While this affective turn has enriched multiple fields, new histories of emotion have at times replicated colonial binaries that divided religious expression into sentimental versus rational forms. For example, in his work on the *Rangila Rasul* controversy, Gilmartin has contrasted the "realm of individual affect" and "expressions of public devotionalism" with "the rationalist realm of 'reformist' debate."[34] This approach, however, risks replicating colonial frameworks which ranked the compatibility of different forms of religion with secular values of neutrality and universality according to their ability to subordinate religious sentiment to rational deliberation.

Moreover, such oppositions between emotion and reason fail to explain critical dimensions of how the Rajpal controversy unfolded. The height of public concern about *Rangila Rasul* unfolded against the backdrop of legal developments in 1927, not after the pamphlet's publication in 1924. The longer chronology of the controversy suggests that Muslim protests were fueled not by feelings of visceral pain sparked by the publication of the pamphlet itself, but by more complex reactions to how the law responded to this injury. The anger Muslim journalists and politicians expressed against *Rangila Rasul* mingled with nuanced criticism of a legal system that many believed failed to protect Muslims. Understanding this interface between law and emotion requires that scholars develop a broader understanding of religious sentiment that does not define it in opposition to rational deliberation.

## Liberty of the Press and Protection of the Prophet

Probing beyond the caricature of Muslim fanaticism that dominated the mainstream and Hindu press in 1927 requires exploring how feelings of attachment to the Prophet intersected with debates about the relationship between law and religious freedom. During that summer,

---

Gilmartin, "Democracy, Nationalism and the Public: A Speculation on Colonial Muslim Politics," *South Asia* 14, no. 1 (1991): 133–5; Ahmed, "Specters of Macaulay," 324.

[33] For examples of this trend in South Asian history, see Rajat Kanta Ray, *Exploring Emotional History: Gender, Mentality and Literature in the Indian Awakening* (New Delhi: Oxford University Press, 2001); Tapan Raychaudhuri, *Perceptions, Emotions, Sensibilities: Essays on India's Colonial and Post-Colonial Experiences* (New Delhi: Oxford University Press, 1999).

[34] Gilmartin, "Partition, Pakistan, and South Asian History," 1078. As work on affect has expanded, scholars have become increasingly sensitive to avoiding direct contrasts with rational thought. Michael Hardt, "Foreword: What Affects Are Good For," in *The Affective Turn: Theorizing the Social*, ed. Patricia Ticineto Clough and Jean Halley (Durham: Duke University Press, 2007), ix.

discussions about Rajpal's trial played out against the backdrop of wider debates about the relationship between communal violence and government censorship. Over the coming months a rich discussion unfolded in the Lahore press about how a government dedicated to liberty should balance competing political and religious rights, a debate in which Muslims took a broad range of views. In this environment Muslim leaders appealed to their coreligionists' love for the Prophet and their common sense of injury at his being insulted to bridge significant differences of opinion about how they should respond to the crisis.

During the summer of 1927 the *Muslim Outlook*, a prominent English-language daily, sparked heated debates about the role that the government should play in regulating the press. In the wake of rioting in Lahore in May, the government targeted the *Outlook* as one of the offending "communal" papers. The confrontation between the government and the *Outlook* came to a head when the paper published an article in June calling on Justice Singh to resign.[35] The Lahore High Court convicted the editor and printer for contempt of court, which only spurred the paper to more vigorous protest against judicial abuse.[36] The *Outlook* also locked horns with members of the Muslim community who shared the government's concerns about the role of the press in instigating intercommunal violence. In May 1927 a group of leaders from different religious communities in the Punjab composed a manifesto urging, "The Government should, in our opinion, take action under the law in order to inspire a sense of responsibility in the minds of those journalists who have failed to realise their responsibility in discharge of their functions."[37] In response the *Muslim Outlook* warned that the manifesto risked further enabling the draconian powers of the government.[38]

The renowned poet and politician Muhammad Iqbal emerged as one of the manifesto's most prominent supporters. Despite their conflicting views, the *Muslim Outlook* interviewed Muhammad Iqbal about his reasons for supporting the manifesto. Iqbal's response captured a vision of liberty that combined individual empowerment with a shared sense of responsibility for protecting the country from strife. Iqbal opened the interview by stating, "he could never make up his mind to believe in absolute liberty in this world." Yet he clarified that his support "should not be understood to mean a desire on my part to suppress the liberty of the

[35] "Resign!," *Muslim Outlook*, June 14, 1927, 3.
[36] Telegram to the Secretary of State, June 26, 1927, NAI, Home/Political/1927/File 132/I, 42.
[37] "Irresponsible Journalists," *Tribune*, May 14, 1927, 6.
[38] "Liberty of the Press: Lahore Editors' Manifesto: Leaders' Interference Resented: Stricture on the Authorities," *Muslim Outlook*, May 24, 1927, 5.

Press which I regard as a most potent factor in the elevation of a people. All that I desire is that the vernacular Press which realizes its power must realize its responsibility." Iqbal insisted that the state had a role to play in enforcing the limits of acceptable speech when publications failed to properly self-regulate.[39]

Despite its differing views on what degree of censorship was necessary, the *Outlook*, like Iqbal, articulated a concept of liberty that balanced political freedom with legal protection against speech that injured other citizens. The *Outlook* advocated limited censorship of publications that overtly propagated intercommunal hatred. As the paper clarified: "We do not want the Government to put the public voice in a hermetically sealed box ... We want the Government to grapple with a definite aggression and tangible danger."[40] The stance that the *Muslim Outlook* took during the summer of 1927, in which it demanded the censorship of works insulting the Prophet but fiercely defended its own right to publish articles criticizing the government, might seem contradictory and self-serving. The paper, however, argued that protests against offensive publications and government inaction soothed rather than enflamed feelings of enmity. Such protests were, the *Outlook* argued, "only a safety valve, which must tend to ease deeply injured feelings."[41]

As both Iqbal and the *Muslim Outlook*'s statements during the controversy suggest, positions that the mainstream press dismissed as communal often articulated a more complex assessment of the relationship between government regulation and liberty. Rather than endorsing absolute liberty of expression, they defended forms of expression that they believed were conducive to social goals. Yet, Muslims in Lahore held widely divergent views about what forms of expression were beneficial or harmful. They also disagreed about the form that government regulation should take and the best strategy for pressing the government to implement change. While Iqbal urged his coreligionists to cooperate with the government to ensure better regulation of the press, other Muslim leaders called for a civil disobedience campaign.

In the face of these divisions, Muslim leaders attempted to use the language of injury to unite Muslims behind a more unified political strategy. In a speech at the Badshahi Masjid with over 10,000 Muslims in attendance, Iqbal proclaimed that Rajpal's book "had wounded the most

[39] "Rights and Responsibilities of Press: Sir Muhammad Iqbal's View: Internal Organisation and Reform First," *Muslim Outlook*, May 25, 1927, 1.
[40] "Ban on Posters and Pamphlets," *Muslim Outlook*, June 5, 1927, 3.
[41] "Amritsar Muslim Meeting," *Muslim Outlook*, June 10, 1927, 3.

delicate part of Muslims' heart."[42] Translated into English, Iqbal's invocation of a wound to the heart, or *qalb*, invokes a visceral sense of emotional injury. In Urdu and Arabic, however, the *qalb* is the seat of both feeling and intellect, an image that translates poorly into a dichotomous construction of reason and emotion.[43] Iqbal tied his appeal to Muslims' sense of injury to an argument about political strategy. He insisted that the Muslim community should unite behind the common goal of curing the insult to the Prophet's honor, rather than embracing a civil disobedience campaign that would fracture the community. Iqbal urged his coreligionists to be patient while the government resolved the problem. In response the crowd shouted in protest, with voices from the audience insisting that the government itself was the problem. Iqbal was forced to cut off his speech with the words, "I value this genuine feeling."[44] As the *Times of India* reported the next day, one of the most powerful figures in Punjabi politics had been "howled down."[45] The public reaction to Iqbal's speech suggested the difficulty of translating uniform outrage into a unified political strategy.

If Iqbal was the voice of moderation during the summer of 1927, Zafar Ali Khan, the editor of the Urdu paper *Zamindar* and a popular poet, was, in the words of one historian, the "most notorious firebrand in the Punjab."[46] Through his poetry Zafar Ali cultivated Muslims' sense of injury and vulnerability. He deftly linked imagery from classical Urdu poetry and popular Islamic epics with jabs at leaders such as B.S. Moonje, Madan Mohan Malaviya, and Lala Lajpat Rai, who were promoting a Hindu-centric vision of national politics. In July 1927 Zafar Ali wrote:

> This rich and powerful, crying and beating *shuddhi*
> Is also becoming the *zambil* of Umar Ayyar
>
> The plan which Moonje and Malaviya strung together[47]
> Is being completed in Lahore
>
> We once regarded Lajpat Rai with a belittling gaze
> Today the falcon is becoming this same small bird

[42] Muhammad Iqbal, "Shahi Masjid men Taqrir," *Inqilab*, July 13, 1927, reprinted in Muhammad Iqbal, *Guftar i-Iqbal*, ed. Muhammad Rafiq Afzal (Lahore: Idarah yi-Tahqiqat i-Pakistan, 1969), 42.
[43] Samira Haj, "Reordering Islamic Orthodoxy: Muhammad Ibn 'Abdul Wahhab," *Muslim World* 92, no. 3–4 (Fall 2002): 351; Irfan Ahmad, "Immanent Critique and Islam: Anthropological Reflections," *Anthropological Theory* 11, no. 1 (March 2011): 115.
[44] Iqbal, "Shahi Masjid men Taqrir," 46.
[45] "Stormy Moslem Meeting at Lahore," *TOI*, July 11, 1927, 10.
[46] S. Qalb-i-Abid, *Muslim Politics in the Punjab, 1921–47* (Lahore: Vanguard, 1992), 95.
[47] This reference is to Balakrishna Shivram Moonje and Madan Mohan Malaviya, two leading figures in the Hindu Mahasabha.

Today Rajpal was acquitted by the court
The law of Islam is being debased[48]

According to Zafar Ali, the Hindus' *shuddhi* (purity) campaign was becoming the *zambil* of Umar Ayyar, a reference to a magical bag owned by the humorous sidekick of the uncle of the Prophet, Amir Hamza, a legendary folk hero. Umar Ayyar could pull anything he wished out of his *zambil*; the reference here implied that *shuddhi* had become a useful tool for accomplishing other ends.

While cultivating his fellow Muslims' mutual sense of injury, Zafar Ali argued that the current crisis stemmed from the lack of sufficient Muslim representation in the Punjab judiciary. In the *Zamindar* Zafar Ali Khan declared that Justice Singh had "heartlessly cut off the limbs of Britain's imperial good policy in the slaughterhouse of his unsound reasoning."[49] Yet he clarified that the presence of only two Muslim judges among the fifteen-judge Lahore High Court posed a greater problem.[50] He insisted that under the current Chief Justice, Sir Shadi Lal, the court was becoming a "Ram Raj," the ideal state of the Hindu god Ram's kingdom, increasingly invoked as a goal of Hindu nationalists.[51]

While Zafar Ali Khan portrayed the decision in Rajpal's case as the product of religious bias within the judiciary, Maulana Muhammad Ali, one of the leaders of the waning Khilafat Movement, publicly defended Justice Singh's decision as an accurate application of existing law. Muhammad Ali argued that the fault was not with the judge, but with the law, and pushed for an amendment to the Indian Penal Code that would cover insults to sacred personalities.[52] When the Maulana publicly locked heads with Zafar Ali Khan over their difference of opinions, he declared that his criticism of his fellow Muslims had been made "out of love." He insisted that he and Zafar Ali "could not disagree on the question of insult to their Prophet."[53] He therefore appealed to the bonds

---

[48] Maulana Zafar Ali Khan, "Salsabil ki Chand Bunden," in *Kulliyat i-Maulana Zafar Ali Khan* (Lahore: ul-Faisal, 2007), 356–7.

[49] Zafar Ali Khan, "Adalat i-Aliya yi-Panjab," *Zamindar*, July 13, 1927, in Zafar Ali Khan, *Anmol Moti: Maulana Zafar Ali Khan ke Mazamin ka Majmu'a*, ed. Sadiq Husain (Lahore: Sadiq Husain, 1968), 165.

[50] Further adding to popular outrage, none of Lahore's many prominent Muslim lawyers were appointed to judgeships in the Lahore High Court. Front matter, AIR Lahore [1927]; Khalid Latif Gauba, *Friends and Foes: An Autobiography* (New Delhi: Indian Book Co., 1974), 212–13.

[51] Khan, "Adalat i-Aliya i-Panjab," 169.

[52] Muhammad Ali, "Rangila Rasul: Qazi ka Qusur ya Qanun ka," *Hamdard*, June 27, 1927, 3. See also Muhammad Ali's various articles published in *Hamdard* between June 28 and July 6, 1927.

[53] "High Court Day: M. Mohd. Ali's Speech at Lahore," *Tribune*, July 24, 1927, 6.

of community, rooted in their shared love for the Prophet, to blunt the impact of the two men's diverging diagnoses of the faults with the judicial system.

Some members of the Muslim community also attempted to use the banner of *sharia* to unify Muslims' protests over the Rajpal decision. Some of these appeals took the form of vague suggestions that, if the government failed to act, Muslims would resort to other means to protect the Prophet. *Al-Jamiat*, the official organ of the *Jamiat Ulama-i-Hind*, a prominent organization of religious scholars, warned, "There is no telling what kinds of dangerous means the religious fervour of the Muslims will be prepared to adopt for its protection." The article added, "The feelings of the Muslims can be correctly ascertained from the fact that under Islam the punishment for insulting the Prophet is death and it is legally permissible to kill those who curse the Prophet."[54]

In mid-September, *Al-Jamiat* clarified earlier statements about the punishments prescribed by the *sharia* for insulting the Prophet. Emphasizing that India was not an Islamic state in which the *sharia* was in force, the paper stated that the purpose of mentioning these punishments was not to advocate for their adoption or to suggest that individual Muslims should take the law into their own hands. Instead, the paper explained, "The purpose of describing this law was simply to bring to the attention of the government the importance of this crime and the delicacy of Muslim religious sentiment."[55] The paper argued that the appeal to *sharia* was meant to prod the government into attending to Muslims' feelings of outrage, not to incite violence. Yet, for all the paper's elaborate explanations, references to *sharia* excited alarmist reports that Muslims were declaring a "Moslem Raj."[56] Few commentators grasped *Al-Jamiat*'s distinction between referencing *sharia* as a source of law under an Islamic government and invoking it as a moral standard in a non-Islamic state. Appealing to *sharia* thus proved to be a precarious strategy that often provoked fear rather than sympathy for the Muslim community.

Calls for *sharia* failed to build unity within the Muslim community, just as appeals to Muslims' religious sentiments did not eliminate differences

---

[54] "Rangila Rasul ka Faisala aur is ke Nata'ij," *Al-Jamiat*, June 2, 1927, 2. The question of the punishment for insulting the Prophet is a matter of debate in Islamic jurisprudence. L. Wiederhold, "Shatm," in *Encyclopaedia of Islam*, 2nd edn, accessed January 20, 2012, http://referenceworks.brillonline.com/entries/encyclopaedia-of-islam-2/shatm-a-SIM_8898.

[55] "Shatim i-Rasul ki Tazir i-Shar'i," *Al-Jamiat*, September 18, 1927, 2.

[56] "Through Indian Eyes: If We Had Moslem Raj," *TOI*, July 19, 1927, 6.

of opinion on the question of how the government should protect Islam from insult. The broad range of views expressed in the Muslim press, and commentators' inability to reach a consensus, reflected the complexity of the issues at stake. Rather than focusing on the black-and-white question of whether or not religion should be involved in politics, the Muslim press debated subtler nuances of how religion should be regulated. These debates weighed the benefits of freedom of expression against the right to protection from injury, focusing on questions of method and degree rather than positing liberty and suppression as diametric opposites. Yet even as the Legislative Assembly moved to allay Muslim concerns by amending the Penal Code, an increasingly vocal chorus of critics argued that religious sentiments had no role in politics. These self-styled "secularists" argued that India would achieve communal harmony not by reconfiguring the ties between religion, law, and politics, but by severing them altogether.

## Indian Penal Code, Section 295A: Debating the Meaning of Indian Secularism

In a seeming recognition of the mounting concern within the Muslim community about Rajpal's acquittal, the central government took steps in the summer of 1927 to introduce new language into the Penal Code that directly criminalized religious insults. In contrast to Section 153A, which had proscribed religious offences only when they promoted enmity between communities, the new Section 295A criminalized any expression made with "deliberate and malicious intentions of outraging the religious feelings of any class."[57] The support that the amendment received in the Legislative Assembly seemed like a victory for Muslims who had demanded more effective legal protection for religious sentiments.[58] Yet despite its passage, commentary on the amendment, both inside and outside the Legislative Assembly, continued to emphasize the unreasonable nature of Muslim protests against *Rangila Rasul*, blunting the potentially conciliatory impact of the bill.

Although Section 295A eventually passed by a relatively wide margin, much of the support it received from Hindu politicians was lukewarm.

---

[57] A Bill Further to amend the Indian Penal Code, in NAI, Home/Political/1927/File 132/I, 75.

[58] Neeti Nair has argued that the bill provides evidence of the ongoing possibility of intercommunal collaboration during the 1920s. "Beyond the 'Communal' 1920s," 317–40. My own analysis is less sanguine; commentary which framed the bill as an unfortunate, but necessary, concession to irrational Muslim sentiment undermined its conciliatory potential.

In his Lahore-based paper *The People*, Lala Lajpat Rai, a leading member
of the Hindu Mahasabha, justified his support for the bill by calling it
"a temporary measure," which was necessary to "satisfy some hyper-
sensitive folk."[59] In a similar vein S. Srinivasa Iyengar argued: "I yield
to none in my love of the Press and in my appreciation of its liberties ...
it is a just law which is necessary to educate people into tolerance."[60]
Srinivasa Iyengar and Lala Lajpat Rai supported an amendment to make
the law expire after 1930, but the amendment was defeated in a close
vote.[61] Despite their failure to make Section 295A temporary, these men
successfully shifted the debate from how to protect religion to how religious expression could be made compatible with a mature secular state.

Some members of the Legislative Assembly went further, opposing the
bill outright and warning that it was a dangerous concession to Muslim
fanaticism. When a committee was appointed to review the proposed
legislation, the majority supported the bill with minor revisions. Five
members of the committee, however, including four Hindu and one
British member, argued against its passage. In a spirited statement of
dissent they described the feelings that the new law purported to protect as "really irreligious feelings." The minute argued: "As we understand it, the inculcation of peace is an essential principle of all the great
religions practised in India, and all departures from this principle are
only manifestations of religious fanaticism." It therefore argued that
"any other form of religion would be anti-social and dangerous – then
it follows that what the original Bill described as religious feelings are
really irreligious feelings."[62] The boundary that the minute drew between
religious and irreligious feelings relied on a distinction between legitimate and illegitimate forms of religious expression. By classifying certain forms of religious expression as "irreligious feelings," opponents of
the bill fostered the notion that Muslims' protests against *Rangila Rasul*
stemmed from a fanaticism that should be discouraged rather than
protected.

The minute of dissent was superficially framed as condemning any
form of religious fanaticism, without reference to whether those feelings
came from the Muslim or Hindu communities. Several members of the
Legislative Assembly, however, used less neutral language. Amar Nath

[59] Lala Lajpat Rai, "Protecting Religions," *The People*, September 15, 1927, in *The Collected Works of Lala Lajpat Rai*, 13: 130.
[60] Extract from the Legislative Assembly Debates, September 16, 1927, in NAI, Home/Political/1927/File 132/I, 138.
[61] Extract from the Legislative Assembly Debates, September 19, 1927, in NAI, Home/Political/1927/File 132/I, 172.
[62] Minutes of Dissent, September 13, 1927, in NAI, Home/Political/1927/File 132/I, 69.

Dutt likened the legislation to "retrograde measures which smack of the favourite wife policy on the part of the Government," referring to the idea that the colonial government cultivated the Muslim community as a political ally against Hindu nationalists.[63] Newspaper commentary insinuated that the bill was a dangerous concession to the intolerance of the Muslim community. The *Leader* commented, "Those who value freedom of speech and writing ... cannot feel happy at the passage of a measure which owed its origin to the intolerance of a section of the Muslim community."[64] The *Bharat Jiwan* declared:

it would have welcomed the Bill if the Government had enacted it either of its own accord, or at the same time when the Muslims had started throwing filth at the religious preceptors of the Hindus, and especially of the Arya Samajists. The enactment of this legislation at the present juncture clearly means that it is due to the fear of the Muslims.[65]

As the comments in *Bharat Jiwan* made clear, more nuanced defenses of freedom of expression often bled into outright efforts to marginalize Muslim political concerns.

During debates about Section 295A, some critics of the amendment embraced the language of political secularism, deploying a vocabulary of binaries that promised to divide religion from politics by distinguishing between private devotion and public communalism, and between reasonable faith and unreasonable fanaticism. In July 1927 the Lahore *Tribune* called for "A Secular Party" whose members would "resent being called Hindus or Muslims in politics."[66] While admitting that the state would have to intervene in certain religious issues, the paper insisted that these issues, "like all other questions within the purview of legislative and executive action, are not only capable of being, but can alone be properly, handled by minds free from theological prepossessions."[67] Advocates for such secular politics usually framed them as religiously neutral, equally open to all Indians who would separate their religious identities from their politics.

Yet, some of the earliest figures to embrace the term secularism linked it with a Hindu-majoritarian discourse that explicitly marginalized Islam, just as critics of Section 295A labelled it a concession to Muslim fanaticism. In September 1927 Lala Lajpat Rai published an article entitled

[63] Extract from the Legislative Assembly Debates, September 16, 1927, in NAI, Home/Political/1927/File 132/I, 133.
[64] "Reactionary Legislation," *Leader*, September 22, 1927, 3.
[65] Notes on the Press, United Provinces of Agra and Oudh, September 3, 1927, 3.
[66] "What Is a Secular Party," *Tribune*, July 28, 1927, 1.
[67] "Wanted a Secular Party," *Tribune*, July 27, 1927, 1.

"'Religionism' v. Secularism" that lamented that India was plagued by an "atmosphere of religionism." Although he admitted that Hindus also sometimes suffered from "religionism," he traced the source of the problem to Muslims. He explained:

> But here also it cannot be denied that some people are actually driven into that position. Hindu intelligentsia may fairly be presumed to belong to this class. Their religionism is of the most flimsy kind. A very large number of them have lost faith in dogmatic or credal [sic] religion, if not in religion itself, but they find that religionism, which is the weapon of the Muslim intelligentsia, can only be met by religionism … The country cannot be saved from the deluge of religionism even if the whole of the Hindu community were to become non-religious, unless and until the Muslims also reach the same intellectual level and substitute merit in place of religion.

Having identified Muslims as primarily responsible for the problem of "religionism," Lajpat Rai suggested that its solution lay first and foremost in changing the mentality of Muslims to embrace a more worldly outlook. He argued that India had to overcome this "stupid religionism" to make "political and economic progress," and he left his reader with little doubt that Muslims – not Hindus – were the crux of the problem.[68]

Lajpat Rai's article demonstrates the intimate relationship between calls for secularism and a majoritarian discourse of Hindu nationalism that demonized Islam. Lajpat Rai's article certainly reflected a more extreme view. Yet, in more subtle ways, much of the commentary during the Rajpal controversy equated Islam with irrational forms of religious sentiment that posed a particular threat to national integration. Thus even as the law constructed religious feelings as worthy of protection, an emerging discourse of Indian secularism delegitimized these emotions when expressed by the Muslim community.

### The Politics of Grieving: An Alternative Approach to Managing Communal Sentiment

Just as the tumultuous debates over Section 295A receded from public attention, a surprising coda to the Rajpal controversy unfolded in 1929. In April a young man named Ilmuddin stabbed and killed Rajpal; he was later tried and executed for murder. While many commentators, Hindu and Muslim alike, worried the assassination and trial would spark further violence, these fears turned out to be largely unfounded. At the trial in Lahore, Ilmuddin was represented by Muhammad Ali Jinnah, later

---

[68] Rai, "'Religionism' vs. Secularism," *The People*, September 8, 1927, in *The Collected Works of Lala Lajpat Rai*, 13: 280–4.

the driving figure behind the founding of Pakistan. While decrying the murder, Jinnah offered a moving, but ultimately unsuccessful, defense of Ilmuddin. In contrast to the demonization of Muslim rage which unfolded during debates about Section 295A, events in 1929 showed how law could foster empathy and how intercommunal alliances could be forged around the right to grieve.

Ilmuddin's trial, and Jinnah's arrival in Lahore to conduct his final appeal, garnered huge public interest, with hundreds of people packing the court's visitor gallery to hear the verdict and further crowds gathering outside.[69] In Ilmuddin's defense Jinnah highlighted contradictions in different witness testimonies and argued that the police had tutored the witnesses. In a final attempt to save Ilmuddin from execution, Jinnah argued that, even supposing that Ilmuddin was guilty, the court should take into consideration his young age and that his action "was prompted by feelings of veneration for the founder of his religion and anger at one who had scurrilously attacked him."[70] Jinnah's defense effectively condemned the act of murder, but still pleaded for mercy on the grounds that Ilmuddin had acted out of feelings of devotion and injury. Although Jinnah failed to sway the judges, the courtroom nonetheless proved a potent space for fusing feelings of injury and calls for mercy with protests against injustice.

The funerals of Rajpal and Ilmuddin drew even larger crowds than the murder trial, providing a weary Lahore with catharsis. The day after Rajpal's murder, despite a standing order forbidding public gatherings, a large crowd of Hindus gathered outside the hospital where his body was kept. When authorities refused to hand over the body, the crowd formed a funeral procession with an empty bier.[71] The police responded by forcibly dispersing the mourners. The Lahore *Tribune* decried the incompetence and brutality of the police, and noted that several Muslim leaders had been willing to accompany the procession to prevent any communal clashes.[72] When the government allowed the funeral to proceed, businesses from all religious communities closed out of respect, and the day proceeded peacefully.[73]

Similarly, after Ilmuddin's execution the Punjab government resisted handing over his body. Hindu newspapers expressed sympathy with the demands of the Muslim community, and the Naujawan Bharat Sabha,

[69] "Rajpal Murder Case," *Tribune*, July 17, 1929, 7.
[70] *Ilam Din v. Emperor* [1930] AIR Lahore 157, 158.
[71] "Funeral Procession with Empty Bier," *TOI*, April 8, 1929, 11.
[72] "The Rajpal Murder," *Tribune*, April 11, 1927, 9.
[73] "Rajpal's Funeral," *TOI*, April 10, 1929, 14.

an anti-colonial leftist youth organization, passed a resolution calling the demands of the Muslim community "just" and condemned the government for withholding the body.[74] On November 14, 1929 the government relented and allowed the Muslim community to bury Ilmuddin in Lahore. The funeral drew an enormous crowd, a mass of people that observers described as "unprecedented."[75] Despite the size of the crowd, the city reported no untoward incidents. After the bitter controversy in 1927, the deaths and funerals of Rajpal and Ilmuddin in 1929 paradoxically strengthened calls for intercommunal cooperation.

The events of 1929 offer an alternative vision of tolerance and plurality, one distinctly at odds with visions of secularism that emphasize the need to separate religious sentiment from politics. The Hindu and Muslim communities found a powerful common cause in fusing respect for devotion and mourning with protests against draconian government action. The delicate consensus that Lahore achieved in 1929 accomplished what deliberation over Section 295A lacked – a vision of religious sentiment that empowered intercommunal collaboration.

### Conclusion

As a midpoint in the transition from colonial to postcolonial politics, events in the 1920s foreshadowed how colonial patterns of secular legal governance would be reworked, rather than discarded, after independence. When Hindu majoritarians demonized Muslim sentiment as irrational while treating their own religious sensibilities as compatible with secular democracy, they eerily echoed colonial discourses that took laws rooted in Christian Europe as universalizable, secular norms. Today the BJP continues this legacy of lopsided secularism by arguing that true secularism requires privileging the religious sensibilities of the Hindu majority rather than providing "pseudo-secular" protection for the Muslim minority.[76]

The postcolonial states of India and Pakistan have also continued the heavy-handed, top-down policing of intercommunal affronts to religious sentiment. As during the colonial period, postcolonial legal regulation of religious sentiment has more often exacerbated than prevented

---

[74] "Muslim Deputation Waits upon Governor," *Tribune*, November 7, 1929, 7; and "Ilam Din's Dead Body," *Tribune*, November 8, 1929, 7.

[75] "Ilmuddin's Body Brought to Lahore and Buried," *Tribune*, November 15, 1929, 3; and "Murder of Rajpal," *TOI*, November 15, 1929, 12.

[76] Tapan Basu, Pradip Datta, Sumit Sarkar, Tanika Sarkar, and Sambuddha Sen, *Khaki Shorts and Saffron Flags: A Critique of the Hindu Right* (New Delhi: Orient Longman, 1993), 37.

violence.[77] This has been true in India, where legal censorship of literary
and academic works has often followed sensational acts or threats of
violence, including the decision to ban the import of Salman Rushdie's
*Satanic Verses* after fourteen people were killed during riots in Bombay in
1988.[78] It has been even more so in Pakistan, where in the 1980s, as part
of a larger program of Islamization, censorship laws inherited from the
colonial state were extended to provide greater protections for the religious sensibilities of the Sunni majority. Unsurprisingly, these provisions,
popularly known as the blasphemy laws, have been disproportionately
used against minorities, including Shias, Christians, and Ahmadiyyas,
an Islamic reform movement declared non-Muslim by the Pakistan government in 1974. The judiciary has often balked at enforcing these draconian and biased laws. Despite the capital penalties mandated under
the laws, no one had been executed under them to date. Once charges
have been brought under the so-called blasphemy laws, however, vigilante justice has often taken over, leading to the murder of minorities and
those who dare to defend them.[79]

The *Rangila Rasul* controversy, however, provides an important
reminder that this carrying forward of colonial legacies was neither inevitable nor uncontested. During debates between Muslims about the
appropriate response to Rajpal's acquittal, during the murder trial of
Ilmuddin, and during the funerals of both men, alternative visions of
intercommunal harmony pivoted around creative rethinking of the relationship between religious sentiment and politics. Rather than contrasting
religion with the rational domains of law and liberal rights, these visions
explored the emotive dimensions of law itself. For example, Jinnah, like
any talented lawyer, strategically deployed the performative possibilities of the courtroom to challenge his audience to empathize with the
motive that drove Ilmuddin to commit murder, even if they deplored
his crime.[80] Jinnah's defense suggested how law might be marshalled to
build empathy between different communities, breaking the pattern of

---

[77] C.S. Adcock, "Violence, Passion, and the Law: A Brief History of Section 295A and Its
Antecedents," *Journal of the American Academy of Religion* 84, no. 2 (June 2016): 337–51.
[78] Mini Chandran, "The Democratisation of Censorship: Books and the Indian Public,"
*Economic and Political Weekly* 45, no. 40 (2010): 28.
[79] Ahmed, "Specters of Macaulay"; Osama Siddique and Zahra Hayat, "Unholy Speech
and Holy Laws: Blasphemy Laws in Pakistan – Controversial Origins, Design Defects,
and Free Speech Implications," *Minnesota Journal of International Law* 17, no. 2
(2008): 303–85.
[80] For an introduction to the considerable body of literature on the narrative and performative aspects of law, see Peter Brooks and Paul D. Gewirtz, eds., *Law's Stories: Narrative
and Rhetoric in the Law* (New Haven: Yale University Press, 1996).

casting religious sentiments as irrational and therefore unknowable to individuals not subscribing to the same beliefs.

Despite the poor record of censorship laws in South Asia, these moments show that law, imaginatively engaged, might still have a critical role to play in promoting intercommunal harmony.[81] But events in 1929 also indicate that the most effective strategies of accomplishing this end will make savvy use of law's own capacity for emotive performance and its entanglements with other forms of politics, from communal grieving to alliance building.

---

[81] My argument here pushes back against the pessimism about legal interventions expressed by such scholars as Saba Mahmood in relation to recent controversies over religious insult and free speech. Mahmood, "Religious Reason and Secular Affect," 64–100.

The renowned poet and philosopher Muhammad Iqbal delivered six lectures in 1928 and 1929, which he later published under the title *The Reconstruction of Religious Thought*. In the lectures he underlined the problematic nature of the "the bifurcation of the unity of man into two distinct and separate realities." Instead, Iqbal argued, "matter is spirit in space-time reference ... The spirit finds its opportunities in the natural, the material, the secular. All that is secular is therefore sacred in the roots of its being."[1] Rebelling against a bifurcated understanding of social life, Iqbal asserted the interdependence of religious and secular life, defying their division within colonial governance. This conviction undergirded his wider interests in the synergies between Islam and contemporary economic thought.[2]

Iqbal was a profoundly creative thinker, but his endeavors unfolded in conversation with a range of contemporary intellectuals and movements. Between the 1910s and 1940s, interest in the material dimensions of Islam surged in India, inspiring trends from Islamic socialism, to the creation of a new academic field of Islamic economics, to broader political calls for Islamic social justice. This chapter traces these ideas across a range of genres, from popular political pamphlets to academic articles in English-language journals to Urdu monographs written by members of the *ulama*. It also moves between intellectual output and legislative campaigns to capture the fluid boundaries that divided scholarship from political and legal activism.[3] The Urdu terminology writers

[1] Mohammad Iqbal, *The Reconstruction of Religious Thought in Islam*, ed. M. Saeed Sheikh (Stanford: Stanford University Press, 2013), 122–3.

[2] On Iqbal's writings on economy, see Ayesha Jalal, "Freedom and Equality: From Iqbal's Philosophy to Sen's Ethical Concerns," in *Arguments for a Better World: Essays in Honor of Amartya Sen*, ed. Kaushik Basu and Ravi Kanbur, vol. 2 (Oxford: Oxford University Press, 2009), 452–69.

[3] This chapter draws together a range of thinkers and movements that have typically been treated separately in the scholarly literature. On the rise of Islamic economics in India, see Timur Kuran, "The Genesis of Islamic Economics: A Chapter in the Politics of Muslim Identity," *Social Research* 64, no. 2 (Summer 1997): 301–38. On writings by the *ulama* on Islamic social justice, see Zaman, *Modern Islamic Thought in a Radical*

used as rough translations for the English word "economy" encouraged Indian Muslims to treat economics, ethics, law, and politics as overlapping categories. While in modern Urdu the terms *iqtisad* and *ma'ashiyyat* have become synonymous with economy and economics, their Arabic roots – *'aish*, life or subsistence, and *qasd*, aim or intent – infused them with broader meanings in the early twentieth century.[4]

While some of these writings drew on older interests in material topics in Islamic thought, they were entangled with contemporary events, both national and global, which were conducive to questioning the specific divisions animating colonial patterns of secular governance.[5] The catastrophic violence of World War I, the double blow to Western capitalism precipitated by the establishment of the Soviet Union and the Great Depression, and the growing influence of anti-colonial nationalism emboldened intellectuals across the colonial world to challenge Western models of development.[6] In echoes of wider trends, Indian Muslims began to assert that Islam offered economic models that could deliver the balanced and equitable growth which British rule had failed to produce. In the process they challenged the ways that secular colonial governance had constricted Islam to the narrow realm of particularistic, communal affairs and domestic life. Instead, this rich body of writing on Islamic economy emphasized Islam's rationalism and its relevance to contemporary life, both for Indian Muslims and wider global and non-Muslim audiences.

Muslims attempted to translate these ideas into legal reforms, first in India in the 1930s and later in Pakistan in the late 1940s and early 1950s, but their efforts failed to gain traction. In both countries Muslims expressed enthusiasm for ideals of Islamic social justice, but when these discussions turned to concrete action, legislators balked at applying religious laws to economic issues, from inheritance of agricultural land

---

*Age*, 221–60. On Muslims' involvement in socialist and communist movements, see Khizar Humayun Ansari, *The Emergence of Socialist Thought among North Indian Muslims, 1917–1947* (Lahore: Book Traders, 1990); Kamran Asdar Ali, "Communists in a Muslim Land: Cultural Debates in Pakistan's Early Years," *Modern Asian Studies* 45, no. 3 (2011): 501–34; Neilesh Bose, "Muslim Modernism and Trans-Regional Consciousness in Bengal, 1911–1925: The Wide World of Samyabadi," *South Asia Research* 31, no. 3 (November 2011): 231–48.

[4] Neither term appears in the most well-known Urdu-Hindi dictionary from the nineteenth century, John Platt's *Dictionary of Urdu, Classical Hindi, and English* (London: WH Allen & Co., 1884).

[5] On Shah Waliullah's influence on twentieth-century writings on Islamic social justice, see Zaman, *Modern Islamic Thought in a Radical Age*, 224–5, 236–8.

[6] On the 1920s and 1930s as generative of radical efforts to reimagine the world order, see Manu Goswami, "Imaginary Futures and Colonial Internationalisms," *The American Historical Review* 117, no. 5 (December 2012): 1461–85.

to finance. Tracing how Islamic economic models continued to be marginalized in this new legal context offers an entry point into a wider story of how critical elements of colonial secular governance – from the association of religion with the family to unitary models of sovereignty – survived the postcolonial transition.

## Revolutionary Religion: Islamic Socialism

During the second decade of the twentieth century, Indians gravitated to socialism and communism to link growing domestic anti-colonial sentiments to wider global critiques of capitalist exploitation. When Muslims joined these movements, they often brought to them a particular interest in exploring the role that Islam might play in inspiring more ethical forms of political economy. For some, participation in the Khilafat Movement, in which Indian Muslims protested against Britain's role in dismantling the Ottoman Empire at the end of War World I, launched them into wider circuits of global radicalism. After several thousand Indian Muslims fled India for Afghanistan as part of Khilafat protests, some continued onto newly declared Soviet territories in Russia and other Eastern European satellite states.[7] Solidifying these global radical links, Khilafat activists joined other Indian expatriate rebels in founding the Communist Party of India in Tashkent in 1920. While some Muslim socialists, in the words of one historian, "converted" from Islam to socialism, others saw the two as mutually reinforcing.[8] They rejected the idea of religion as an opiate of the masses, instead arguing that Islam's commitment to equality could infuse socialism with spiritual depth.

The writings of two figures, Mushir Hosain Kidwai and Maulana Barakatullah, capture the *zeitgeist* of this intellectual movement.[9] Born in 1878 into a family of landowners, Kidwai traveled to London to study law at Lincoln's Inn. He spent over a decade and a half abroad, receiving an honorary appointment from the Ottoman Sultan and serving as the secretary of the Pan-Islamic Society in London along the way. After returning to India in 1920, Kidwai became a Khilafat activist and a member of the United Provinces Legislative Assembly. He also wrote a series of books, including *Islam and Socialism* (c. 1912), *The Abolition of Personal Ownership of Property* (n.d.), and *Pan-Islamism and Bolshevism*

---

[7] Gail Minault, *The Khilafat Movement: Religious Symbolism and Political Mobilization in India* (New York: Columbia University Press, 1982), 106.
[8] K.H. Ansari, "Pan-Islam and the Making of the Early Indian Muslim Socialists," *Modern Asian Studies* 20, no. 3 (January 1986): 528–9.
[9] For a discussion of Obaidullah Sindhi, another important theorist of Islamic socialism, see Zaman, *Modern Islamic Thought in a Radical Age*, 223–30.

(1937).[10] Mirroring their author's itinerant path, Kidwai's books also traveled widely, including through adaptations carried out by H.O.S. Tjokroaminoto, a mentor to Sukarno, Indonesia's first president.[11]

In *Islam and Socialism* Kidwai argued that while Islam shared many of socialism's values, it rejected its secular orientation. According to Kidwai, the Prophet and early Muslims had anticipated the egalitarian ethos of modern socialism by prohibiting *riba*, or interest; collecting *zakat*, a tax on wealth which was used for charitable purposes; and giving basic rights to slaves.[12] Kidwai also praised the Prophet's efforts to promote direct government by the people, which he compared to state socialism, and which he argued allowed the early Islamic state to avoid the "bureaucratism" that plagued modern governments. As Kidwai explained, "Their administration was not bureaucratic in any sense. There were no departments, no portfolios. The Muslims' leaders could not be as independent of public opinion as are the Cabinets and ministers of the present-day democratic governments of the West."[13] Kidwai's efforts to link Islamic socialism to a critique of modern state forms foreshadowed how writings on Islamic economy more generally challenged colonial modes of governance rooted in unitary understandings of sovereignty.

Kidwai's disdain for centralized, hierarchical state power led him to emphasize the importance of cultivating socialist values from the bottom up and opposing violent revolution from above. Because European communists had focused exclusively on the material dimensions of socialism while embracing violent revolution, they had, according to Kidwai, failed to build a truly socialist society. He argued that, even if European revolutionaries succeeded in forcibly nationalizing land and capital, "they cannot better the condition of the people or advance the cause of Socialism so long as the people of the State do not improve morally." Instead, true socialism required that society cultivate ethical values from the bottom up, including respect for the "sovereign rights

---

[10] S. Tanvir Wasti, "Mushir Hosain Kidwai and the Ottoman Cause," *Middle Eastern Studies* 30, no. 2 (1994): 252–61.

[11] I am deeply grateful to Kevin W. Fogg for sharing his ongoing research on H.O.S. Tjokroaminoto, including his manuscript paper "Islamic Socialism from South Asia to Indonesia." Fogg has shown that Tjokroaminoto's Indonesian work *Islam dan Socialisme* (1924) drew heavily on Kidwai's *Islam and Socialism*; translated passages from Kidwai constitute the bulk of the text. Tjokroaminoto also sent his son Harsono to South Asia to study Islam and Muslim culture in a society in which Muslims were a minority.

[12] Mushir Hosain Kidwai, *Islam and Socialism* (London: Luzac, c. 1912), ii–v. For a more in-depth discussion of debates about the meaning of *riba*, which have been central to debates about the legality of charging interest in contemporary Pakistan, see Fazlur Rahman, "Riba and Interest," *Islamic Studies* 3, no. 1 (March 1964): 1–43.

[13] Kidwai, *Islam and Socialism*, iii.

of individuals" and "sentiments of mutual harmony and brotherhood."
Kidwai believed that Asia, rather than Europe, would pioneer true
socialism because Asia possessed the "great moral stamina and spiritual strength which Europe lacks." Kidwai therefore concluded that
Buddhists and Hindus would "be our best allies and associates in the
sacred cause of advancing Socialism."[14]

While written in an accessible manner, Kidwai's book was directed
at an elite, English-speaking audience. In contrast, Barakatullah, one of
the great swashbuckling revolutionaries of his time, fomented socialist
revolution among the Muslim masses. Born in the Indian princely
state of Bhopal in the middle of the nineteenth century (the exact date
is unknown), Barakatullah traveled between Bombay, London, Tokyo,
Istanbul, Cairo, San Francisco, Kabul, Moscow, and Berlin, among
other places. He used his international travels to establish anti-colonial
journals in multiple languages and was a leading member of the Ghadar
Party, an anti-colonial movement organized by Indian immigrants to
North America.[15]

In Tashkent in 1919, Barakatullah published a Persian pamphlet,
"Bolshevism and the Islamic Body-Politic," that argued for the synergies between struggles against imperialism and capitalism.[16] While
Barakatullah's pamphlet was more propaganda than intellectual discourse, it addressed similar themes as Kidwai's book. Like Kidwai,
Barakatullah found in Islamic history predecessors to modern socialism
such as the *bait-ul-mal*, a public fund devoted to the general welfare. The
thrust of Barakatullah's message, however, urged an alliance between
Muslims and the Soviets to fight British injustice. Barakatullah called on
"the Muhammedans of the world and Asiatic nations to understand the
noble principles of Russian Socialism and to embrace it seriously and
enthusiastically."[17] While the international revolution that Barakatullah
hoped for did not materialize, in the 1920s a sustained network of collaboration developed between Indian nationalists and the Soviets.
Meanwhile, a rising interest in socialism among Indian Muslims focused
attention on how to interpret the economic message of Islam.

---

[14] Ibid., vi–vii, xi.
[15] For additional details on Barakatullah's biography, see Ansari, *Emergence of Socialist
Thought*, 239–41; Maia Ramnath, *Haj to Utopia: How the Ghadar Movement Charted
Global Radicalism and Attempted to Overthrow the British Empire* (Berkeley: University of
California Press, 2011).
[16] An English translation of the pamphlet was preserved in British surveillance records.
"Translation of a pamphlet by Barkatulla on 'Bolshevism & Islam," IOR/L/PS/10/836.
[17] Ibid., 61.

## The Academic Challenge: Islamic Economics in Hyderabad

The field of Islamic economics developed against the backdrop of larger trends in academia and Indian politics in the early twentieth century. During this period, the disciplinary boundaries of economics remained fluid and receptive to explicitly normative projects, offering a hospitable environment for research on religion and economics.[18] In the Indian context, nationalist politics reinforced disciplinary openness, as Indian academics looked for indigenous alternatives to what many viewed as exploitative systems of Western capitalism. Reflecting these intersecting cross-currents, *The Indian Journal of Economics*, which was founded in 1916, published articles on such topics as "The Religious Base in Indian Economy" and "The Hindu Taxation System."[19] In this context, a group of scholars at Osmania University in Hyderabad forged Islamic economics as a new field of study as a way to explore their interest in Islam's social message. The researchers at Osmania looked to Islamic institutions as a means to temper economic inequality and volatility while preserving private enterprise.

The princely state of Hyderabad offered a hospitable environment for Muslim intellectuals exploring modernist alternatives to Western models of development. As a protectorate rather than a formal colony, the sprawling princely state enjoyed a degree of autonomy even while it remained subject to a British resident who monitored its administrative affairs. Hyderabad also played a key role in global Muslim circuits, hosting itinerant intellectuals, including the renowned Muslim internationalist Sayyid Jamaluddin-al-Afghani.[20] Wilfred Scawen Blunt, the poet and anti-colonial activist, described the city as "after Cairo the most

---

[18] For an overview of the development of the field of economics, see Emma Rothschild, "Political Economy," in *The Cambridge History of Nineteenth-Century Political Thought*, ed. Gareth Stedman Jones and Gregory Claeys (Cambridge: Cambridge University Press, 2011), 748–79; Marion Fourcade, *Economists and Societies: Discipline and Profession in the United States, Britain, and France, 1890s to 1990s* (Princeton: Princeton University Press, 2009).

[19] See, for example, B.G. Bhatnagar, "The Religious Base in Indian Economy," *Indian Journal of Economics* [hereafter *IJE*] 5 (1924–5): 73–86; Dr. Balkrishna, "The Hindu Taxation System," *IJE* 8 (1927–8): 27–40, 89–117; Prem Chand Malhotra, "Scope of Economics: A Discussion of the Relation between Economics and Ethics," *IJE* 20 (1939–40): 451–8; G.D. Karwal, "Is Economics Non-Moral," *IJE* 24 (1943–4): 75–80; and Shri Narayan Agarwala, "A Religious Interpretation of Economics," *IJE* 26 (1945–6): 299–301.

[20] Niki R. Keddie, *An Islamic Response to Imperialism: Political and Religious Writings of Sayyid Jamal Ad-Din "Al-Afghani"* (Berkeley: University of California Press, 1983), 21–3.

gay and busy in the Mohammedan East."[21] Drawing on these regional, colonial, and Islamic influences, Hyderabad fostered social experiments in fields from public education to urban infrastructure.[22]

This spirit of innovation was embodied in the founding of Osmania University in 1918 as India's first university dedicated to providing modern education in an Indian vernacular language. Osmania sponsored Urdu translations and textbooks to make global fields of knowledge accessible to its students.[23] As part of this larger project, the university published Urdu translations of classic and contemporary works of economics in the 1920s and 1930s, including J.S. Mill's *Utilitarianism*, William Stanley Jevon's *Money and the Mechanism of Exchange*, and Romesh Dutt's *The Economic History of India*.[24] The translation bureau also produced two economic textbooks, *Usul-i-Ma'ashiyyat* (Principles of Economics) and *Ma'ishat-ul-Hind* (The Economy of India).[25] Reflecting the university's rising status as a center of Muslim intellectual life, Iqbal delivered portions of his lectures on the *Reconstruction of Religious Thought* at Osmania.[26] His challenge to the "bifurcation of the unity of man" into sacred and secular spheres resonated with the university's mission.[27] By promoting Urdu, which was associated with Indo-Islamic religious learning, as a medium for spreading modern, scientific knowledge, Osmania emphasized the capacity of Indian Muslims to embrace secular fields.[28]

Drawing on these wider trends, three members of the Osmania faculty – Muhammad Hamidullah, a professor of international law, Maulana Ahsan Gilani, the head of the theology department, and Anwar Iqbal Qureshi, the head of the Osmania economics department – looked to specifically integrate Islam with the modern field of economic research. The three men were exceptionally well networked across a range of

---

[21] Wilfrid Scawen Blunt, *India under Ripon: A Private Diary* (London: T. Fisher Unwin, 1909), 60.

[22] Eric Lewis Beverley, *Hyderabad, British Indian, and the World: Muslim Networks and Minor Sovereignty, c. 1850–1950* (Cambridge: Cambridge University Press, 2015); John Roosa, "The Quandary of the Qaum: Indian Nationalism in a Muslim State, Hyderabad, 1850–1948" (Ph.D., University of Wisconsin, 1998).

[23] Kavita Datla, *The Language of Secular Islam: Urdu Nationalism and Colonial India* (Honolulu: University of Hawai'i Press, 2013).

[24] *Literary Services of the Compilation and Translation Bureau, Osmania University, Hyderabad-Deccan, 1917–1946* (Hyderabad: Osmania University Press, 1946).

[25] Muhammad Ilyas Barni, *Usul-i-Ma'ashiyyat* (Hyderabad: Jami'ah Usmaniyah, 1922); *Ma'ishat-ul-Hind* (Hyderabad: Jami'ah Usmaniyah, 1929).

[26] Masudul Hasan, *Life of Iqbal: General Account of His Life*, 1st edn (Lahore: Ferozsons, 1978), 1: 238–9.

[27] Iqbal, *The Reconstruction of Religious Thought in Islam*, 122.

[28] Datla, *The Language of Secular Islam*.

secular and Islamic educational institutions.[29] Links between scholars
in Hyderabad also extended beyond India. The Egyptian scholar Sayyid
Rashid Rida purportedly wrote his Arabic treatise *Riba wa-al-muamalat
fi al-Islam* (Riba and Commercial Dealings in Islam), in response to a
query from an unnamed scholar in Hyderabad.[30]

Hamidullah's training and career epitomized these diverse intellec-
tual networks. Hamidullah received a traditional Islamic education in
Hyderabad before embarking on advanced studies in international
law, eventually earning doctorates from the Universities of Bonn and
Paris.[31] In 1936 he published an article in the Hyderabad journal *Islamic
Culture* entitled "Islam's Solution of the Basic Economic Problems."[32]
Hamidullah opened his essay by reflecting on how economists had
struggled to simultaneously maximize private gains and social welfare.
Hamidullah was critical of *laissez-faire* economics, which he argued had
produced a system in which "poverty like a tragic spectre has haunted
the ceaselessly toiling humanity."[33] On the other hand, he criticized communism for hindering "the moral development which the exercise of
personal choice in connection with private property makes possible."[34]
Hamidullah argued that the Islamic practice of distributing *zakat* to
the needy would temper the capitalist exploitation of workers by providing them with a guaranteed basic level of subsistence. Similarly, he
suggested that implementing an Islamic prohibition on interest would
prevent the violent boom-bust cycles to which free-market capitalism
was prone, a conclusion he linked to the work of the American economist
Irving Fisher on debt deflation. Hamidullah explained that Islam would
check irresponsible speculation by forcing investors to share financial
risk through partnerships.

Manazir Ahsan Gilani joined the faculty at Osmania after studying
and teaching *hadith* at the *madrasa* at Deoband.[35] In the introduction to

---

[29] Muhammad Hamidullah, "Haidarabad's Contribution to Islamic Economic Thought
and Practice," *Die Welt Des Islams* 4, no. 2/3 (January 1955): 78.

[30] Rida's Arabic text was published by an Egyptian press in 1960, purportedly over thirty
years after he received the query from Hyderabad. *Dr. M. Alsam Khaki and Others
v. Syed Muhammad Hashim and Others* [2000] All Pakistan Legal Decisions 52 231,
cited at 410.

[31] Muhammad al-Ghazali, "Dr Muhammad Hamidullah (1908–2002)," *Islamic Studies* 42,
no. 1 (April 2003): 183–7; Mahmud Rifat Kademoglu, "Remembering Muhammad
Hamidullah," *Islam and Science* 1, no. 1 (June 2003): 143–52.

[32] M. Hamidullah, "Islam's Solution of the Basic Economic Problems," *Islamic Culture* 10,
no. 2 (April 1936): 213–33.

[33] Ibid., 213.

[34] Ibid., 218.

[35] Muhammad Qasim Zaman, "Studying Hadith in a Madrasa in the Early Twentieth
Century," in *Islam in South Asia in Practice*, ed. Barbara D. Metcalf (Princeton: Princeton
University Press, 2009), 225–39.

his Urdu monograph, *Islami Ma'ashiyyat* (Islamic Economics), which was published in the mid-1940s, Gilani lamented that Islamic scholars had neglected economics and claimed that his book was the first significant work on the topic in Urdu or Arabic.[36] While this statement was not strictly true – the Delhi-based scholar Hifz-ul-Rahman Seoharvi published a work titled *Islam ka Iqtisadi Nizam* (The Economic System of Islam) in 1939 – it captured Gilani's sense of the novelty of the topic.[37]

Gilani argued that the struggle for material prosperity was central to an Islamic conception of piety, describing economic struggle (*ma'ashi jid-o-jahad*) as a form of conducting *jihad* in the cause of Allah. He cited the *surah muzzammil*, a passage of the Quran that describes the conditions under which Muslims should perform *tahajjud*, the voluntary performance of prayer at night. A portion of the *surah* specified that these prayers should not become a burden because "He [God] knows that some of you will be sick, some of you traveling through the land seeking God's bounty, some of you fighting in God's way: recite as much as is easy for you."[38] By arguing that the reference to seeking God's bounty could refer to economic endeavors, Gilani assured his readers that Islam recognized efforts to secure material prosperity as an expression of devotion to God.[39]

Gilani also connected abstract research to the immediate concerns facing Indian Muslims, including whether it might be permissible for Muslims to receive interest payments on bank deposits. In an extended article published in 1945, he drew on Islamic jurisprudence that differentiated between *dar-ul-Islam* (a territory under Muslim rule) and *dar-ul-harb* (a territory under non-Muslim rule) to argue that Indian Muslims were permitted to receive interest in their transactions with non-Muslims. Gilani emphasized that Islamic law provided this exception to enable Muslims to adjust to the demands of life under non-Muslim rule and to ensure that "they will be protected from being gobbled up by different communities when they enter into the international struggles of the financial world."[40]

Hamidullah and Gilani's colleague Anwar Iqbal Qureshi brought the most specialized economic expertise to the project. Qureshi studied as a

---

[36] Sayyid Manazar Ahsan Gilani, *Islami Ma'ashiyyat* (Lahore: Sang-i-Mill, 2007), 7. Gilani's introduction to the first edition is dated September 1945.

[37] Zaman, *Modern Islamic Thought in a Radical Age*, 234.

[38] Abdel Haleem, M.A.S., trans., "Enfolded," in *The Qur'an. Oxford Islamic Studies Online*, accessed August 30, 2012, www.oxfordislamicstudies.com/article/book/islam106./islam-9780192831934-chapter-73?astart=1&asize=20.

[39] Gilani, *Islami Ma'ashiyyat*, 28.

[40] Sayyid Manazar Ahsan Gilani, "Masalah-yi-Sod Muslim aur Harbi men," in *Maqalat-i-Gilani* (Lahore: Shaikh Zayid Islamic Center, 2004), quoted on 152.

M.A. and Ph.D. student in London and Dublin before publishing a range of comparative research on agricultural debt and state banking in India, Australia, New Zealand, South Africa, and the United States.[41] While serving as the head of the economics department at Osmania, he also advised the Hyderabad government and served in the Agricultural Credit Department of the State Bank of India.[42] Influenced by his colleagues at Osmania, Qureshi turned to Islam for further insight into problems of finance and debt. In *Islam and the Theory of Interest* (1946), Qureshi argued that research on finance, driven by the upheaval of the Great Depression and World War II, was moving towards the same conclusions as the Islamic prohibition on interest. He noted that researchers such as John Maynard Keynes had shown that the amount of individual savings was largely determined by fluctuations in income, not interest rates, and that excessive savings might hinder economic growth by hoarding capital. Qureshi insisted that Keynes's research underlined the economic benefits of prohibiting interest, and that only Keynes's environment prevented him from "condemn[ing] outright the charging of interest."[43]

Hamidullah, Gilani, and Qureshi crafted a body of scholarship in the late 1930s and early 1940s that suggested that Islamic alternatives could merge the benefits of capitalism and communism while protecting against each system's excesses – a recurring theme in future work on Islamic economics. They also mentored students who pursued research on topics ranging from Islamic principles of partnership to indigenous and cooperative banking networks.[44] These students connected research on Islamic economy to wider currents of nationalist thought, including

---

[41] Anwar Iqbal Qureshi, *The Farmer and His Debt: Being a Study of Farm Relief in Australia, New Zealand and South Africa, with Suggestions for India* (London: Indian Rural Reconstruction League, 1934); *Agricultural Credit: Being a Study of Recent Developments in Agricultural Credit Administration in the United States of America* (London: Sir Isaac Pitman & Sons, 1936); *The State and Economic Life: Being a Study of the Methods of State Intervention in Economic Life in the Leading Countries of the World* (Bombay: New Book Company, n.d., preface dated 1938); *State Banks for India: Being a Study of State Banks and Land Mortgage Credit Institutions in Australia, New Zealand, South Africa and the United States of America, with Suggestions for Establishing Similar Banks in India* (London: Macmillan, 1939).

[42] I have drawn the biographical information on Qureshi from materials provided in his publications.

[43] Anwar Iqbal Qureshi, *Islam and the Theory of Interest* (Lahore: Shaikh M. Ashraf, 1946), 16–17.

[44] One of Gilani and Qureshi's students, Muhammad Yusufuddin, produced another major work in Urdu on Islamic economy, *Islam ke ma'ashi nazariye* (Hyderabad: Matba-yi-Ibrahimiyah, 1950). Osmania's own archives include a rich body of student work on topics related to Islamic economics, including Wahidullah Khan, "Islami Qanun-i-Shirakat ke Usul ka Muqabala Hyderabad ke Qawanin se" (M.A., Osmania University, 1944); and Ram Autar, "Hyderabad men Desi Bank Kari" (M.A., Osmania University, 1947).

Gandhi's interest in reinvigorating Indian forms of economic production and governance.

One topic, however, remained strikingly absent from their budding research program on Islamic economics: the widespread agrarian unrest unfolding in Hyderabad in the 1940s. While this absence was possibly due to Osmania's ties to the state government, it also reflected the project's emphasis on ideals rather than pragmatic policy recommendations.[45] It is impossible to know whether the scholars at Osmania might eventually have turned their attention to this issue because their endeavors were cut short in 1948 when India invaded and forcibly integrated Hyderabad. In subsequent years, Qureshi migrated to Pakistan, where he served as an economic advisor to the government, while Hamidullah was stranded as a stateless refugee in Paris after India cancelled his passport because of his protests against the occupation of Hyderabad. Hamidullah would later lament in an article on Hyderabad's contribution to Islamic economics: "All this has also suffered on account of the upheaval that has come about."[46]

## Mawdudi's Economic Thought

Despite the demise of the princely state, the scholarship produced in Hyderabad gained a degree of longevity and popularity through the work of Sayyid Abu A'la Mawdudi, even as he took it in new directions. Mawdudi worked at the Osmania translation bureau from 1931 to 1937.[47] After leaving Hyderabad, in 1941 he founded the Jama'at-i-Islami, which would grow into one of the most significant Islamic movements in South Asia. As a leading theorist of political Islam, Mawdudi also garnered a wider global audience, inspiring the work of Hassan al-Banna and Sayyid Qutb in Egypt and Ruhollah Khomeini in Iran.[48]

Mawdudi delivered one of his earliest statements on Islamic economics in an address at Aligarh Muslim University in October 1942. In the early 1940s, when Mawdudi gave his speech, the Aligarh campus

---

[45] John Roosa, "Passive Revolution Meets Peasant Revolution: Indian Nationalism and the Telangana Revolt," *The Journal of Peasant Studies* 28, no. 4 (July 2001): 57–94.

[46] "Anwar Iqbal Qureshi," in Ahmad Saeed, *Muslim India, 1857–1947: A Biographical Dictionary* (Lahore: Institute of Pakistan Historical Research, 1997), 85. Hamidullah, "Haidarabad's Contribution to Islamic Economic Thought and Practice," 78. In the 1950s Hamidullah briefly served on a committee of Islamic scholars that provided guidance during the drafting of the first Pakistani constitution, but he later resigned.

[47] Seyyed Vali Reza Nasr, *Mawdudi and the Making of Islamic Revivalism* (New York: Oxford University Press, 1996), 23–4.

[48] Roy Jackson, *Mawlana Mawdudi and Political Islam: Authority and the Islamic State* (London: Routledge, 2011), 2.

was teeming with socialist and anti-colonial politics.[49] In his address Mawdudi infused academic research on Islamic economy with spirited populism. He opened by criticizing the discipline of economics for its "magic of professional complications" and "rigmarole of terminology." He proposed instead to examine economic problems in their "plain and natural simplicity."[50] He argued that economics must be studied from an ethical and practical perspective, taking into account both the spiritual and material needs of humankind. The essential problem, he told his audience, was to figure out "how should economic distribution be arranged so as to keep men supplied with the necessities of life and see that every individual in a society is provided with opportunities adequate to the development of his personality."[51] Mawdudi's solution to this problem revolved around balancing man's social and individualistic impulses. He argued that inequalities of wealth, which were rooted in men's different capacities, were natural, but that the rich should not be allowed to tyrannize the poor. He insisted that if man "finds himself possessing more of these means than his requirements justify, it only implies that a surplus which was really the portion of others reached him."[52] He therefore was morally obligated to give the surplus to those in need.

Mawdudi also insisted that economic development should be directed towards increasing human welfare, both material and psychological, rather than solely towards increasing the volume of production. Yet he condemned communism for pursuing these goals by subjecting people to a centralized authority in which individual diversity was reduced to a "soulless uniformity."[53] Mawdudi insisted: "What human personality needs above everything else for its evolution and advancement is that it should have freedom, it should have some means at its disposal which it may use in accordance with its own discretion and its own will and choice and in so doing develop its hidden potentialities."[54] The communist state, according to Mawdudi, squashed this freedom by monopolizing economic decision-making.

Mawdudi concluded by explaining how Islam, unlike capitalism or communism, was able to balance human freedom with social protection

[49] Mushirul Hasan, "Aligarh Muslim University: Recalling Radical Days," *India International Centre Quarterly* 29, no. 3/4 (December 2002): 53.
[50] Sayyed Abulala Maudoodi, *The Economic Problem of Man and Its Islamic Solution*, 2nd edn (Lahore: Maktaba-e-Jama'at-e-Islami, 1955), 3. For an Urdu edition of the address, see Syed Abulala Maudoodi, *Insan ka Ma'ashi Masalah aur us ka Islami Hal* (Lahore: Markazi Maktabah-yi-Jama'at-i-Islami, 1953).
[51] Maudoodi, *The Economic Problem of Man and Its Islamic Solution*, 12.
[52] Ibid., 25.
[53] Ibid., 43.
[54] Ibid., 40.

because it cultivated man's moral nature rather than a top-down program of state control. He insisted, "the authority and pressure of law and the coercive power of government should not be used except when it becomes inevitable to do so." Mawdudi explained that Islam maintained "that man should be free to strive for his livelihood, that he should retain the right of ownership over whatever he earns by his labour, and that disparity must exist between various men due to their varying abilities and circumstances." Yet Mawdudi clarified that while Islam gave considerable free rein to organic economic development, it also introduced "certain restrictions on its actual practice so that it may not be misused and made a means of exploiting and oppressing the weaker sections of society."[55]

Anyone familiar with Mawdudi's later political career in postcolonial Pakistan will hear notes of irony in his cautions against depending too heavily on "the coercive power of government" to accomplish Islamic ideals. From the 1950s through the 1970s, Mawdudi used his influence as a political activist and scholar to push for greater state Islamization, eventually supporting Zia-ul-Haq, who after seizing power in a military coup in 1977, instituted an authoritarian program of "Shariazation." Mawdudi thus came to support the very centralized and top-down modes of governance that he had criticized in his earlier work on Islamic economy.[56] Frustrated with the pace of bottom-up moral reform, Mawdudi looked to the state to accelerate the process of change. Mawdudi was not alone in his retreat from earlier ideals. As proponents of Islamic economy turned to concrete policy-making, they repeatedly made concessions to political expediency that threatened to marginalize their idealistic commitments.

### Reverting to Colonial Secular Governance: The Muslim Personal Law (Shariat) Act of 1937

Some of the earliest indications of these challenges occurred during deliberations over the Muslim Personal Law (Shariat) Act, passed by the Indian Legislative Assembly in 1937. Proponents of the act sought to curtail the recognition of custom to bring all Indian Muslims under a uniform body of religious personal laws, which they equated with the divine *sharia*. In arguing for the act, Muslim legislators emphasized that the *sharia* ensured a wider distribution of wealth by mandating that estates be divided among male and female family members, albeit in

[55] Ibid., 46–7.
[56] On the growing top-down, statist orientation of Mawdudi's thought see, Nasr, *Mawdudi and the Making of Islamic Revivalism.*

unequal shares. Reflecting their growing interest in integrating Islam into contemporary socio-economic discourse, legislators alternatively praised Islam for its socialist values or suggested that it offered a critical middle ground between capitalism and communism. Yet despite this emphasis on Islam's material injunctions, the Legislative Assembly ultimately acceded to the demands of elite landlords by inserting wide exemptions for inheritance, particularly of agricultural land, thereby severely limiting the act's economic impact.

The Muslim Personal Law (Shariat) Act was one of several legislative interventions passed in the decades leading up to independence that sought to reform the colonial administration of religious law. As growing numbers of Indians were elected to provincial and national legislative assemblies, direct government intervention in religious law became more palatable. Muhammad Ali Jinnah, who at the time was a promising young lawyer anxious to make a name for himself on the national stage, led the first such major legislative campaign, for the Mussalman Wakf Validating Act of 1913. Historically Muslims used the legal vehicle of *waqf* to set aside property as an inalienable endowment, the proceeds of which could be dedicated to various social services specified by the donor. In 1894 the Privy Council ruled that *waqf*s were invalid if they primarily benefitted the "private" interests of an individual family rather the general interests of the wider "public."[57] Jinnah joined other prominent Muslims in arguing that the decision, which became the law of British India, distorted Islamic laws governing *waqf* by interpreting them through the prism of English legal concepts of charity rather than through Islamic jurisprudence. With the passage of the 1913 act, Muslim leaders celebrated a crucial victory in asserting the rights of members of Indian communities, as opposed to colonial institutions, to interpret their own religious laws.[58]

The 1913 act, however, also foreshadowed the ways in which core stereotypes about religious law would survive the transition of power from British to Indian leadership. Proponents of the act insisted that there was a uniform law governing Islamic endowments, which the British had misinterpreted. Yet in practice, *waqf*, which was not mentioned directly in the Quran, had evolved as a pragmatic tool that gave Muslims greater flexibility in dividing their estates. While the Quran mandated

---

[57] In her work on contemporaneous debates about Hindu endowments and trusts, Ritu Birla has linked the growing emphasis on the need for charities to serve the "public" to the simultaneous mapping of the market as distinct from a private sphere of the family. Ritu Birla, *Stages of Capital: Law, Culture, and Market Governance in Late Colonial India* (Durham: Duke University Press, 2009), 104–42.

[58] Kozlowski, *Muslim Endowments and Society in British India*, 96–191.

that two-thirds of all estates be divided between family members in fixed proportions, Muslim jurists developed *waqf*, alongside gift and fictitious sale, to allow Muslims to circumvent the proscribed division of estates, even as some of their peers criticized these practices as unethical.[59] In a testament to the historical flexibility with which Muslim jurists had responded to shifting socio-economic needs, norms governing *waqf* also differed between the different schools of Islamic law and regions.[60] In pressing for legislative intervention, however, Jinnah and his supporters described family *waqf* as rooted in ancient and immutable holy law. They therefore reinforced the colonial construction of Muslim law as a unified code rather than emphasizing its diversity and adaptability.[61]

The campaign for the Muslim Personal Law (Shariat) Act, which Jinnah also led, followed a similar pattern of reiterating colonial stereotypes about Muslim law even as it challenged the authority of British legal institutions. The act originated in a more limited bill passed by the Punjab Legislative Assembly in 1931 that sanctioned customs of primogeniture within the powerful Tiwana family. During debates about the bill, several legislators complained that concessions to custom deprived Muslim women of their legal right to an inheritance as mandated under the *sharia*. Pir Akbar Ali, a rural representative from Ferozepore, declared:

In India as well as in other countries a great stress is being laid on granting equal rights to women. The spirit of the times is towards democracy, but alas! in this Council, in this responsible House, we are passing measures which will not only deprive women of their due share but throw them also on the whim and mercy of the eldest member of the House.[62]

Some of the bill's most vocal opponents argued that the economic rights that Islam extended to women reflected the faith's socialist spirit. Arguing that concentrating wealth in the hands of a few individuals was contrary to Islam, Shaikh Muhammad Sadiq of Amritsar explained: "Islam being a socialistic religion, further enjoins that the property of an individual

---

[59] David S. Powers, "The Islamic Inheritance System: A Socio-Historical Approach," *Arab Law Quarterly* 8, no. 1 (1993): 13–29; Jon E. Mandaville, "Usurious Piety: The Cash Waqf Controversy in the Ottoman Empire," *International Journal of Middle East Studies* 10, no. 3 (1979): 289–308.

[60] For examples of divergences between different schools of law on questions related to *waqf*, see Murat Çizakça, *A History of Philanthropic Foundations: The Islamic World from the Seventh Century to the Present* (Istanbul: Boğaziçi University Press, 2000), 19–25; David S. Powers, "The Islamic Family Endowment (Waqf)," *Vanderbilt Journal of Transnational Law* 32 (October 1999): 1186–7.

[61] Kozlowski, *Muslim Endowments and Society in British India*, 186.

[62] Punjab Legislative Council Debates, November 30, 1931, vol. 20: 189.

should in no case descend to one person who may jealously guard it
and sit over it like a snake."[63] Raising the banner of socialism, however,
did not prove a successful strategy in a legislative body dominated by
rural landowners. As Khan Bahadur Shaikh Din Muhammad sarcastic-
ally replied: "This is really a very funny argument. Will my friend kindly
let us know whether he has ascertained that the province ... is prepared
to adopt bolshevism?"[64]

While the Tiwana bill passed, one of its opponents, Malik Muhammad
Din, introduced a second, broader bill that sought to eliminate customary
exemptions to the application of Muslim personal laws.[65] The bill quickly
failed – unsurprisingly given the critical role that concessions to custom
played in undergirding the colonial development of Punjab's agrarian
economy.[66] Some representatives, however, remained committed to the
bill's ideals.

Hafiz Abdullah introduced the Muslim Personal Law (Shariat) Act in
the Indian Legislative Assembly in an attempt to achieve at the center what
his peers had failed to accomplish in the Punjab.[67] During the discussion
of the bill, its supporters again framed the act's ethical importance in
terms of its economic impact, citing the role of Islamic inheritance laws
in preventing extreme concentrations of wealth. At the all-India level,
the idea of Islam as offering a middle ground gained support, as when
Mr. A. O. Koreshi, a representative from Bombay, praised it for preventing
"the destructive extremes of Capitalism and Communism."[68] Similarly,
Khan Bahadur Shaikh Fazl-i-Haq Piracha from the Punjab argued that
the bill offered a critical opportunity to make economic reforms that
would reduce the threat of violent socialist revolution.[69]

Despite its advocates' repeated references to the act's economic
benefits, however, its symbolic importance, and, ultimately, its contents,
shifted as legislative efforts made the journey from the Punjab to New
Delhi. Muhammad Ali Jinnah saw the act primarily as an opportunity to
craft a unified pan-Indian Muslim agenda out of the divergent interests

---

[63] Punjab Legislative Council Debates, November 26, 1931, vol. 20: 62–3.
[64] Ibid., 201.
[65] David Gilmartin, "Kinship, Women, and Politics in Twentieth-Century Punjab," in *The Extended Family: Women and Political Participation in India and Pakistan*, ed. Gail Minault (Delhi: Chanakya Publications, 1981), 167.
[66] For more on the structure of the agrarian economy in Punjab and its underpinnings in colonial laws such as the Alienation of Land Act (1901), see David Gilmartin, *Empire and Islam: Punjab and the Making of Pakistan* (London: Tauris, 1988), esp. 170.
[67] "Statement of Objects and Reasons," IOR/L/P+J/7/943.
[68] Legislative Assembly Department, Opinions on the Muslim Personal Law (Shariat) Application Act, Paper No. II, 25, IOR/L/P+J/7/943.
[69] Legislative Assembly Debates, April 1, 1937, vol. 3: 2539.

of Muslims in different regions. He recognized that opposition to the original bill in the Punjab grew out of its threat to the region's rural landlords. Anxious to court this powerful elite, Jinnah pointed out that, under the provisions of the Government of India Act of 1935, the new legislation could not cover agricultural land, and also introduced an amendment that excluded adoption, wills, and legacies. Muslims in regions such as the Punjab where custom predominated could voluntarily sign a declaration that would bind future generations to divide inherited property in accordance with the *sharia*. Powerful landholding families, who had a strong interest in keeping their estates intact, however, were unlikely to take this option.[70] Through deft legislative maneuvering, Jinnah was thus able to craft a bill that could serve as a symbol of Muslim unity but which did little to address actual economic inequalities among Muslims. This compromise, which Jinnah used to gain support for the bill among Punjab's influential Muslim landlords, ensured its successful passage.

Jinnah's critics castigated the legislature for passing a "crippled measure which gives nothing but a name."[71] Even the bill's supporters admitted that it was primarily symbolic, since 99.5 percent of all property in India was classified as agricultural lands and therefore exempt. Pointing out the discrepancy between the act's original inspiration and its eventual form, Fazl-i-Haq Piracha warned that the legislature had done nothing to stem "the increasing temptation of an agrarian revolt."[72]

Despite contemporary awareness of the act's limited practical impact, subsequent scholarly and popular accounts have credited it with the monumental achievement of "codifying" Muslim personal law.[73] This assessment is surely overstating the case. The act did, however, create

---

[70] Gilmartin, "Democracy, Nationalism and the Public: A Speculation on Colonial Muslim Politics," 169–74; Jalal, *Self and Sovereignty*, 384–5; Eleanor Newbigin, "Personal Law and Citizenship in India's Transition to Independence," *Modern Asian Studies* 45, no. 1 (2011): 27.

[71] Legislative Assembly Debates, September 16, 1937, vol. 5: 1854.

[72] Legislative Assembly Debates, September 9, 1937, vol. 5: 1443.

[73] For examples of scholars using the terms codification or codify in describing the Shariat Act, see Rajeswari Sunder Rajan, *The Scandal of the State: Women, Law, and Citizenship in Postcolonial India* (Durham: Duke University Press, 2003), 46; Vrinda Narain, *Gender and Community: Muslim Women's Rights in India* (Toronto: University of Toronto Press, 2001), 23; Elora Shehabuddin, *Reshaping the Holy: Democracy, Development, and Muslim Women in Bangladesh* (New York: Columbia University Press, 2012), 44. This language is also used in more popular discussions of the act, often in connection with ongoing debates about the status of Muslim personal law in postcolonial India. For example, *The Indian Express* recently described the Shariat Act as formulating "an Islamic law code for Indian Muslims." Adrija Roychowdhury, "Shariat and Muslim Personal Law: All Your Questions Answered," *The Indian Express*, last updated October 13, 2016, http://indianexpress.com/article/research/shariat-muslim-personal-law-sharia-history-shayara-bano-shah-bano-triple-talaq-personal-laws-religious-laws-uniform-civil-code-2784081/.

a sense of closure. After the passage of the Dissolution of Muslim Marriages Act in 1939, which broadened the conditions under which Muslim women could petition for divorce, India's lawmakers introduced no additional national legislation on Muslim personal law for almost a half-century.[74] In contrast, in the realm of Hindu personal law, the Indian Legislative Assembly appointed a Hindu Law Committee in 1941, which embarked on a massive project to codify religious laws. These efforts culminated after Indian independence in the passage in 1955 and 1956 of major reforms to Hindu marriage, succession, minority status, guardianship, adoption, and maintenance.[75] Further modifications of Hindu personal law followed, including amendments in 1964 and 1976 that expanded Hindus' access to divorce. In 2005, another set of amendments gave Hindu daughters and sons equal rights in ancestral property.[76]

The diverging paths of legislative interventions in Muslim and Hindu personal laws in postcolonial India were the product of the unequal representation of the two religious communities in the politics of the new nation. In the years after independence, Hindus could feel far more confident that their religious interests would be adequately represented in the seat of government; in contrast, the Muslim minority in India, whose numbers were further diminished after partition, was fearful about its ability to retain control over legislative interventions in Muslim personal laws. Yet these trends had already begun even before partition. In the decades leading up to independence, Hindus increasingly emphasized the secular, progressive nature of Hindu law and its adaptability to changing historical circumstances.[77] The secular position proved more difficult for Muslims to occupy, even as Muslim economists promoted the religion's commitment to socio-economic equality. In the course of debates about the Sharia Act, the need to assert Muslim unity through portraying the *sharia* as ancient and unchanging drowned out its relevance to current problems of inequality besetting the Indian economy as a whole. After independence, many Muslims who remained in India

[74] Subsequent judicial interpretation of the act, however, has in important instances widened Muslim women's right to maintenance after divorce. Narendra Subramanian, "Legal Change and Gender Inequality: Changes in Muslim Family Law in India," *Law and Social Inquiry* 33, no. 3 (September 2008): 631–72.
[75] For a history of the Hindu Law Acts that emphasizes the limits of their progressive impact on Hindu women, see Newbigin, *The Hindu Family and the Emergence of Modern India.*
[76] Werner Menski, *Modern Indian Family Law* (London: Routledge, 2013), 48; Newbigin, *The Hindu Family and the Emergence of Modern India,* 227.
[77] Newbigin has also argued that the ability to portray Hindu law as more adaptable grew from colonial discourses portraying Muslim law as more dependent on textual sources. Newbigin, "Personal Law and Citizenship in India's Transition to Independence."

felt further pressure to defend the religious distinctiveness of Muslim personal laws in order to wall them off from a secular democratic politics that felt stacked against them.

## Pakistan: "Laboratory of Applied Islam"[78]

In comparison to postcolonial India, Pakistan at first seemed to offer more fertile ground to implement Islamic economic models and, more generally, to challenge colonial patterns of secular governance. In the 1940s a growing alliance between the Muslim League and the Communist Party of India brought economic questions to the forefront of the Pakistan movement. Young Muslim members of the Communist Party pushed the Muslim League towards left-leaning economic policies while campaigning on its behalf among the rural poor and urban working class.[79] In the years following the creation of Pakistan, intellectuals interested in Islamic economy looked to the new state to put their ideas into practice, producing a flood of pamphlets, newspaper articles, and books on the topic in the late 1940s and early 1950s. These writings tied calls for economic reform to broader questions of citizenship and sovereignty. Knitting together positive and negative conceptions of freedom, they advocated forms of political economy that would both protect individual rights and ensure social well-being.

Despite the brutal violence that accompanied the partition of the subcontinent and the considerable fiscal and security challenges that Pakistan faced, many of its new citizens expressed an optimistic, even utopian, enthusiasm about nation building. They believed that Pakistan could encourage political and economic innovations that would serve as an example for both the Muslim and non-Muslim world. As one writer from East Pakistan explained, crafting an Islamic constitution was the new nation's "moral, as well as, Islamic duty, because its very inception was to serve as [a] laboratory for the Islamic way of life."[80]

Dr. Ishtiaq Husain Qureshi, a historian of medieval India who also served in Pakistan's Constituent Assembly, expanded on these sentiments in a pamphlet entitled *The Future Development of Islamic Polity*, published on the eve of independence in 1946. Qureshi expressed almost euphoric excitement about the project of "fashioning the future of Muslim society."

[78] Altaf Husain, foreword to *The Spirit of Pakistan*, by Fareed S. Jafri (Karachi: Ansari, 1951), 5.

[79] Ali, "Communists in a Muslim Land," 508–10.

[80] Ali Ahmad Khan, *Why Islamic Constitution Only?* (Dacca: Jahan-e-Nau Publications, 1955), 22.

Yet he also urged "mature and calm deliberation." Using the same metaphor of the new nation as a "laboratory," Qureshi argued that the new nation would provide an opportunity to test political theories against the "crucible" of "human experience."[81] He urged that Islam should be the guiding force in this endeavor while sharply rejecting a rigid separation of religion and politics. He insisted, "our religion is not an organized church but the idealism that governs our entire life. How can we separate the two?"[82]

Qureshi elaborated a concept of freedom grounded in Islam's commitment to human development. He argued that a truly Islamic democracy would focus on eliminating poverty as a source of human oppression. As he explained, "Islam believes in the fullest growth of man; it gives him freedom to enable him to attain his fullest stature, but not to indulge in meaningless and destructive pleasure or wield an unhealthy influence upon society."[83] For Qureshi, this conception of human liberty made Islam incompatible with capitalism. Equating capitalism with tyranny, Qureshi argued, "Tyranny whether of power or of money cramps the human soul; hunger, poverty, starvation reduce the human being to the level of an animal. These demons cannot be allowed to exist in the world of Islam."[84] Qureshi believed that the route to eliminating economic oppression lay through what he termed, "State Capitalism," in which the government engaged in economic planning. He argued that Soviet Russia provided a model for combining rapid development with social justice, but rejected its doctrine of "materialistic dialectics."[85]

In an address to the All-Pakistan Political Science Conference, held in Peshawar in 1951 and later published as a pamphlet in English and Urdu, Qureshi addressed the question of the nature of sovereignty in an Islamic democracy.[86] He attempted to clarify the heavily debated question by distinguishing between political, legal, and real sovereignty. He argued that the people of Pakistan should hold political sovereignty while the law of Islam should hold legal sovereignty. Real sovereignty, however, lay with "those innumerable forces which sway the life of a nation and direct its activities."[87] Qureshi emphasized that the critical

---

[81] Ishtiaq Husain Qureshi, *The Future Development of Islamic Polity* (Lahore: Shaikh Muhammad Ashraf, 1946), 1.

[82] Ibid., 7.

[83] Ibid., 18.

[84] Ibid., 19.

[85] Ibid., 23.

[86] Ishtiaq Husain Qureshi, *Pakistan: An Islamic Democracy* (Lahore: Institute of Islamic Culture, n.d.); *Pakistan: Ek Islami Jumhuriyat* (Lahore: Idarah-yi-Saqafat-i-Islami, n.d.).

[87] Qureshi, *Pakistan: An Islamic Democracy*, 16.

question was how these different forms of sovereignty would interact. While emphasizing the legal sovereignty of the *sharia*, Qureshi argued that Islamic jurisprudence needed to be reinterpreted in light of modern conditions. The legislature had to shoulder this responsibility because "as the supreme representative of the people, the legislature alone can speak for them and accept on their behalf."[88] Qureshi allowed the *ulama* a role in these discussions, but insisted that their views should not be treated as sacrosanct. By differentiating between political, legal, and real sovereignty, Qureshi added depth to the concept of Islamic democracy, portraying sovereignty in terms of a dynamic relationship between Islam, the citizens of Pakistan, and the law.

Pakistan's vigorous press played a major role in debates about the place of Islam in the new nation. In 1951, Fareed S. Jafri, the editor of the *Civil and Military Gazette*, wrote a short book entitled *The Spirit of Pakistan*.[89] The book lacked the measured reasoning of Qureshi's writings, but Jafri infused the text with excitement about constructing a new nation founded on Islam. He periodically burst into capitalized text, visually splashing his enthusiasm across the page. The book reviewed the strengths and weaknesses of various forms of democracy, including Western democracy, capitalist-controlled democracy, cooperative democracy, and communist democracy. Jafri exhorted his fellow Muslim to "accept all that is gold from these rich and productive mines, for Islam encourages evolution." Yet he cautioned: "But at the same time, we must not forget that everything that glitters is not gold."[90] The text that followed presented an eclectic mix of references, drawing on the works of Abraham Lincoln and Oscar Wilde to Turkish scholarship on the founding of the Republic. Ultimately, Jafri argued that Islam itself provided a model of "spiritual democracy" that was richer than any existing model offered by the West, whether capitalist or communist.[91]

Books like Jafri's were directed both at the Pakistani public and wider international audiences, as debates in Pakistan intersected with Cold War politics. While visiting England in 1953, Jafri lectured at the Royal Central Asian Society on communism and Islam. Jafri argued that, if the Islamic world was to return to "basic Islamic democracy," which

---

[88] Ibid., 23.
[89] During World War II Jafri served as a war correspondent for Reuters in Cairo; in the late 1940s he worked as the London correspondent for the Karachi newspaper *Dawn*. The back covers of some of Jafri's publications provided basic biographical information. Fareed S. Jafri, *Yugoslavia Today* (Place and Publisher Unknown, 1964); Fareed S. Jafri, *Eyewitness: Modern Sudan* (Lahore: Ferozsons, 1964).
[90] Fareed S. Jafri, *The Spirit of Pakistan* (Karachi: Ansari, 1951), 25.
[91] Ibid., 102.

promoted economic equality, it could avoid the perils of communism. Jafri insisted that if in 1946 the British and Americans had created a "Chinese Pakistan," 50 million Muslims in China would have become a "great bulwark for democracy."[92] In the early 1950s other Pakistani intellectuals similarly attracted international attention as potential critics of communism. In an atmosphere of growing tension between the United States and the Soviet Union, many Western observers became interested in the role that the Muslim states might play as a counterweight against the rise of communism.

Another Pakistani, Mazheruddin Siddiqi, briefly became a hit on the international academic circuit in the 1950s after publishing a book denouncing the dangers of communism. Siddiqi became interested in Islam and socialism while living in Hyderabad, where he wrote a book in Urdu comparing the philosophy of Marx and Hegel to Islam. While completing the book, he met Mawdudi, who mentored his research.[93] In the English work *Marxism or Islam?* (1954), Siddiqi urged that Islam offered a better means of furthering social justice than Marxism, which relied too heavily on the power of the state. Marxism, according to Siddiqi, "left an extremely narrow field of action for the exercise of free choice by men and women and for self-regulation, which is the essence of morality." In contrast, Siddiqi explained, Islam relied primarily on moral instruction. The state, by ensuring peace and order, merely laid the foundation for the free moral development of individuals and society.[94]

In 1953 Siddiqi attended the Harvard International Seminar, a program that Henry Kissinger organized with covert funding from the CIA to bring emerging international leaders to the United States.[95] While the seminar's annual report declared that its purpose was not to propagandize, the participants were taken on a carefully curated tour emphasizing the prosperity and benevolence of the U.S. economy, including stops at a Ford factory, the Council of Industrial Organization, and Goodwill Industries.[96] After the Harvard program, Siddiqi attended the

[92] Fareed Jafri, "Communism in the Muslim World," *Journal of the Royal Central Asian Society* 40, no. 2 (April 1953): 161–8, quoted 162, 166.
[93] Mazheruddin Siddiqi, *Hegel, Marx aur Islami Nizam*, 2nd edn (Pathankot: Tarjuman-ul-Quran, 1945), 28.
[94] Mazheruddin Siddiqi, *Marxism or Islam?*, 2nd edn (Lahore: Orientalia, 1954), quoted on iii, 141.
[95] Hugh Wilford, *The Mighty Wurlitzer: How the CIA Played America* (Cambridge: Harvard University Press, 2009), 124–8; Inderjeet Parmar, *Foundations of the American Century: The Ford, Carnegie, and Rockefeller Foundations in the Rise of American Power* (New York: Columbia University Press, 2015), 103–8.
[96] "Report of the 1953 Harvard International Seminar," Summer School of Arts and Sciences and of Education, Special Programs Files, International Seminar: General Records, Harvard University Archives, UAV813.141.25, Part I: 1. See also Siddiqi's

Colloquium on Islamic Culture at Princeton, a conference funded by the State Department's International Information Administration.[97]

Although Siddiqi wrote enthusiastically about his experience, his correspondence from the period suggests a certain dissonance between his outlook and that of his hosts. In a letter he wrote after the Harvard International Seminar, Siddiqi thanked Kissinger for his "extreme tolerance of my ideological aggressiveness." He assured Kissinger that although he might have mistaken Siddiqi for a "fanatic or proselytizer," he was actually "a believer in American democracy." Siddiqi concluded by informing Kissinger that he had recommended him as a speaker at the Colloquium on Islamic Culture at Princeton. In a jocular final sentence, he encouraged Kissinger to attend and assured him: "You need not fear being converted, I think you have sufficient grit."[98] Despite Siddiqi's polite tone, the letter suggested that the two men had not seen eye-to-eye on the question of the relationship between Islam and American democracy. While Siddiqi's trip to the United States prefigured the growth of a Cold War alliance between Pakistan and the United States, the strategic alliance that developed between an increasingly autocratic Pakistani state and the United States was a far cry from the partnership that Siddiqi had imagined, founded in the two nations' common liberal commitments.

In the early years of its existence, Pakistan was a rich laboratory for critical thinking about the form and purpose of the state. Many of the ideas that emerged during this period about the relationship between Islam, democracy, and economic development defy stereotypes about Islamist political thought. Existing scholarship on "Islamization" has associated it with rising authoritarianism, tracing its development through the state-centered projects that unfolded between the late 1960s and late 1980s in Pakistan, Egypt, and Malaysia.[99] Reaching back further into the

---

own account of the trip, Mazheruddin Siddiqi, *Impressions of the United States* (Lahore: Orientalia, 1955).

[97] Department of State Memorandum from Wilson S. Compton to David K.E. Bruce, "Colloquium on Islamic Culture to Be Held in September, 1953, under the Joint Sponsorship of the Library of Congress and Princeton University," January 13, 1953, U.S. National Archives, Records of the Department of State, Decimal Files, 1950–4, reproduced in "Documentation on Early Cold War U.S. Propaganda Activities in the Middle East," National Security Archives, George Washington University, Document 89, accessed June 1, 2017, http://nsarchive.gwu.edu/NSAEBB/NSAEBB78/propaganda%20089.pdf.

[98] Mazheruddin Siddiqi to Mr. Kissinger, September 1, 1953, in "Report of the 1953 Harvard International Seminar," Appendix A.

[99] On the state-centered focus of Islamist politics, see Seyyed Vali Reza Nasr, *Islamic Leviathan: Islam and the Making of State Power* (Oxford: Oxford University Press, 2001). For a more recent account of Islamists' growing interest in civil society, see Humeira Iqtidar, "Secularism beyond the State: The 'State' and the 'Market' in Islamist Imagination," *Modern Asian Studies* 45, no. 3 (2011): 535–64.

early years of Pakistan's existence, however, reveals an alternative trajectory for political Islam. In contrast to later movements, writings from this period warned that excessive state power threatened core Islamic values.[100] They emphasized the need for forms of governance that would allow for the free development of individuals' moral and economic capacities while reigning in their excesses. In subsequent years, however, Pakistanis struggled to translate these aspirations into coherent policies. These challenges quickly became apparent as the new nation turned to drafting its first constitution.

## A Constitution for the Islamic Republic: Delayed and Enfeebled

While India had a constitution in place by the beginning of 1950, Pakistan took almost a decade to draft its first constitution. Though the question of the role of Islam in the new state was not the only source of delay, lack of consensus on the point exacerbated existing disagreements.[101] During this period Pakistan had to juggle intersecting crises, including war with India, shortages of financial and infrastructural resources, and the breakdown of the Muslim League. In this environment the new state's democratic institutions were increasingly overwhelmed by the rising ascendance of the military and civilian bureaucracy.[102] By the time that Pakistan eventually ratified a constitution in 1956, the early optimism about forging a new experiment in Islamic democracy had dimmed. Among the most marked casualties of this period was a rapid retreat from the new nation's early commitment to Islamic social justice.

When Pakistan's Constituent Assembly passed an Objectives Resolution in March 1949, the first stage in drafting a new constitution, calls for Islamic social justice occupied center stage. The resolution recognized God as the ultimate source of sovereignty while committing the new state to working through the chosen representatives of the people. It resolved that the nation should observe "the principles of democracy, freedom, equality, tolerance and social justice, as enunciated by Islam."[103] In introducing the Objectives Resolution, Liaquat Ali Khan,

---

[100] On the relationship between Islamism and the growing power of the state, see Nasr, *Islamic Leviathan*.

[101] On debates about the role of Islam in Pakistan's constitution, see Leonard Binder, *Religion and Politics in Pakistan* (Berkeley: University of California Press, 1961).

[102] Ayesha Jalal, *The State of Martial Rule: The Origins of Pakistan's Political Economy of Defence* (Cambridge: Cambridge University Press, 1990); Ian Talbot, *Pakistan: A Modern History* (London: C. Hurst, 1998), 125–47.

[103] Constituent Assembly of Pakistan Debates, March 9, 1949, vol. 5, no. 3, 39.

Pakistan's first prime minister, highlighted the importance of the material dimensions of Islamic social justice to its positive and enabling conception of freedom. As the prime minister explained, "Islam envisages a society in which social justice means neither charity nor regimentation. Islamic social justice is based upon fundamental laws and concepts which guarantee to man a life free from want and rich in freedom."[104] Further elaborating on the relationship between Pakistan's commitment to Islam and its economic objectives, Liaquat Ali Khan declared, "It is our intention to build up an economy on the basic principles of Islam which seeks a better distribution of wealth and the removal of want. Poverty and backwardness – all that stands in the way of the achievement of his fullest stature by man – must be eradicated from Pakistan."[105]

Yet in subsequent years the Constituent Assembly devoted almost no attention to translating this theoretical commitment into a practical platform of economic reform. This retreat was facilitated by the political missteps of the Left and the *ulama,* who might otherwise have united around a shared platform of Islamic social justice. The Communist Party of Pakistan alienated potential allies by rejecting appeals to Islam as retrogressive.[106] Meanwhile Mawdudi's Jama'at-i-Islami castigated socialism as a threat to Islam.[107] While the Left and the *ulama* foreclosed the possibility of mutual collaboration, they also provoked official wrath. The Communist Party of Pakistan was implicated in the failed Rawalpindi Conspiracy of 1951, which involved a plot to overthrow the government with support from the military.[108] In 1954 the Party was outlawed, a move that coincided with Pakistan's strengthening alliance with the United States. During the same period the *ulama* fomented violence against the Ahmadis, a controversial Muslim sect.[109] When the government refused to declare the Ahmadis a non-Muslim minority, Mawdudi and his associates helped lead anti-Ahmadi riots in Lahore and other regions of the Punjab. In response the government declared Pakistan's first martial law regime in 1953, an ominous first step in the state's descent into

---

[104] Constituent Assembly of Pakistan Debates, March 7, 1949, vol. 5, no. 1, 4.

[105] Ibid., 6.

[106] Ali, "Communists in a Muslim Land," 514–22.

[107] Nasr, *Mawdudi and the Making of Islamic Revivalism,* 105. The Jama'at press also printed the Urdu version of Mazheruddin Siddiqi's *Ishtirakiyyat aur Nizam i-Islam* in 1949.

[108] There have been significant debates about which, if any, of the allegations against members of the Communist Party were true. Ali, "Communists in a Muslim Land," 529.

[109] Some Sunni Muslims believed that Mirza Ghulam Ahmad, who founded the Ahmadi sect in the late nineteenth century, committed apostasy by claiming Prophethood. For a nuanced account of Ahmadis' beliefs, see Yohanan Friedmann, *Prophecy Continuous: Aspects of Ahmadi Religious Thought and Its Medieval Background* (Berkeley: University of California Press, 1989).

authoritarianism. For his role in the agitations Mawdudi was initially
sentenced to death, later commuted to two years in prison.[110] Mutually
at odds with each other, outlawed, and imprisoned, the Left and the
*ulama* were by the mid-1950s in no position to mount a campaign for
meaningful policies of Islamic social justice.

Instead, by the time the reconstituted Constituent Assembly finally
ratified a constitution in 1956, the ambitious project of fostering Islamic
social justice was largely reduced to symbolic, but nonetheless divisive,
assertions of the new nation's Islamic identity. One of the more controversial provisions in the new constitution was the requirement that
the head of state be Muslim. The constitution also included a so-called
"repugnancy clause," which declared that no laws should be passed that
contravened the Quran or *sunnah*, and that all existing laws would be
amended to conform to Islamic injunctions. This provision, however,
excluded "fiscal and monetary measures, laws relating to banking, insurance, provident funds, loans, and other matters affecting the existing
economic, financial and credit system."[111] Although the constitution
specified that after twenty-five years a commission should consider how
these areas could be brought in line with the injunctions of the Quran
and *sunnah*, the exemption effectively removed economic matters from
the state's program of Islamic reform. The exemptions recalled the economic exclusion included in the Shariat Bill of 1937. Even as Pakistan
rejected a division between religion and politics, it largely maintained a
practical boundary between religious values and economic policies that
perpetuated a hidden legacy of colonial secular governance.

A few voices of protest bemoaned the gap between the vision of social
justice that originally animated calls for Islamic legislation and the retreat
to maintaining a status quo of poverty and inequality under the guise of
Islamic governance. Abdul Kasem Khan of East Bengal upbraided his
peers for failing to live up to the promise of what he somewhat ambigu-
ously termed "Islamic sociology":

We have preached from many platforms and the Press that we want to give the
people Islamic sociology, which means certainly a better distribution of wealth in
the country. But, have we made in the last six years any conscious effort to secure

---

[110] Mawdudi was sentenced to death for instigating "feelings of enmity and hatred between different groups," although his sentence was later commuted to two years in prison. Binder, *Religion and Politics in Pakistan*, 259–303; Sadia Saeed, "Political Fields and Religious Movements: The Exclusion of the Ahmadiyya Community in Pakistan," *Political Power and Social Theory* 23 (August 2012): 202–7.
[111] Constituent Assembly of Pakistan Debates, November 3, 1953, vol. 15, no. 21, 669–70.

to our people the benefits of a better distribution of wealth in the country? Not to my knowledge ... But I can tell you that the people will not be satisfied if we fail in securing for them the substances of Islam, the substance of freedom.[112]

As Abdul Kasem Khan foreshadowed, the demand to realize the promise of Islamic social justice through a penetrating program of economic reform retained popular appeal. In the 1970s the populist Zulfikar Ali Bhutto ran on a platform promising to promote Islamic socialism. In the 1980s, under the military government of General Muhammad Zia ul-Haq, the officially appointed Islamization Committee recommended an extensive program of economic reform to address rampant social inequality. Yet in practice, with the exception of largely symbolic programs to establish an interest-free banking system and *zakat* distribution, Zia's program of Islamization focused instead on the punitive enforcement of a narrow code of Islamic morality.[113]

## Conclusion

In both postcolonial India and Pakistan, class and gender hierarchies inherited from the economic policies of the colonial government, rather than Islamic norms of social justice, have dominated. The marginalization of Islamic economy from political discourse in postcolonial India has meant that appeals to Islam have remained limited to "communal" affairs, including personal law, while remaining largely cut off from more universal causes, such as fighting inequality. In contrast, Hindus have successfully appealed to their religion as an ethos of tolerance, which they argue all Indians should embrace. In postcolonial Pakistan, the hollowing out of calls for Islamic social justice into symbolic gestures affirming the nation's Islamic unity has derailed critical efforts to reevaluate Islamic theology and law in light of contemporary challenges. In both cases the retreat from earlier calls for Islamic economy has left intact crucial features of colonial secular governance, including limiting Islam to a narrow field of communal affairs and downplaying its diversity and adaptability to changing historical conditions.

How are we to account for the frailty of Islamic economy and the perverse longevity of colonial patterns of secular governance? Answering this question requires looking to wider global contexts. Visions of Islamic economy and social justice evolved alongside a wave of creative efforts

---

[112] Constituent Assembly of Pakistan Debates, October 22, 1953, vol. 15, no. 11, 283.
[113] Nasr, *Islamic Leviathan*, 76–9; 144–6.

to rethink modern social and political institutions that swept across Asia, Africa, and the Middle East in the decades immediately preceding and following the creation of postcolonial nations. Yet as postcolonial leaders grappled with the practical challenges of securing independence, building new states, and navigating Cold War geopolitics, they often backed away from their earlier ambitions to experiment with new political forms. Instead they found themselves replicating the forms of top-heavy, centralized bureaucracy and Western strategies of economic development that they had earlier criticized. As scholars in regions from Africa to South and Southeast Asia have observed, the acute pressures that accompanied the moment of independence often proved surprisingly inhospitable to the lofty aspirations which had animated anticolonial imaginaries.[114]

While Islamic economy was the victim of the structural constraints that accompanied its infancy during the late colonial and early postcolonial period, its demise offers insight into the conditions that might have proved more fertile to its development. Between the 1820s and 1860s, the formation of colonial secular governance was propelled by the growing power of unitary conceptions of sovereignty. Early writings on Islamic economy were remarkably perceptive in reconceptualizing the relationship between Islam and secular economy and in rejecting established state forms. From Mushir Hosain Kidwai's outcry against "bureaucratism" to Ishtiaq Husain Qureshi's tripartite structure of sovereignty, their writings sought to imagine different forms of governance. Yet these ideas had limited practical impact on legislative and constitutional deliberations, either in late colonial India or early postcolonial Pakistan. Instead, in both contexts Muslim leaders equated political power, whether as a community or as a nation, with the ability to project a unified religious identity – an emphasis that made tackling socio-economic divisions seem ill-advised. Their focus on Muslim consensus mirrored the unitary forms of sovereignty that undergirded secular legal governance under the British. Without challenging these

---

[114] Frederick Cooper, "Possibility and Constraint: African Independence in Historical Perspective," *Journal of African History* 49, no. 2 (2008): 167–96; Sugata Bose, "Instruments and Idioms of Colonial and National Development," in *International Development and the Social Sciences: Essays on the History and Politics of Knowledge*, ed. Frederick Cooper and Randall M. Packard (Berkeley: University of California Press, 1997), 45–63. My thinking on these questions has also been shaped by collaboration on the volume, *The Postcolonial Moment in South and Southeast Asia*, edited by Gyan Prakash, Nikhil Menon, and Michael Laffan (forthcoming from Bloomsbury), in which I reflect further on these questions. I also benefitted from related conversations as part of a workshop, "Recalling Democracy: Lineages of the Present," organized by Manu Goswami and Mrinalini Sinha at the University of Michigan in 2014.

underlying political forms, attempts to rethink the relationship between Islam and the economy faltered, revealing the entrenched legacy of colonial secular governance. Today, however, with postcolonial states more firmly established, there might as yet be opportunities to return to early twentieth-century visions of Islamic social justice – particularly their emphasis on rethinking basic structures of governance.

# Conclusion

As I was finishing this book in the spring of 2017, controversy erupted in Dhaka over the statue of a *sari*-clad Lady Justice. This formidable figure – constructed out of two-and-a-half tons of cold steel – had recently been erected in front of the Supreme Court of Bangladesh. The statue mirrors the image of protesting Muslim women with which this book opened. The women in New Delhi embodied this visual metaphor as a medium of protest, but in Dhaka, Lady Justice found herself the target of protest.[1] The Islamist group Hifazat-i-Islam (Protection of Islam) denounced the statue for contravening Islamic prohibitions on idolatry. Prime Minister Sheikh Hasina added fuel to the fire when she blamed the Hindu Chief Justice for erecting the statue, which she derided as "half Greek, half Bengali."[2]

In pre-dawn darkness on the morning of May 26, the beginning of the month of Ramazan, workers removed the statue from the courtyard in front of the Supreme Court. The global press widely portrayed the decision as a major concession to Islamists.[3] The sculptor Mrinal Haque, echoed that interpretation, declaring that the statue's removal was a "defeat for the freedom-loving, secular people of the country."[4] Two days later, however, the statue was re-erected inside the confines of the court.

---

[1] Julfikar Ali Manik and Ellen Barry, "Statue of Woman Removed from Bangladesh's Supreme Court," *The New York Times*, May 26, 2017, www.nytimes.com/2017/05/26/world/asia/bangladesh-statue-justice-supreme-court-islam.html.

[2] "Hasina Slams Critics of Bid to Remove Statue from Supreme Court Premises," *bdnews24.com*, April 25, 2017, http://bdnews24.com/bangladesh/2017/04/25/hasina-slams-critics-of-bid-to-remove-statue-from-supreme-court-premises.

[3] "Bangladesh PM Backs Islamists over Statue Controversy," *Free Malaysia Today*, April 12, 2017, www.freemalaysiatoday.com/category/world/2017/04/12/bangladesh-pm-backs-islamists-over-statue-controversy/; "In Bangladesh, A Movement against a Statue of Lady Justice Reveals the Dangers of Rising Islamism," *Scroll.in*, April 23, 2017, https://scroll.in/article/835086/in-bangladesh-a-movement-against-a-statue-of-lady-justice-reveals-the-dangers-of-rising-islamism; Michael Safi, "Lady Justice Statue in Bangladesh Is Removed after Islamist Objections," *The Guardian*, May 26, 2017, www.theguardian.com/world/2017/may/26/lady-justice-statue-bangladesh-removed-islamist-objections.

[4] Manik and Barry, "Statue of Woman Removed."

184

Local media reported that the compromise removed the statue from the sight-lines of the nearby National Eidgah, where Muslim worshippers would mark the end of the holy month.[5]

The fate of Lady Justice – maligned and toppled only to rise again, veiled from view – captures the phenomenon of the simultaneous instability and persistence of secularism at the heart of this book. Entrenched during the colonial period, these patterns have adapted to the new contours of postcolonial politics. In India, Pakistan, and Bangladesh the relationship between religion and secularism has remained a continuous site of political debate. Purportedly the most secular of the three, India's constitution, when introduced in 1950, recognized the right to freedom of conscience and banned religious discrimination, but did not explicitly invoke secularism. In a move that challenges easy equations between secularism and democracy, the term "secular" was first introduced to the Indian constitution in an amendment in 1976 under Indira Gandhi's Emergency government, which oversaw a temporary suspension of civil liberties and rule by executive fiat. Today India's secular commitments remain far from settled. Testifying to the protean ties between secularism and religion, Prime Minister Narendra Modi seized a major electoral victory in 2014 on a joint platform of liberal economic development and Hindu majoritarianism.[6]

Across the border in Pakistan, longer and more overt campaigns to find alternatives to secular institutions have produced an equally contested relationship between politics and religion. In 1956 Pakistan's first constitution declared the country an Islamic Republic. A revised constitution, introduced under the leadership of General Ayub Khan in 1962, omitted the term, only for it to be quickly re-introduced the following year by the National Assembly as part of an amendment that sought to "Islamize" the new government.[7] In 1973, the third and current constitution named Islam as the state religion.[8] Yet the role of Islam in Pakistani politics continues to ebb and flow (as does the overall government's vacillation between democracy and authoritarianism). As a recent special issue on "Secularism and the State in Pakistan" noted, Pakistan attracts global

[5] "Statue of Lady Justice Reinstalled before SC Annex Building," *The Daily Star*, May 27, 2017, www.thedailystar.net/city/statue-lady-justice-being-reinstalled-1411747.
[6] Christophe Jaffrelot, "India's Democracy at 70: Toward a Hindu State?," *Journal of Democracy* 28, no. 3 (July 2017): 52–63.
[7] Lawrence Ziring, "From Islamic Republic to Islamic State in Pakistan," *Asian Survey* 24, no. 9 (1984): 934–5; Fazlur Rahman, "Islam and the Constitutional Problem of Pakistan," *Studia Islamica* 32 (1970): 275–87.
[8] Jeffrey A. Redding, "Constitutionalizing Islam: Theory and Pakistan," *Virginia Journal of International Law* 44, no. 3 (2004): 759–828.

attention both as an epicenter of Islamist threats and "as a critical site for the redemptive power of secularism."[9]

Echoing these same instabilities, Bangladesh's original constitution of 1972 enshrined secularism as a core principle, only to see it removed in 1979 after a military coup seized power. Most recently in 2011, after a ruling by the Supreme Court, Bangladesh's parliament reinstated the original reference to secularism from the 1972 constitution.[10]

Seven decades after independence, the meaning and fate of secularism, and its relationship to religion, thus remains deeply ambiguous and unsettled in South Asia. Yet despite this volatility, debates about religion in all three countries have adhered to remarkably similar patterns, with common roots in their shared colonial past. Over and over, women's issues and bodies have been the core sites of battle. The fact that Dhaka's Lady Justice became the subject of controversy was thus completely predictable. Hifazat-i-Islam, which led the protests against the statue, has repeatedly gravitated towards issues of gender. The group first garnered national attention in 2009 when it mobilized protests against the government's Women's Development Policy, which proposed giving women and men equal inheritance rights.[11] In 2013, after a wave of anti-Islamist protests in which urban women played a leading role, Hifazat issued a thirteen-point manifesto that called for banning public mixing of men and women.[12]

Women have also been at the fulcrum of debates about religion and secularism in India and Pakistan. In India sustained fallout from the Shah Bano verdict of 1985 and the Muslim Women (Protection of Rights on Divorce) Act of 1986 have contributed to heightened communal tensions. The case and legislation pivoted around the question of whether a Muslim woman's right to receive maintenance after divorce would be governed by secular statute or religious personal law. The Hindu Right decried the 1986 act, which favored personal law, as a concession to

[9] Humeira Iqtidar and David Gilmartin, "Secularism and the State in Pakistan: Introduction," *Modern Asian Studies* 45, no. 3 (2011): 491.

[10] Jahid Hossain Bhuiyan, "Secularism in the Constitution of Bangladesh," *Journal of Legal Pluralism and Unofficial Law* 49, no. 2 (2017): 204–27.

[11] Toufique Imrose Khalidi, "Behind the Rise of Bangladesh's Hifazat," *Al Jazeera*, May 9, 2013, www.aljazeera.com/indepth/features/2013/05/201356134629980318.html.

[12] The 2013 protests, popularly known as the Shahbag Movement, demanded that a leading member of Bangladesh's Jamaat-i-Islami be executed after his conviction for war crimes. Nusrat Chowdhury, "Muslim Women and Violent Protest: Bangladesh," *Encyclopedia of Women and Islamic Cultures*, ed. Suad Joseph (Brill Online, 2014), http://referenceworks. brillonline.com/entries/encyclopedia-of-women-and-islamiccultures/muslim-women-and-violent-protest-bangladesh-COM_002008; Fahmida Zaman, "Agencies of Social Movements: Experiences of Bangladesh's Shahbag Movement and Hefazat-e-Islam," *Journal of Asian and African Studies* (2016): 1–11.

Muslim separatism, ensuring that the legal governance of marriage has remained a key site of contest in India's ongoing struggle to define the meaning of postcolonial secularism.[13]

Across the border in Pakistan, women were also among the most visible targets of Zia-ul-Haq's Islamization policies in the 1980s. These included requirements that women veil on television, in government employment, and in schools. Even more controversially, in a number of prominent cases women were charged with adultery or fornication after accusing men of raping them. The vast majority of their male attackers were acquitted under new "Islamized" laws of evidence, which required that a rape be confirmed by four male witnesses to the crime. Unable to prove charges of rape against their male assailants, the women, especially if pregnant, were sometimes convicted of engaging in extramarital sex or of making false accusations – an extreme version of blaming rape victims for their own injuries.[14] Women were also among the most vocal protesters against Zia's policies, culminating in the police beating back crowds of women who gathered under the auspices of the Women's Action Forum in February 1983.[15]

Echoes of colonial patterns have also reverberated through the unequal ways in which postcolonial nations have treated majority and minority religious sensibilities. Just as the British recast evangelicalism as a secular program of civilizational conversion, today religious majorities in India, Pakistan, and Bangladesh equate public recognition of their own religious traditions with nationalism. Meanwhile secularism's binary "Other," communalism, which was first deployed by an ascendant Hindu majority in British India, has also been repurposed by Sunni Muslim majorities in Pakistan and Bangladesh to marginalize minorities, whether non-Muslim, Shia, or Ahmadiyya.

This repeated repurposing of colonial patterns of secularism into new forms in postcolonial South Asia can make the possibility of meaningful change seem all but impossible. Colonial secularism, and its postcolonial adaptations, have failed to deliver on its core promises, whether to protect women or to reduce religious violence. But the contradictions and ambiguities within secular governance have only seemed to endow it with adaptive perseverance. My emphasis on secularism's wily powers of

---

[13] *Mohd. Ahmed Khan v. Shah Bano Begum and Others* [1985] Supreme Court Cases 2 556–74; Sumit Ganguly, "The Crisis of Indian Secularism," *Journal of Democracy* 14, no. 4 (October 2003): 17–18.

[14] Afshan Jafar, "Women, Islam, and the State in Pakistan," *Gender Issues* 22, no. 1 (Winter 2005): 35–55.

[15] Ayesha Jalal, *The Struggle for Pakistan: A Muslim Homeland and Global Politics* (Cambridge: Harvard University Press, 2014), 250.

persistence may sit at odds with the current moment. At present many in South Asia fear (or celebrate) the imminent demise of secularism, whether in the guise of the victory of Hindutva in India or Islamism in Pakistan and Bangladesh. As a historian, however, I think that these forecasts are probably premature. Instead secularism's future, mirroring its past, is likely to be riven with ambiguities and tensions. Yet, as this book has shown, secularism's inbuilt contradictions have more often strengthened than weakened its powers of adaptability. Secularism, Hindutva, and Islamism have also historically evolved as dialectic triplets – mutually reinforcing each others' worst impulses rather than one vanquishing the others. Thus I remain equally skeptical of secularism's ability to deliver on its normative promises and even more terrified by many of the forces that appear to oppose it.

This may sound like a gloomy conclusion. But this book has also tried to draw out the possibilities for an alternative politics which operates through strategic traverses of secularism's logics rather than head-on collisions. Turning back to Lady Justice, her quiet reinstallation just days after her removal points to how South Asians can use ambiguities within the relationship between secularism and religion to forge strategic compromises. Resurrecting the statue inside the confines of the court grounds both emphasized the judiciary's status as a sanctuary for secular rule-of-law and accommodated the religious sensibilities of the Muslims who gathered for Eid prayers across the street. Neither hardline secularists nor Islamists were satisfied by this compromise. But the decision allowed the rest of Dhaka to move on – no small victory in the increasingly feverish climate of contemporary religious-secular contests.[16]

The compromise in Dhaka relied on cutting across the oppositional logics which pit secular law against religious sensibilities. What would it mean to forge a broader politics out of such strategic traverses? The book has shown how the most powerful critiques of colonial secularism have weaved across its binary divides, between family and economy, religion and reason, community and state. Negotiations in Dhaka also showed the importance of engaging with law's multiple sites and modalities of contest. Attention to the affective, embodied power of the statue of Lady Justice brings to mind other historic engagements with law – including Jinnah's memorable defense of the murderer Ilmuddin and the intercommunal cooperation that accompanied his funeral and that of his Hindu victim. Turning these moments into a more sustained politics

---

[16] For a similar argument about the productivity of the compromise, see K. Anis Ahmed, "Bangladesh Puts Lady Justice in Her Place," *The New York Times*, June 9, 2017, www.nytimes.com/2017/06/09/opinion/bangladesh-islamists-secularists.html.

requires navigating between official and unofficial spheres of legal adjudication. Already women's NGOs in India are embracing such a strategy by offering legal advice alongside other services, from community-based arbitration to childcare.[17] Legal historians also have a role to play in these politics. When we widen our studies to embrace multiple discursive registers, from theatrics of the courtroom to out-of-court negotiations, we contribute to more savvy engagements with law in the present.

Leveraging these potentials within the law is unlikely to solve secularism's crises, nor will it lead directly to a revolutionary alternative. Instead, it is a way to work the trap that we are already in, to return to Judith Butler's phrasing.[18] My perspective as a historian gives me a degree of optimism that working the trap might someday lead to more radical change, although the timing and content of that change are unpredictable. Over the course of the nineteenth century, colonial governance entrenched a new concept of religion that would have been equally unrecognizable to both Britons and Indians a century before. Looking forward, the findings of this book suggest that if we keep working this trap, we might one day break free of its claws.

---

[17] Sylvia Vatuk, "Islamic Feminism in India: Indian Muslim Women Activists and the Reform of Muslim Personal Law," *Modern Asian Studies* 42, no. 2–3 (March 2008): 489–518.

[18] "The Body You Want: Liz Kotz Interviews Judith Butler," *Artforum* 31, no. 3 (November 1992): 84.

# Select Bibliography

## MANUSCRIPT PRIMARY SOURCES

### BRITISH LIBRARY, ASIAN AND AFRICAN STUDIES
"Radd-i Wahhabiyah," Urdu MS IO 4297 (i)

### BRITISH LIBRARY, INDIA OFFICE RECORDS
Bengal Public Consultations
Bengal Regulations
Bombay Regulations
Home Legislative Proceedings
Indian Legislative Consultations
Moorshedabad Factory Records
Political and Secret Department Records
Public and Judicial Department Records
Quarterly Catalogue of Books for Bengal, North-Western Provinces, Punjab, and Oudh

### NATIONAL ARCHIVES OF INDIA
Home Judicial Proceedings
Home Political Proceedings
Legislative Department Proceedings

### PRIVY COUNCIL RECORDS
Printed Cases in Indian and Colonial Appeals (Privy Council Offices, Downing Street, Lincoln's Inn, and The British Library)

### HARVARD UNIVERSITY ARCHIVES
Summer School of Arts and Sciences and of Education, Conference files, 1948–85

### U.S. NATIONAL ARCHIVES AND RECORDS ADMINISTRATION
Records of the Department of State, Decimal Files, 1950–4

OTHER GOVERNMENT DOCUMENTS IN DIGITAL
OR MICROFILM FORMAT

Abstract of the Proceedings of the Council of the Governor General of India
Constituent Assembly of Pakistan Debates
House of Commons Parliamentary Papers
Indian Legislative Assembly Debates
Notes on the Press, United Provinces of Agra and Oudh
Notes on the Punjab Press
Punjab Legislative Council Debates
Report on Native Papers, Bengal
Report on Newspapers and Periodicals in Bengal

## PUBLISHED PRIMARY SOURCES

LAW REPORTS

All India Reporter
All Pakistan Legal Decisions
Criminal Law Journal of India
English Reports
Indian Law Reports
Judgments of the Privy Council on Appeals from India
Madras High Court Reports
Punjab Record
Reports of Cases Heard and Determined by the Judicial Committee, and The
    Lords of Her Majesty's Most Honourable Privy Council, on Appeal from the
    Supreme and Sudder Dewanny Courts in the East Indies
Supreme Court Cases, India

NEWSPAPERS

*Al-Jamiat* (Delhi)
*Civil and Military Gazette* (Lahore)
*Hamdard* (Delhi)
*Haryana Tilak* (Rohtak)
*Leader* (Allahabad)
*Madras Mail* (Madras)
*Milap* (Lahore)
*Muslim Outlook* (Lahore)
*Pioneer* (Allahabad)
*Times of India* (Bombay)
*Tribune* (Lahore)

URDU, PERSIAN, AND HINDI MATERIALS

Abbas, Ghulam. *Anandi. Tab-i-Jadid.* Lahore: Maktabah-yi-Jadid, 1968.
Ahmad Gangohi, Rashid. *Fatawa-yi-Rashidiyah (Kamil).* Karachi: Muhammad
    Ali Karkhanah-yi-Islami Kutub, 1987.

Ali Jaunpuri, Karamat. *Miftah-ul-Jannat*. Reprint Lucknow: Nawal Kishor, 1916.

Autar, Ram. "Hyderabad men Desi Bank Kari." M.A. Thesis. Osmania University, 1947.

Barni, Muhammad Ilyas. *Ma'ishat-ul-Hind*. Hyderabad: Jami'ah Usmaniyah, 1929.
*Usul-i-Ma'ashiyyat*. Hyderabad: Jami'ah Usmaniyah, 1922.

Bilhauri, Khurram Ali. *Nasihat-ul-Musalmin*. Reprint Lucknow: Darulisha'at-i-Islamiyah, 1964.

*Fatuhat-i-Ahl-i-Hadith*. Amritsar: Roz Bazar Steam Press, 1914.

Gilani, Sayyid Manazar Ahsan. *Islami Ma'ashiyyat*. Lahore: Sang-i-Meel, 2007.
"Masalah-yi-Sod Muslim aur Harbi men." In *Maqalat-i-Gilani*. Lahore: Shaikh Zayid Islamic Center, 2004.

Hasan, Sayyid Ahmad. *Talkhis-ul-Anzar Fi Ma Buniya-Ilah-yi-ul-Intisar*. Delhi: Faruqi Press, 1290 H. [1873 or 1874].

Husain, Muhammad Irshad. *Intisar-ul-Haqq*. 1873; Reprint Rampur, 1318.

Husain, Sayyid Amir. *Barahin-i-Isna-Ashar*. Delhi: Faruqi Press, 1874.

Husain, Sayyid Nazir. *Meyar-ul-Haqq*. Reprint Lahore: Maktabah Naziriyah, 1965.

Iqbal, Muhammad. *Guftar-i-Iqbal*. Edited by Muhammad Rafiq Afzal. Lahore: Idarah-yi-Tahqiqat-i-Pakistan, 1969.

Ismail, Shah Muhammad. *Taqwiyat-ul-Imam*. Reprint Lucknow: Nami Press, 1967.

Ismail Gangohi, Muhammad. *Javab-i-Ishtihar-i-Ghair Muqallidin*. Ludhiana: Rahmani Press, 1294 H. [1877 or 1878].

Khairabadi, Fazl-i-Haq. *Tahqiq-ul-Fatwa fi Ibtal-ul-Tughwa*. Urdu and Persian. Edited and translated by Muhammad Abdul Hakim Sharf Qadiri. Lahore: Maktabah-yi- Qadiriyah Shah Abdul Haq Muhaddis Dihlawi Academy, 1979.

Khan, Abu Yahya Imam. *Tarajim-i-Ulama-yi-Hadith-i-Hind*. 1938; Reprint Lahore: Markazi Jamiyyat-i-Talabahyi Ahl-i-Hadith, 1971.

Khan, Sayyid Ahmad. "Rah-i-Sunnat aur Radd-i-Bidat." In *Maqalat-i-Sar Sayyid*, edited by Muhammad Ismail, 2nd edn. Lahore: Majlis-i-Taraqqi Adab, 1990.

Khan, Sayyiduddin. *Tanqid fi Bayan-ul-Taqlid*. Delhi: Akmal-ul Matabe, 1869.

Khan, Wahidullah. "Islami Qanun-i-Shirakat ke Usul ka Muqabala Hyderabad ke Qawanin se." M.A. Thesis. Osmania University, 1944.

Khan, Zafar Ali. *Anmol Moti: Maulana Zafar Ali Khan Ke Mazamin Ka Majmu'a*. Edited by Sadiq Husain. Lahore: Sadiq Husain, 1968.
*Kulliyat-i-Maulana Zafar Ali Khan*. Lahore: al-Faisal, 2007.

Mawdudi, Sayyid Abul Ala. *Insan ka Ma'ashi Masalah aur us ka Islami Hal*. Lahore: Markazi Maktabah-yi-Jama'at-i-Islami, 1953.

Muhammad, Maulvi. *Intisar-ul-Islam*. Ludhiana: Rahmani Press, 1294 H. [1877 or 1878].

Qureshi, Ishtiaq Husain. *Pakistan: Ek Islami Jumhuriyat*. Lahore: Idarah-yi-Saqafat-i-Islami, n.d.

Qutbuddin, Muhammad. *Taufir-ul-Haqq*. [Lahore]: Ganesh Press, 1869.

*Rangila Rasul*. Banaras: Baldev Prasad Sharma, n.d.

Shah, Muhammad. *Madar-ul-Haqq fi Radd Meyar-ul-Haqq ma Rasa'il Urvat-ul-Vusqa*. 1869; Reprint Lahore: Jamiyyat Ahl-i-Sunnat, 1991.
*Urvat-ul-Vusqa*. n.d.; Reprinted in *Madar-ul-Haqq*.

Shauq, Ahmad Ali Khan. *Tazkirah-yi-Kamilan-i-Rampur*. 1929; Reprint Patna: Khuda Baksh Oriental Public Library, 1986.
Siddiqi, Mazheruddin. *Hegel, Marx aur Islami Nizam*. 2nd edn. Pathankot: Tarjuman-ul-Quran, 1945.
*Ishtirakiyyat aur Nizam-i-Islam*. Lahore: Markazi Maktabah-yi-Jama'at-i-Islami, 1949.
Usmani, Aziz-al-Rahman. *Fatawa Dar-ul-Ulum Deoband*. 13 vols. Edited by Muhammad Zafir-ul-Din. Modern Computer Edition. Karachi: Shakil Press, 2002.
Yusafi, Maulana Khalil-ul-Rahman. *Risala-yi-Fatiha dar Radd-i-Wahhabiyah*. Bombay, 1261 H. [1845].
Yusufuddin, Muhammad. *Islam ke Ma'ashi Nazarye*. Hyderabad: Matba-yi-Ibrahimiyah, 1950.

BOOKS AND ARTICLES IN ENGLISH

Ali, Syed Ameer. *Mahommedan Law, Compiled from Authorities in the Original Arabic*. 2nd edn. Calcutta: Thacker, Spink, 1892.
Baillie, John. *A Digest of Mohummudan Law According to the Tenets of the Twelve Imams* .... Calcutta: Hon. Company's Press, 1805.
Baillie, Neil B.E. *Digest of Moohummudan Law on the Subjects to Which It Is Usually Applied by British Courts of Justice in India* .... London: Smith, Elder & Co., 1865.
*The Land Tax of India: According to the Moohummudan Law*. London: Smith Elder & Co., 1853.
*The Moohummudan Law of Sale, According to the Huneefeea Code: From the Futawa Alumgeeree, a Digest of the Whole Law*. London: Smith Elder, 1850.
Blunt, Wilfrid Scawen. *India under Ripon: A Private Diary*. London: T. Fisher Unwin, 1909.
Dutt, Romesh Chunder. *The Peasantry of Bengal: Being a View of Their Condition under the Hindu, the Mahomedan, and English Rule, and a Consideration of the Means Calculated to Improve Their Future Prospects*. Calcutta: Thacker, Spink & Co., 1874.
Elberling, Francis E. *A Treatise on Inheritance, Gift, Will, Sale and Mortgage: With an Introduction on the Laws of the Bengal Presidency*. Serampore: Serampore Press, 1844.
Galloway, Archibald. *Observations on the Law and Constitution of India: On the Nature of Landed Tenures, and on the System of Revenue and Finance, as Established by the Moohummudum Law and Moghul Government*.... London: Kingsbury, Parbury, and Allen, 1825.
*Gazetteer of the Central Provinces, Part 1*. Nagpore: Chief Commissioner's Office Press, 1867.
Grady, Standish Grove, and W.H. Macnaghten. *A Manual of the Mahommedan Law of Inheritance and Contract, Comprising the Doctrines of the Soonee and Sheea Schools* .... London: W.H. Allen, 1869.

Hamidullah, M. "Haidarabad's Contribution to Islamic Economic Thought and Practice." *Die Welt Des Islams* 4, no. 2/3 (January 1955): 73–8.

"Islam's Solution of the Basic Economic Problems." *Islamic Culture* 10, no. 2 (April 1936): 213–33.

Iqbal, Mohammad. *The Reconstruction of Religious Thought in Islam*. Edited by M. Saeed Sheikh. Stanford: Stanford University Press, 2013.

Jafri, Fareed S. *The Spirit of Pakistan*. Karachi: Ansari, 1951.

Khan, Ali Ahmad. *Why Islamic Constitution Only?* Dacca: Jahan-e-Nau Publications, 1955.

Khan, Sayyid Ahmad. *Review on Dr. Hunter's Indian Musalman's: Are They Bound in Conscience to Rebel against the Queen?* Benares: Medical Hall Press, 1872.

*Literary Services of the Compilation and Translation Bureau, Osmania University, Hyderabad-Deccan, 1917–1946*. Hyderabad: Osmania University Press, 1946.

Macaulay, Thomas Babington. "Gladstone on Church and State (1839)." In *Critical and Historical Essays: Contributed to the Edinburgh Review*. London: Longmans, Green, Reader, and Dyer, 1883.

Maine, Henry Sumner. *Ancient Law: Its Connection with the Early History of Society, and Its Relation to Modern Ideas*. 3rd American edn. New York: Henry Holt and Company, 1875.

*Village-Communities in the East and West: Six Lectures Delivered at Oxford, to Which Are Added Other Lectures, Addresses, and Essays*. 3rd edn. London: J. Murray, 1876.

Maudoodi, Sayyed Abulala. *The Economic Problem of Man and Its Islamic Solution*. 2nd edn. Lahore: Maktaba-e-Jama'at-e-Islami, 1955.

Mukerjee, J.N. and N.N. Mukerjee. *The Law Relating to Pardanashins in British India (Civil and Criminal)*. Calcutta: R. Cambray, 1906.

Mulla, Sir Dinshah Fardunji. *Principles of Mahomedan Law*. 2nd edn. Bombay: Thacker & Company, 1907.

"Notice of the Peculiar Tenets Held by the Followers of Syed Ahmed, Taken Chiefly from the 'Sirat-Ul-Mustaqim,' a Principal Treatise of That Sect, Written by Maulvi Mahommed Ismail." *Journal of the Asiatic Society of Bengal* 1, no. 11 (November 1832): 479–95.

Perry, Sir Erskine. *Cases Illustrative of Oriental Life and the Application of English Law to India, Decided in H.M. Supreme Court at Bombay*. London: S. Sweet, 1853.

Qureshi, Anwar Iqbal. *Agricultural Credit: Being a Study of Recent Developments in Agricultural Credit Administration in the United States of America*. London: Sir Isaac Pitman & Sons, 1936.

*Islam and the Theory of Interest*. Lahore: Shaikh M. Ashraf, 1946.

*State Banks for India: Being a Study of State Banks and Land Mortgage Credit Institutions in Australia, New Zealand, South Africa and the United States of America, with Suggestions for Establishing Similar Banks in India*. London: Macmillan, 1939.

*The Farmer and His Debt: Being a Study of Farm Relief in Australia, New Zealand and South Africa, with Suggestions for India*. London: Indian Rural Reconstruction League, 1934.

*The State and Economic Life: Being a Study of the Methods of State Intervention in Economic Life in the Leading Countries of the World.* Bombay: New Book Company, n.d.

Qureshi, Ishtiaq Husain. *Pakistan: An Islamic Democracy.* Lahore: Institute of Islamic Culture, n.d.

*The Future Development of Islamic Polity.* Lahore: Shaikh Muhammad Ashraf, 1946.

Rahman, Fazlur. "Islam and the Constitutional Problem of Pakistan." *Studia Islamica* 32 (1970): 275–87.

"Riba and Interest." *Islamic Studies* 3, no. 1 (March 1964): 1–43.

Rahman, Nawab A.F.M. Abdur. *Institutes of Mussalman Law: A Treatise on Personal Law According to the Hanafite School, with References to Original Arabic Sources and Decided Cases from 1795 to 1906.* Calcutta: Thacker, Spink and Company, 1907.

Rai, Lala Lajpat. *The Collected Works.* 15 vols. Edited by B.R. Nanda. New Delhi: Manohar, 2003–10.

Rankin, George. "Custom and the Muslim Law in British India." *Transactions of the Grotius Society* 25 (January 1939): 89–118.

Rattigan, William. "The Parda Nashin Woman and Her Protection by British Courts of Justice." *Journal of the Society of Comparative Legislation* 3, no. 2, New Series (January 1901): 259–60.

"Review Judgement on Riba: The Supreme Court of Pakistan (Shari'at Appellate Bench)." *Islamic Studies* 41, no. 4 (December 2002): 705–24.

Roe, Charles Arthur. *Tribal Law in the Punjab: So Far as It Relates to Right in Ancestral Land.* Lahore: Civil and Military Gazette Press, 1895.

Roy, Rammohun. "Questions and Answers on the Judicial System of India." In *The English Works of Raja Rammohun Roy. ...* Allahabad: Panini Office, 1906.

Roy, Sripati. *Customs and Customary Law in British India.* Calcutta: Hare Press, 1911.

Savigny, Friedrich Karl von. *The History of the Law during the Middle Ages.* Translated by E. Cathcart. Edinburgh: Adam Black, 1829.

*Von Savigny's Treatise on Possession: Or, The Jus Possessionis of the Civil Law.* Translated by Erskine Perry. London: S. Sweet, 1848.

Shurreef, Jaffur. *Qanoon-E-Islam, or the Customs of the Moosulmans of India: Comprising a Full and Exact Account of Their Various Rites and Ceremonies, from the Moment of Birth till the Hour of Death.* London: Parbury, Allen, and Co., 1832.

Siddiqi, Mazheruddin. *Impressions of the United States.* Lahore: Orientalia, 1955.

*Marxism or Islam?* 2nd edn. Lahore: Orientalia, 1954.

Sorabji, Cornelia. "Safeguards for Purdahnishins." *Imperial and Asiatic Quarterly Review and Oriental and Colonial Record,* Third Series 15, no. 29–30 (April 1903): 69–78.

Thomas, Babington Macaulay. *Speeches of Lord Macaulay, Corrected by Himself.* London: Longmans, Green, and Co., 1866.

Wilson, Roland Knyvet. *A Digest of Anglo-Muhammadan Law: Setting Forth in the Form of a Code, with Full References to Modern and Ancient Authorities, the*

*Special Rules Now Applicable to Muhammadans as Such by the Civil Courts of British India*. London: W. Thacker, 1895.

## SECONDARY SOURCES

### UNPUBLISHED DISSERTATIONS, THESES, AND MANUSCRIPTS IN PROCESS

Ahmed, Asad. "Adjudicating Muslims: Law, Religion and the State in Colonial India and Post-Colonial Pakistan." Ph.D. Dissertation, University of Chicago, 2006.

De, Rohit. "Litigious Citizens, Constitutional Law and Everyday Life in the Indian Republic." Manuscript under preparation, n.d.

Guenther, Alan M. "Syed Mahmood and the Transformation of Muslim Law in British India." Ph.D., McGill University, 2005.

Khan, Fareeha. "Traditionalist Approaches to Shari'ah Reform: Mawlana Ashraf 'Ali Thanawi's Fatwa on Women's Right to Divorce." Ph.D., University of Michigan, 2008.

Lemons, Katherine. "At the Margins of Law: Adjudicating Muslim Families in Contemporary Delhi." Ph.D., University of California, 2010.

Masud, Muhammad Khalid. "Trends in the Interpretation of Islamic Law as Reflected in the Fatawa Literature of Deoband School." M.A., McGill University, 1969.

Roosa, John. "The Quandary of the Qaum: Indian Nationalism in a Muslim State, Hyderabad, 1850–1948." Ph.D., University of Wisconsin, 1998.

Stubenrauch, Joseph. "Faith in Goods: Evangelicalism, Materiality, and Consumer Culture in Nineteenth-Century Britain." Ph.D., Indiana University, 2011.

### PUBLISHED ARTICLES AND BOOKS

Adcock, C.S. *The Limits of Tolerance: Indian Secularism and the Politics of Religious Freedom*. New York: Oxford University Press, 2014.

"Violence, Passion, and the Law: A Brief History of Section 295A and Its Antecedents." *Journal of the American Academy of Religion* 84, no. 2 (June 2016): 337–51.

Agrama, Hussein Ali. *Questioning Secularism: Islam, Sovereignty, and the Rule of Law in Modern Egypt*. Chicago: University of Chicago Press, 2012.

Ahmed, Asad Ali. "Specters of Macaulay: Blasphemy, the Indian Penal Code, and Pakistan's Postcolonial Predicament." In *Censorship in South Asia: Cultural Regulation from Sedition to Seduction*, edited by Raminder Kaur and William Mazzarella. Bloomington: Indiana University Press, 2009.

Alavi, Seema. *Muslim Cosmopolitanism in the Age of Empire*. Cambridge: Harvard University Press, 2015.

Ali, Kamran Asdar. "Communists in a Muslim Land: Cultural Debates in Pakistan's Early Years." *Modern Asian Studies* 45, no. 3 (2011): 501–34.

Al-Qattan, Najwa. "Dhimmis in the Muslim Court: Legal Autonomy and Religious Discrimination." *International Journal of Middle East Studies* 31, no. 3 (August 1999): 429–44.

Amin, Shahid. "Gandhi as Mahatma: Gorakhpur District, Eastern UP, 1921." In *Selected Subaltern Studies*, edited by Ranajit Guha and Gayatri Chakravorty Spivak. New York: Oxford University Press, 1988.

Anderson, Michael R. "Islamic Law and the Colonial Encounter in British India." In *Institutions and Ideologies: A SOAS South Asia Reader*, edited by Peter Robb and David Arnold. Richmond, Surrey: Curzon Press, 1993.

Ansari, Khizar Humayun. "Pan-Islam and the Making of the Early Indian Muslim Socialists." *Modern Asian Studies* 20, no. 3 (January 1986): 509–37.

*The Emergence of Socialist Thought among North Indian Muslims, 1917–1947*. Lahore: Book Traders, 1990.

Asad, Talal. *Formations of the Secular: Christianity, Islam, Modernity*. Stanford: Stanford University Press, 2003.

*Genealogies of Religion: Discipline and Reasons of Power in Christianity and Islam*. Baltimore: Johns Hopkins University Press, 1993.

Aziz, Ahmad. "Political and Religious Ideas of Shah Wali-Ullah of Delhi." *Muslim World* 52, no. 1 (1962): 22–30.

Balijon, J.M.S. *Religion and Thought of Shah Wali Allah Dihlawi, 1703–1762*. Leiden: E.J. Brill, 1986.

Basu, Tapan, Pradip Datta, Sumit Sarkar, Tanika Sarkar, and Sambuddha Sen. *Khaki Shorts and Saffron Flags: A Critique of the Hindu Right*. New Delhi: Orient Longman, 1993.

Bayly, C.A. *Empire and Information: Intelligence Gathering and Social Communication in India, 1780–1870*. Cambridge: Cambridge University Press, 1996.

*Indian Society and the Making of the British Empire*. Cambridge: Cambridge University Press, 1988.

*Rulers, Townsmen, and Bazaars: North Indian Society in the Age of British Expansion, 1770–1870*. Cambridge: Cambridge University Press, 1983.

Bentley, James. *Ritualism and Politics in Victorian Britain: The Attempt to Legislate for Belief*. Oxford: Oxford University Press, 1978.

Benton, Lauren A. *Law and Colonial Cultures: Legal Regimes in World History, 1400–1900*. Cambridge: Cambridge University Press, 2002.

Bhargava, Rajeev, ed. *Secularism and Its Critics*. New Delhi: Oxford University Press, 1998.

Bhuiyan, Jahid Hossain. "Secularism in the Constitution of Bangladesh." *Journal of Legal Pluralism and Unofficial Law* 49, no. 2 (2017): 204–27.

Binder, Leonard. *Religion and Politics in Pakistan*. Berkeley: University of California Press, 1961.

Birla, Ritu. *Stages of Capital: Law, Culture, and Market Governance in Late Colonial India*. Durham: Duke University Press, 2009.

Bose, Neilesh. "Muslim Modernism and Trans-Regional Consciousness in Bengal, 1911–1925: The Wide World of Samyabadi." *South Asia Research* 31, no. 3 (November 2011): 231–48.

Bose, Sugata. *A Hundred Horizons: The Indian Ocean in the Age of Global Empire*. Cambridge: Harvard University Press, 2006.

"Instruments and Idioms of Colonial and National Development." In *International Development and the Social Sciences: Essays on the History and Politics of Knowledge*, edited by Frederick Cooper and Randall M. Packard. Berkeley: University of California Press, 1997.

"Nation, Reason and Religion: India's Independence in International Perspective." *Economic and Political Weekly* 33, no. 31 (1998): 2090–7.

*Peasant Labour and Colonial Capital: Rural Bengal since 1770.* Cambridge: Cambridge University Press, 1993.

Brooks, Peter, and Paul D. Gewirtz, eds. *Law's Stories: Narrative and Rhetoric in the Law.* New Haven: Yale University Press, 1996.

Brown, Daniel W. *Rethinking Tradition in Modern Islamic Thought.* Cambridge: Cambridge University Press, 1996.

Brown, Ford K. *Fathers of the Victorians: The Age of Wilberforce.* Cambridge: University Press, 1961.

Butler, Judith. *Gender Trouble: Feminism and the Subversion of Identity.* 2nd edn. New York: Routledge, 1999.

*Undoing Gender.* New York: Routledge, 2004.

Chandra, Sudhir. *Enslaved Daughters: Colonialism, Law and Women's Rights.* Delhi: Oxford University Press, 1998.

Chandran, Mini. "The Democratisation of Censorship: Books and the Indian Public." *Economic and Political Weekly* 45, no. 40 (2010): 27–31.

Chatterjee, Indrani. *Gender, Slavery, and Law in Colonial India.* Oxford: Oxford University Press, 1999.

Chatterjee, Nandini. "Reflections on Religious Difference and Permissive Inclusion in Mughal Law." *Journal of Law and Religion* 29, no. 3 (October 2014): 396–415.

*The Making of Indian Secularism: Empire, Law and Christianity, 1830–1960.* Basingstoke: Palgrave Macmillan, 2011.

Chatterjee, Partha. *A Princely Impostor?: The Kumar of Bhawal and the Secret History of Indian Nationalism.* Delhi: Permanent Black, 2002.

*Nationalist Thought and the Colonial World: A Derivative Discourse.* Minneapolis: University of Minnesota Press, 1993.

*The Nation and Its Fragments: Colonial and Postcolonial Histories.* Princeton: Princeton University Press, 1993.

Chatterjee, Piya. *A Time for Tea: Women, Labor, and Post/Colonial Politics on an Indian Plantation.* Durham: Duke University Press, 2001.

Çizakça, Murat. *A History of Philanthropic Foundations: The Islamic World from the Seventh Century to the Present.* Istanbul: Boğaziçi University Press, 2000.

Cohn, Bernard. "From Indian Status to British Contract." *The Journal of Economic History* 21 (1961): 613–28.

"Law and Colonial State in India." In *Colonialism and Its Forms of Knowledge.* Princeton: Princeton University Press, 1996.

"Representing Authority in Victorian Britain." In *An Anthropologist Among the Historians and Other Essays.* Delhi: Oxford University Press, 1987.

"Some Notes on Law and Change in North India." *Economic Development and Cultural Change* 8 (1959): 79–93.

"The Census, Social Structure, and Objectification in South Asia." In *An Anthropologist among the Historians and Other Essays.* New Delhi: Oxford University Press, 1987.

Cooper, Frederick. "Possibility and Constraint: African Independence in Historical Perspective." *Journal of African History* 49, no. 2 (2008): 167–96.

Cuno, Kenneth M. "Disobedient Wives and Neglectful Husbands: Marital Relations and the First Phase of Family Law Reform in Egypt." In *Family, Gender, and Law in a Globalizing Middle East and South Asia*, edited by Kenneth M. Cuno and Manisha Desai. Syracuse: Syracuse University Press, 2009.

Curtis, Dennis E., and Judith Resnik. "Images of Justice." *The Yale Law Journal* 96, no. 8 (July 1987): 1727–72.

Darnton, Robert. "Literary Surveillance in the British Raj: The Contradictions of Liberal Imperialism." *Book History* 4 (January 2001): 133–76.

Datla, Kavita. *The Language of Secular Islam: Urdu Nationalism and Colonial India.* Honolulu: University of Hawai'i Press, 2013.

De, Rohit. "Mumtaz Bibi's Broken Heart: The Many Lives of the Dissolution of Muslim Marriages Act, 1939." *Indian Economic and Social History Review* 46, no. 1 (2009): 105–30.

Derrett, J. Duncan M. *Religion, Law and the State in India.* London: Faber, 1968.
"The Administration of Hindu Law by the British." *Comparative Studies in Society and History* 4, no. 1 (November 1961): 10–52.

Devji, Faisal. *Muslim Zion: Pakistan as a Political Idea.* London: Hurst & Company, 2013.

Fadel, Mohammad. "The Social Logic of Taqlid and the Rise of the Mukhatasar." *Islamic Law and Society* 3, no. 2 (January 1996): 193–233.

Fernando, Mayanthi L. *The Republic Unsettled: Muslim French and the Contradictions of Secularism.* Durham: Duke University Press, 2014.

Fisch, Jörg. *Cheap Lives and Dear Limbs: The British Transformation of the Bengal Criminal Law, 1769–1817.* Wiesbaden: F. Steiner, 1983.

Ford, Lisa. *Settler Sovereignty: Jurisdiction and Indigenous People in America and Australia, 1788–1836.* Cambridge: Harvard University Press, 2010.

Fourcade, Marion. *Economists and Societies: Discipline and Profession in the United States, Britain, and France, 1890s to 1990s.* Princeton: Princeton University Press, 2009.

Freitag, Sandria B. *Collective Action and Community: Public Arenas and the Emergence of Communalism in North India.* Berkeley: University of California Press, 1989.
"Crime in the Social Order of Colonial North India." *Modern Asian Studies* 25, no. 2 (May 1991): 227–61.
"Enactments of Ram's Story and the Changing Nature of 'The Public' in British India." *South Asia: Journal of South Asian Studies* 14, no. 1 (June 1991): 65–90.

Friedmann, Yohanan. *Prophecy Continuous: Aspects of Ahmadi Religious Thought and Its Medieval Background.* Berkeley: University of California Press, 1989.

Fyzee, Asaf A.A. *Cases in the Muhammadan Law of India, Pakistan and Bangladesh.* Edited by Tahir Mahmood. 2nd edn. New Delhi: Oxford University Press, 2005.

Gaborieau, Marc. "A Nineteenth-Century Indian 'Wahhabi' Tract against the Cult of Muslim Saints: Al-Balagh Al-Mubin." In *Muslim Shrines in India: Their Character, History, and Significance*, edited by Christian W. Troll. Delhi: Oxford University Press, 1989.

"Late Persian, Early Urdu: The Case of 'Wahhabi' Literature (1818–1857)." In *Confluence of Cultures: French Contributions to Indo-Persian Studies*, edited by Françoise Nalini Delvoye. New Delhi: Manohar, 1994.

Galanter, M. "The Displacement of Traditional Law in Modern India." *Journal of Social Issues* 24, no. 4 (October 1968): 65–90.

Ganguly, Sumit. "The Crisis of Indian Secularism." *Journal of Democracy* 14, no. 4 (October 2003): 11–25.

Ghosh, Durba. *Sex and the Family in Colonial India: The Making of Empire*. Cambridge: Cambridge University Press, 2006.

Ghosh, Papiya. "Muttahidah Qaumiyat in Awalliat Bihar: The Imarat I Shariah, 1921–1947." *Indian Economic and Social History Review* 34, no. 1 (1997): 1–20.

Gilmartin, David. *Blood and Water: The Indus River Basin in Modern History*. Berkeley: University of California Press, 2015.

"Customary Law and Shariat in British Punjab." In *Shariat and Ambiguity in South Asian Islam*, edited by Katherine P. Ewing. Berkeley: University of California Press, 1988.

"Democracy, Nationalism and the Public: A Speculation on Colonial Muslim Politics." *South Asia* 14, no. 1 (1991): 123–40.

*Empire and Islam: Punjab and the Making of Pakistan*. London: Tauris, 1988.

"Kinship, Women, and Politics in Twentieth-Century Punjab." In *The Extended Family: Women and Political Participation in India and Pakistan*, edited by Gail Minault. Delhi: Chanakya Publications, 1981.

"Partition, Pakistan, and South Asian History: In Search of a Narrative." *The Journal of Asian Studies* 57, no. 4 (November 1998): 1068–95.

Giunchi, Elisa. "The Reinvention of Shari'a under the British Raj: In Search of Authenticity and Certainty." *The Journal of Asian Studies* 69, no. 4 (2010): 1119–42.

Gooptu, Suparna. *Cornelia Sorabji: India's Pioneer Woman Lawyer*. New Delhi: Oxford University Press, 2006.

Goswami, Manu. "Imaginary Futures and Colonial Internationalisms." *The American Historical Review* 117, no. 5 (December 2012): 1461–85.

Gould, William. *Hindu Nationalism and the Language of Politics in Late Colonial India*. Cambridge: Cambridge University Press, 2004.

Green, Nile. *Bombay Islam: The Religious Economy of the West Indian Ocean, 1840–1915*. New York: Cambridge University Press, 2011.

Gupta, Charu. *Sexuality, Obscenity, Community: Women, Muslims, and the Hindu Public in Colonial India*. Delhi: Permanent Black, 2001.

Hallaq, Wael B. *Authority, Continuity and Change in Islamic Law*. Cambridge: Cambridge University Press, 2001.

"From Fatwas to Furu: Growth and Change in Islamic Substantive Law." *Islamic Law and Society* 1, no. 1 (1994): 29–65.

*The Impossible State: Islam, Politics, and Modernity's Moral Predicament*. New York: Columbia University Press, 2013.

"Was the Gate of Ijtihad Closed?" *International Journal of Middle East Studies* 16, no. 1 (March 1984): 3–41.

Halley, Janet, and Kerry Rittich. "Critical Directions in Comparative Family Law: Genealogies and Contemporary Studies of Family Law

Exceptionalism." *The American Journal of Comparative Law* 58, no. 4 (October 2010): 753–75.

Hasan, Farhat. *State and Locality in Mughal India: Power Relations in Western India, c. 1572–1730*. Cambridge: Cambridge University Press, 2004.

Hasan, Mushirul. "Aligarh Muslim University: Recalling Radical Days." *India International Centre Quarterly* 29, no. 3/4 (December 2002): 47–59.

Hilton, Boyd. *The Age of Atonement: The Influence of Evangelicalism on Social and Economic Thought, 1795–1865*. Oxford: Clarendon Press, 1988.

Hoeflich, Michael H. "Savigny and His Anglo-American Disciples." *The American Journal of Comparative Law* 37, no. 1 (January 1989): 17–37.

Holcombe, Lee. *Wives and Property: Reform of the Married Women's Property Law in Nineteenth-Century England*. Toronto: University of Toronto Press, 1983.

Iqtidar, Humeira. "Secularism beyond the State: The 'State' and the 'Market' in Islamist Imagination." *Modern Asian Studies* 45, no. 3 (2011): 535–64.

*Secularizing Islamists?: Jama'at-e-Islami and Jama'at-ud-Da'wa in Urban Pakistan*. Chicago: University of Chicago Press, 2011.

Iqtidar, Humeira, and David Gilmartin. "Secularism and the State in Pakistan: Introduction." *Modern Asian Studies* 45, no. 3 (2011): 491–9.

Jackson, Roy. *Mawlana Mawdudi and Political Islam: Authority and the Islamic State*. London: Routledge, 2011.

Jafar, Afshan. "Women, Islam, and the State in Pakistan." *Gender Issues* 22, no. 1 (Winter 2005): 35–55.

Jaffrelot, Christophe. "India's Democracy at 70: Toward a Hindu State?" *Journal of Democracy* 28, no. 3 (July 2017): 52–63.

Jalal, Ayesha. *Democracy and Authoritarianism in South Asia: A Comparative and Historical Perspective*. Cambridge: Cambridge University Press, 1995.

"Exploding Communalism: The Politics of Muslim Identity in South Asia." In *Nationalism, Democracy, and Development: State and Politics in India*, edited by Sugata Bose and Ayesha Jalal. Delhi: Oxford University Press, 1997.

"Freedom and Equality: From Iqbal's Philosophy to Sen's Ethical Concerns." In *Arguments for a Better World: Essays in Honor of Amartya Sen*, edited by Kaushik Basu and Ravi Kanbur. Oxford: Oxford University Press, 2009.

*Partisans of Allah: Jihad in South Asia*. Cambridge: Harvard University Press, 2008.

*Self and Sovereignty: Individual and Community in South Asian Islam since 1850*. New York: Routledge, 2000.

*The State of Martial Rule: The Origins of Pakistan's Political Economy of Defence*. Cambridge: Cambridge University Press, 1990.

*The Struggle for Pakistan: A Muslim Homeland and Global Politics*. Cambridge: Harvard University Press, 2014.

Johansen, Baber. *Contingency in a Sacred Law: Legal and Ethical Norms in the Muslim Fiqh*. Leiden: Brill, 1999.

Jones, Justin. *Shi'a Islam in Colonial India: Religion, Community and Sectarianism*. Cambridge: Cambridge University Press, 2011.

Katznelson, Ira, and Gareth Stedman Jones, eds. *Religion and the Political Imagination*. Cambridge: Cambridge University Press, 2010.

Keddie, Niki R. *An Islamic Response to Imperialism: Political and Religious Writings of Sayyid Jamal Ad-Din "Al-Afghani."* Berkeley: University of California Press, 1983.

Kennedy, Duncan. "Savigny's Family/Patrimony Distinction and Its Place in the Global Genealogy of Classical Legal Thought." *American Journal of Comparative Law* 58, no. 4 (2010): 811–41.

"Three Globalizations of Law and Legal Thought: 1850–2000." In *The New Law and Economic Development: A Critical Appraisal*, edited by David M. Trubek and Alvaro Santos. Cambridge: Cambridge University Press, 2006.

Kolsky, Elizabeth. *Colonial Justice in British India*. Cambridge: Cambridge University Press, 2010.

"Forum: Maneuvering the Personal Law System in Colonial India: Introduction." *Law and History Review* 28, no. 4 (2010): 973–8.

Kozlowski, Gregory C. *Muslim Endowments and Society in British India*. Cambridge: Cambridge University Press, 1985.

Kugle, Scott Alan. "Framed, Blamed and Renamed: The Recasting of Islamic Jurisprudence in Colonial South Asia." *Modern Asian Studies* 35 (2001): 257–313.

Kuran, Timur. "The Discontents of Islamic Economic Morality." *The American Economic Review* 86, no. 2 (May 1996): 438–42.

"The Genesis of Islamic Economics: A Chapter in the Politics of Muslim Identity." *Social Research* 64, no. 2 (Summer 1997): 301–38.

Lelyveld, David. *Aligarh's First Generation: Muslim Solidarity in British India*. 1978; Reprint New Delhi: Oxford University Press, 1996.

Lokhandwalla, S. T. "Islamic Law and Ismaili Communities (Khojas and Bohras)." *Indian Economic and Social History Review* 4, no. 2 (April 1967): 155–76.

Mahmood, Saba. "Rehearsed Spontaneity and the Conventionality of Ritual: Disciplines of Salat." *American Ethnologist* 28, no. 4 (November 2001): 827–53.

*Religious Difference in a Secular Age: A Minority Report*. Princeton: Princeton University Press, 2015.

"Religious Reason and Secular Affect: An Incommensurable Divide?" In *Is Critique Secular?*, edited by Talal Asad, Wendy Brown, Judith Butler, and Saba Mahmood. Berkeley: University of California Press, 2009.

Maier, Charles S. "Consigning the Twentieth Century to History: Alternative Narratives for the Modern Era." *The American Historical Review* 105, no. 3 (June 2000): 807–31.

"Transformations of Territoriality 1600–2000." In *Transnationale Geschichte: Themen, Tendenzen und Theorien*, edited by Gunilla Budde, Sebastian Conrad, and Oliver Janz. Göttingen: Vandenhoeck & Ruprecht, 2006.

Majumdar, Rochona. *Marriage and Modernity: Family Values in Colonial Bengal*. Durham: Duke University Press, 2009.

Mallampalli, Chandra. "Escaping the Grip of Personal Law in Colonial India: Proving Custom, Negotiating Hindu-ness." *Law and History Review* 28, no. 4 (2010): 1043–65.

*Race, Religion, and Law in Colonial India: Trials of an Interracial Family*. Cambridge: Cambridge University Press, 2011.

Mandaville, Jon E. "Usurious Piety: The Cash Waqf Controversy in the Ottoman Empire." *International Journal of Middle East Studies* 10, no. 3 (1979): 289–308.

Mantena, Karuna. *Alibis of Empire: Henry Maine and the Ends of Liberal Imperialism*. Princeton: Princeton University Press, 2010.

Masselos, J.C. "The Khojas of Bombay: The Defining of Formal Membership Criteria during the Nineteenth Century." In *Caste and Social Stratification among the Muslims*, edited by Imtiaz Ahmad. Delhi: Manohar Book Service, 1973.

Masud, Muhammad Khalid. "Apostasy and Judicial Separation in British India." In *Islamic Legal Interpretation: Muftis and Their Fatwas*, edited by Muhammad Khalid Masud, Brinkley Morris Messick, and David Stephan Powers. Cambridge: Harvard University Press, 1996.

"The Significance of Istiftā' in the Fatwā Discourse." *Islamic Studies* 48, no. 3 (Autumn 2009): 341–66.

Mathew, Johan. *Margins of the Market: Trafficking and Capitalism across the Arabian Sea*. Oakland: University of California Press, 2016.

Menski, Werner. *Hindu Law: Beyond Tradition and Modernity*. New Delhi: Oxford University Press, 2003.

*Modern Indian Family Law*. London: Routledge, 2013.

Metcalf, Barbara D. *Islamic Revival in British India: Deoband, 1860–1900*. 1982; Reprint New Delhi: Oxford University Press, 2002.

"Two Fatwas on Hajj in British India." In *Islamic Legal Interpretation: Muftis and Their Fatwas*, edited by Muhammad Khalid Masud, Brinkley Morris Messick, and David Stephan Powers. Cambridge: Harvard University Press, 1996.

Metcalf, Thomas R. *Ideologies of the Raj*. 1994: Reprint Cambridge: Cambridge University Press, 2008.

*The Aftermath of Revolt: India, 1857–1870*. Princeton: Princeton University Press, 1964.

Minault, Gail. *The Khilafat Movement: Religious Symbolism and Political Mobilization in India*. New York: Columbia University Press, 1982.

"Women, Legal Reform, and Muslim Identity." *Comparative Studies of South Asia, Africa and the Middle East* 17, no. 2 (September 1997): 1–10.

Mody, Perveez. "Love and the Law: Love-Marriage in Delhi." *Modern Asian Studies* 36, no. 1 (2002): 223–56.

Mufti, Aamir. *Enlightenment in the Colony: The Jewish Question and the Crisis of Postcolonial Culture*. Princeton: Princeton University Press, 2007.

Mukherjee, Mukul. "Impact of Modernisation on Women's Occupations: A Case Study of the Rice-Husking Industry of Bengal." In *Women in Colonial India: Essays on Survival, Work, and the State*, edited by J. Krishnamurty. Delhi: Oxford University Press, 1989.

Nair, Neeti. "Beyond the 'Communal' 1920s: The Problem of Intention, Legislative Pragmatism, and the Making of Section 295A of the Indian Penal Code." *Indian Economic and Social History Review* 50, no. 3 (July 2013): 317–40.

*Changing Homelands: Hindu Politics and the Partition of India*. Cambridge: Harvard University Press, 2011.

Nasr, Seyyed Vali Reza. *Islamic Leviathan: Islam and the Making of State Power*. Oxford: Oxford University Press, 2001.

*Mawdudi and the Making of Islamic Revivalism*. New York: Oxford University Press, 1996.

Nelson, Matthew J. *In the Shadow of Shari'ah: Islam, Islamic Law, and Democracy in Pakistan*. New York: Columbia University Press, 2011.

Newbigin, Eleanor. "Personal Law and Citizenship in India's Transition to Independence." *Modern Asian Studies* 45, no. 1 (2011): 7–32.

*The Hindu Family and the Emergence of Modern India: Law, Citizenship and Community*. Cambridge: Cambridge University Press, 2013.

Pandey, Gyanendra. *The Construction of Communalism in Colonial North India*. Delhi: Oxford University Press, 1990.

Parker, Kunal M. "'A Corporation of Superior Prostitutes' Anglo-Indian Legal Conceptions of Temple Dancing Girls, 1800–1914." *Modern Asian Studies* 32, no. 3 (July 1998): 559–633.

Parmar, Inderjeet. *Foundations of the American Century: The Ford, Carnegie, and Rockefeller Foundations in the Rise of American Power*. New York: Columbia University Press, 2015.

Peters, Rudolph. "From Jurists' Law to Statute Law or What Happens When the Shari'a Is Codified." *Mediterranean Politics* 7, no. 3 (2002): 82–95.

"Idjtihad and Taqlid in 18th and 19th Century Islam." *Die Welt Des Islams* 20, no. 3/4 (January 1980): 131–45.

Poovey, Mary. "Covered but Not Bound: Caroline Norton and the 1857 Matrimonial Causes Act." *Feminist Studies* 14 (1988): 467–85.

Porter, Andrew. "'Commerce and Christianity': The Rise and Fall of a Nineteenth-Century Missionary Slogan." *The Historical Journal* 28 (1985): 597–621.

Powers, David S. "The Islamic Family Endowment (Waqf)." *Vanderbilt Journal of Transnational Law* 32 (October 1999): 1167–90.

"The Islamic Inheritance System: A Socio-Historical Approach." *Arab Law Quarterly* 8, no. 1 (1993): 13–29.

Purohit, Teena. *The Aga Khan Case: Religion and Identity in Colonial India*. Cambridge: Harvard University Press, 2012.

Rai, Mridu. *Hindu Rulers, Muslim Subjects: Islam, Rights, and the History of Kashmir*. Princeton: Princeton University Press, 2004.

Rajan, Rajeswari Sunder. *The Scandal of the State: Women, Law, and Citizenship in Postcolonial India*. Durham: Duke University Press, 2003.

Ramnath, Maia. *Haj to Utopia: How the Ghadar Movement Charted Global Radicalism and Attempted to Overthrow the British Empire*. Berkeley: University of California Press, 2011.

Rao, Anupama. *The Caste Question: Dalits and the Politics of Modern India*. Berkeley: University of California Press, 2009.

Ray, Rajat Kanta. *Exploring Emotional History: Gender, Mentality and Literature in the Indian Awakening*. New Delhi: Oxford University Press, 2001.

Raychaudhuri, Tapan. *Perceptions, Emotions, Sensibilities: Essays on India's Colonial and Post-Colonial Experiences*. New Delhi: Oxford University Press, 1999.

Redding, Jeffrey A. "Constitutionalizing Islam: Theory and Pakistan." *Virginia Journal of International Law* 44, no. 3 (2004): 759–828.

Rizvi, Saiyid Athar Abbas. *Shah Wali-Allah and His Times: A Study of Eighteenth Century Islam, Politics and Society in India*. Canberra, Australia: Ma'rifat, 1980.

Robb, Peter. *Ancient Rights and Future Comfort: Bihar, the Bengal Tenancy Act of 1885, and British Rule in India*. Richmond, Surrey: Curzon Press, 1997.

Robinson, Francis. "Islamic Reform and Modernities in South Asia." *Modern Asian Studies* 42, no. 2/3 (2008): 259–81.

"Strategies of Authority in Muslim South Asia in the Nineteenth and Twentieth Centuries." *Modern Asian Studies* 47, no. 1 (2013): 1–21.

"Technology and Religious Change: Islam and the Impact of Print." *Modern Asian Studies* 27, no. 1 (February 1993): 229–51.

Roosa, John. "Passive Revolution Meets Peasant Revolution: Indian Nationalism and the Telangana Revolt." *The Journal of Peasant Studies* 28, no. 4 (July 2001): 57–94.

Rothschild, Emma. "Political Economy." In *The Cambridge History of Nineteenth-Century Political Thought*, edited by Gareth Stedman Jones and Gregory Claeys. Cambridge: Cambridge University Press, 2011.

Royle, Edward. "Secularists and Rationalists, 1800–1940." In *A History of Religion in Britain: Practice and Belief from Pre-Roman Times to the Present*, edited by Sheridan Gilley and W.J. Sheils. Oxford: Blackwell, 1994.

Saeed, Sadia. "Political Fields and Religious Movements: The Exclusion of the Ahmadiyya Community in Pakistan." *Political Power and Social Theory* 23 (August 2012): 189–223.

Sanyal, Usha. *Devotional Islam and Politics in British India: Ahmad Riza Khan Barelwi and His Movement, 1870–1920*. Delhi: Oxford University Press, 1996.

Sartori, Andrew. *Bengal in Global Concept History: Culturalism in the Age of Capital*. Chicago: University of Chicago Press, 2008.

"The Resonance of 'Culture': Framing a Problem in Global Concept-History." *Comparative Studies in Society and History* 47, no. 4 (October 2005): 676–99.

Schlossberg, Herbert. *Conflict and Crisis in the Religious Life of Late Victorian England*. New Brunswick: Transaction Publishers, 2009.

Sen, Samita. "Offences against Marriage: Negotiating Custom in Colonial Bengal." In *A Question of Silence?: The Sexual Economies of Modern India*, edited by Mary E. John and Janaki Nair. New Delhi: Kali for Women, 1998.

"Unsettling the Household: Act VI (of 1901) and the Regulation of Women Migrants in Colonial Bengal." In *Peripheral Labour: Studies in the History of Partial Proletarianization*, edited by Shahid Amin and Marcel van der Linden. Cambridge: Cambridge University Press, 1997.

Sharafi, Mitra. "Justice in Many Rooms since Galanter: De-Romanticizing Legal Pluralism through the Cultural Defense." *Law and Contemporary Problems* 71 (2008): 139–46.

*Law and Identity in Colonial South Asia: Parsi Legal Culture, 1772–1947*. New York: Cambridge University Press, 2014.

"The Marital Patchwork of Colonial South Asia: Forum Shopping from Britain to Baroda." *Law and History Review* 28, no. 4 (2010): 979–1009.

"The Semi-Autonomous Judge in Colonial India: Chivalric Imperialism Meets Anglo-Islamic Dower and Divorce Law," *Indian Economic and Social History Review* 46, no. 1 (2009): 57–81.

Shehabuddin, Elora. *Reshaping the Holy: Democracy, Development, and Muslim Women in Bangladesh*. New York: Columbia University Press, 2012.

Sherman, Taylor C. *State Violence and Punishment in India*. London: Routledge, 2010.

Siddique, Osama, and Zahra Hayat. "Unholy Speech and Holy Laws: Blasphemy Laws in Pakistan – Controversial Origins, Design Defects, and Free Speech Implications." *Minnesota Journal of International Law* 17, no. 2 (2008): 303–85.

Singha, Radhika. *A Despotism of Law: Crime and Justice in Early Colonial India*. Delhi: Oxford University Press, 1998.

"Making the Domestic More Domestic: Criminal Law and the 'Head of the Household', 1772–1843." *Indian Economic and Social History Review* 33, no. 3 (1996): 309–43.

Sinha, Mrinalini. *Specters of Mother India: The Global Restructuring of an Empire*. Durham: Duke University Press, 2006.

Sivaramakrishanan, K. *Modern Forests: Statemaking and Environmental Change in Colonial Eastern India*. Stanford: Stanford University Press, 1999.

Skuy, David. "Macaulay and the Indian Penal Code of 1862: The Myth of the Inherent Superiority and Modernity of the English Legal System Compared to India's Legal System in the Nineteenth Century." *Modern Asian Studies* 32, no. 3 (1998): 513–57.

Solanki, Gopika. *Adjudication in Religious Family Laws: Cultural Accommodation, Legal Pluralism, and Gender Equality in India*. Cambridge: Cambridge University Press, 2011.

Sreenivas, Mytheli. *Wives, Widows, and Concubines: The Conjugal Family Ideal in Colonial India*. Bloomington: Indiana University Press, 2008.

Stanley, Brian. *The Bible and the Flag: Protestant Missions and British Imperialism in the Nineteenth and Twentieth Centuries*. Leicester, England: Apollos, 1990.

Stein, Burton. *Vijayanagara*. Cambridge: Cambridge University Press, 1989.

Stephens, Julia. "An Uncertain Inheritance: The Imperial Travels of Legal Migrants, from British India to Ottoman Iraq." *Law and History Review* 32, no. 4 (November 2014): 749–72.

"The Phantom Wahhabi: Liberalism and the Muslim Fanatic in Mid-Victorian India." *Modern Asian Studies* 47, no. 1 (2013): 22–52.

Stokes, Eric. *The English Utilitarians and India*. 1959; Reprint Delhi: Oxford University Press, 1982.

Strawson, John. "Islamic Law and English Texts." *Law and Critique* 6, no. 1 (1995): 21–38.

Sturman, Rachel. *The Government of Social Life in Colonial India: Liberalism, Religious Law, and Women's Rights*. Cambridge: Cambridge University Press, 2012.

Subramanian, Narendra. "Legal Change and Gender Inequality: Changes in Muslim Family Law in India." *Law & Social Inquiry* 33, no. 3 (September 2008): 631–72.

*Nation and Family: Personal Law, Cultural Pluralism, and Gendered Citizenship in India*. Stanford: Stanford University Press, 2014.

Sullivan, Robert E. *Macaulay: The Tragedy of Power*. Cambridge: Belknap Press, 2009.

Surkis, Judith. *Sexing the Citizen: Morality and Masculinity in France, 1870–1920*. Ithaca: Cornell University Press, 2006.

Talbot, Ian. *Pakistan: A Modern History*. London: C. Hurst, 1998.

Tambe, Ashwini. *Codes of Misconduct: Regulating Prostitution in Late Colonial Bombay*. Minneapolis: University of Minnesota Press, 2009.

Tejani, Shabnum. *Indian Secularism: A Social and Intellectual History, 1890–1950*. Bloomington: Indiana University Press, 2008.

Thursby, Gene R. *Hindu-Muslim Relations in British India: A Study of Controversy, Conflict, and Communal Movements in Northern India 1923–1928*. Leiden: Brill, 1975.

Travers, Robert. *Ideology and Empire in Eighteenth Century India: The British in Bengal*. Cambridge: Cambridge University Press, 2007.

Tucker, Judith E. *In the House of the Law: Gender and Islamic Law in Ottoman Syria and Palestine*. Berkeley: University of California Press, 1998.

Van der Veer, Peter. *Imperial Encounters: Religion and Modernity in India and Britain*. Princeton: Princeton University Press, 2001.

"The Secularity of the State." In *The State in India: Past and Present*, edited by Masaaki Kimura and Akio Tanabe. New Delhi: Oxford University Press, 2006.

Vatuk, S. "Islamic Feminism in India: Indian Muslim Women Activists and the Reform of Muslim Personal Law." *Modern Asian Studies* 42, no. 2–3 (March 2008): 489–518.

"Shurreef, Herklots, Crooke, and Qanoon-E-Islam: Constructing an Ethnography of 'The Moosulmans of India.'" *South Asian Research* 19, no. 1 (1999): 5–28.

Vikør, Knut S. *Between God and the Sultan: A History of Islamic Law*. London: Hurst & Co., 2005.

Viswanath, Rupa. *The Pariah Problem: Caste, Religion, and the Social in Modern India*. New York: Columbia University Press, 2014.

Viswanathan, Gauri. *Masks of Conquest: Literary Study and British Rule in India*. New York: Columbia University Press, 1989.

*Outside the Fold: Conversion, Modernity, and Belief*. Princeton: Princeton University Press, 1998.

Washbrook, D.A. "Law, State and Agrarian Society in Colonial India." *Modern Asian Studies* 15 (1981): 649–721.

Wilford, Hugh. *The Mighty Wurlitzer: How the CIA Played America*. Cambridge: Harvard University Press, 2009.

Wilson, Jon E. *The Domination of Strangers: Modern Governance in Eastern India, 1780–1835*. Basingstoke: Palgrave Macmillan, 2008.

Wolffe, John. *God and Greater Britain: Religion and National Life in Britain and Ireland, 1843–1945*. London: Routledge, 1994.

Yaduvansh, U. "The Decline of the Role of the Qadis in India, 1793–1876." *Studies in Islam* 6 (1969): 155–71.

Zaman, Muhammad Qasim. *Modern Islamic Thought in a Radical Age: Religious Authority and Internal Criticism*. Cambridge: Cambridge University Press, 2012.

"Studying Hadith in a Madrasa in the Early Twentieth Century." In *Islam in South Asia in Practice*, edited by Barbara D. Metcalf. Princeton: Princeton University Press, 2009.

*The Ulama in Contemporary Islam: Custodians of Change*. Princeton: Princeton University Press, 2002.

Ziring, Lawrence. "From Islamic Republic to Islamic State in Pakistan." *Asian Survey* 24, no. 9 (1984): 931–46.

# Index

*Abdul Kadir* v. *Salima*, 70
Abdullah, Hafiz, 170
*Abolition of Personal Ownership of Property,*
*The* (Kidwai), 157
adoption, 45
adultery (*zina*), 82
Afghanistan, 157
agency, 4, 15, 89, 96
Agrama, Hussein Ali, 18
agriculture, 31, 92n18
Ahl-i-Hadith sect, 105, 116, 118,
123, 130
suspicion of *aql* (human reason), 121
*taqlid* debate and, 126
Ahmad, Sayyid, 112
Ahmadis (Ahmadiyya), 153, 179, 187
Akbar Ali, *Pir*, 169
Aligarh Muslim University, 165–66
Ali Khan, Liaquat, 178–79
Ali, Maulana Muhammad, 145
Allahabad High Court, 70, 73, 126,
137, 138
Ameer Ali, Syed, 73
*Ancient Law* (Maine, 1861), 86, 89
Arabic legal texts, 24, 27, 29, 33, 37
*Hidaya*, 31, 62, 71, 72, 73
lack of accessibility to wider reading
public, 72
shift toward vernacular publishing and, 118
with Urdu translation, 122
Asad, Talal, 5
Assam Labour and Emigration Act
(1901), 103
Ayub Khan, Muhammad, 185
Aziz, Shah Abdul, 122

Babri Masjid, destruction of (1992),
1, 2, 3
Baillie, John, 22, 23
Baillie, Neil, 22–23, 31, 32
Bangladesh, 20, 184–88
Banna, Hassan al-, 165

*Barahin-i-Isna-Ashar* [Twelve Arguments]
(Amir Husain, 1874), 121
Barakatullah, Maulana, 157, 159
Barelwi, Sayyid Ahmad, 115, 116
Barelwi sect, 105, 116–17
Bayly, E.C., 54
Bengal, 28, 35, 42–43, 100, 117
East India Company rule in, 6, 25
Hastings's 1772 Plan in, 30
marriage law in, 101
*nikah* marriage custom in, 98
Tajpore case in, 105
women laborers recruited in, 102
Bentham, Jeremy, 89
Bentinck, Lord W.C., 34, 35, 37, 43
Benton, Lauren, 13
Bharatiya Janata Party (BJP), 134, 152
Bhutto, Zulfikar Ali, 181
*bidat* (heretical innovations), 114, 116, 119, 123
Birla, Ritu, 52
blasphemy laws, 153
Blunt, Wilfred Scawen, 160–61
"Bolshevism and the Islamic Body-Politic"
(Barakatullah, 1919), 159
Bombay High Court, 64
Britain, 9, 10, 53, 130
British Raj, 52
Buddhists, 159
Butler, Judith, 15, 18, 189

Calcutta High Court, 62, 65, 128–29
*Calvin's Case* (1608), 44–45
Cameron, C.H., 43–44, 47, 48
canon law, 62–63
capitalism, 156, 157
boom-bust cycles of, 162
indigenous alternatives to, 160
Islamic economics and, 164, 168, 174
case law, 17, 49
Company legal reform and, 29
law reporting and, 32
*mahr* payments and conflicts in, 69–74

case law (*cont.*)
  patriarchy and, 68
  on ritual, 108
caste, 9, 17, 23, 30
  Indian Law Commission and, 52
  *lex loci* and, 48
  marriage customs and, 97, 98, 99, 103
Caste Disabilities Removal Act (1850), 41
censorship, 19, 20, 154
  communal violence and, 142, 153
  debate over, 143
  Penal Code and, 133
Chatterjee, Nandini, 7, 26
children, 71, 90, 92, 102, 103
  ritual and, 112
  unpaid labor output of, 88
  women and custody of, 9
China, Muslims in, 176
Christianity, 10, 23, 153
  Church of England, 106
  evangelical, 38–40, 46–48
civilization, 39, 48
civil law, 11, 15, 30, 104
  *lex loci* and, 42, 47
  marital property and, 57
Code of Civil Procedure, 63, 64n17
Cohn, Bernard, 13
Coke, Edward, 44–45
Cold War, 175, 177, 182
colonial courts, 7, 29, 73, 76–77
  custom and, 88
  disputes settled outside of, 74–84
  divorces granted to Muslim women, 83
  economic-domestic boundaries and,
    19, 67
  enforcement of husband's conjugal
    rights by, 79
  local customs supported by, 11–12
  as mediator of Muslim ritual
    differences, 105–6
  Muslim law assistants to, 60
  "nonintervention" in religious law, 53
  *pandit* and *qazi* advisers to, 52, 80
  *taqlid* and, 130–31
  women's relation to property and, 66, 69
colonial law, 8, 13, 88
  ambiguity and malleability of, 5
  conjugal rights in, 64
  internal tensions of, 9
  oppositions mapped out by, 10
  paradoxical workings of, 1
  patriarchy and, 87, 103
  personal law as core organizing principle
    of, 19
  religious difference and, 7

stasis and fluidity in, 84
  *taqlid* and, 124–30
  vernacular legal culture and, 12
colonial rule, British: "Age of Reform,"
  23, 34, 38
  as parody of secular governance, 9–10
  "rubber-band" state, 10–15, 69
  transfer from Company to Crown rule
    (1857), 23
commercial codes, 9, 56
communalism, 1, 17, 107
  "communal 1920s," 134–36
  intercommunal violence, 134
  intra-communal disputes, 12, 108
  Muslim law communalized, 23
  as "Other" of secularism, 4, 187
  personal law and, 9
  sexual politics and, 135–37
communism/communists, 158, 164, 166,
  168, 175–76
Communist Party of India, 157, 173
Communist Party of Pakistan, 179
community, 15, 50, 188
  as category of governance, 108
  as unit of governance, 12, 107, 108
conjugal rights, 59n2, 60, 63
  *mahr* payments and, 71–72, 73,
    74, 84, 85
  Privy Council opinion on, 62
contracts, 7, 23, 55
Cornwallis, Lord, 28
Cornwallis Code (Permanent
  Settlement), 28–29
"counter conducts," 14
criminal law, 7, 11, 31, 69, 103
  Company administration of Muslim
    law, 27
  *lex loci* and, 42
custom, 12, 14, 19, 68
  curtailed recognition of, 167
  "immoral," 93–97
  as source of law, 86
customary law, 37, 49, 85, 94
  disinheritance of daughters and, 88–93
  economic-domestic boundaries and, 87
  Indian Law Commission and, 86
  patriarchy and, 104
  secular governance and, 103

*dar-ul-ifta* (*fatwa*-issuing department), at
  Deoband, 75–76, 77, 78, 80, 84
debts, 31, 33, 87, 92
democracy, 152, 174, 175–76, 177, 185
Deobandi sect, 105, 116
Deoband *madrasa*, 12, 19, 77, 83, 85, 162

debate over *taqlid* and, 116
establishment of (1866), 75, *see also*
    *dar-ul-ifta*
Derrett, J.D.M., 27
*Digest of Anglo-Muhammadan Law, A*
    (Wilson, 1895), 73
*Digest of Moohummudan Law* (Baillie,
    1865), 22, 23, 32
*Digest of Muhammadan Law, A* (Baillie,
    1805), 22, 23
Din, Malik Muhammad, 170
Din Muhammad, Khan Bahadur
    Shaikh, 170
discipline, Foucault's concept of, 14
Dissolution of Muslim Marriage Act
    (1939), 83, 172
divorce, 9, 31, 59, 80–81, 99, 186
    Dissolution of Muslim Marriage Act
        (1939), 83, 172
    *iddat* waiting period after, 78
    Indian Law Commission and, 23
    *lex loci* and, 45
    by official decree (*tafriq*), 81–82
*diwani* (civil) courts, 25
Dowla, Mussammat, 4
Duff, Alexander, 39
Dutt, Amar Nath, 148–49
Dutt, Romesh, 99, 161

East India Company, 6, 7, 56
    Company courts, 32
    *lex loci* and, 41
    Mughal law and, 25–29
    Rebellion of 1857 and, 51, 52
    sovereignty and, 35
economic-domestic binary, 53–56, 84,
    87, 107
    *mahr* payments and, 69–74
    Ruheem case and, 57, 58
*Economic History of India, The* (Dutt), 161
economy/economics, 15, 155, 156, 188
    emergence as distinct social sphere, 5
    interest payments on bank deposits, 163
    Islamic economics in Hyderabad, 160–65
    of Mawdudi, 165–67
    Pakistan as "laboratory of applied
        Islam," 173–78
Elberling, F.E., 32
English law, 41, 42, 44, 45–46
    domestic and economic independence of
        women and, 68
    marriage contract and, 62–63

Fadel, Mohamamd, 127
family, 10, 15, 29, 157, 188

delegitimization of non-normative
    families, 93–97
domestic household as "Other" of
    capitalist market, 17
extended families, 74
family-law exceptionalism, 6
patriarchal, 89–90
religious laws associated with, 23
transformations in, 5
*Fatuhat-i-Ahl-i-Hadith* (Victories of the
    Ahl-i-Hadith), 130
*fatwa*s, 4, 12, 60, 122
    curtailed use in criminal trials, 35
    on marriage, 74–84, 99
    non-binding nature of, 75
    vernacular legal culture and, 19
*faujdari* courts, 25
Fazl-i-Haq Piracha, Khan Bahadur Shaikh,
    170, 171
*Fazl Karim v. Maula Baksh*, 105
feudalism/feudal law, 8, 36
fines, 31
*fiqh* (orthodox Islamic jurisprudence), 7,
    8n19, 117, 120
Fisher, Irving, 162
Foucault, Michel, 13–14
*Future Development of Islamic Polity, The*
    (Qureshi, 1946), 173

Galloway, Archibald, 44
gambling, 77
Gandhi, Mohandas K., 133, 134, 165
Gangohi, Maulana Rashid Ahmad, 3
Ganguli, Amulya, 2
gender, 181, 186
    custom and female inheritance, 88–93
    performative nature of, 15
Ghadar Party, 159
*Ghasiti v. Umrao Jan*, 95–96
gifts, 31
Gilani, Manazir Ahsan, 162–63, 164
Gilmartin, David, 140, 141
Gladstone, William, 40
Gladwin, Francis, 31
governmentality, 13, 14, 15
Government of India Acts, 133, 171
Grady, Standish Grove, 32
Great Depression, 156, 164
*Guru Ghantal* (Hindu newspaper), 135

*hadith* (traditions of the Prophet), 109,
    113, 162
    changing historical circumstances and, 121
    direct consultation of, 116
    *taqlid* debate and, 119, 120, 123, 124

Halley, Janet, 6
Hamidullah, Muhammad, 161, 162,
    164, 165
Hamilton, Charles, 27, 31
Hanafi school, 22, 31, 63n15, 71
    *tafriq* (divorce by decree) and, 81–82
    *taqlid* debate and, 117, 124, 125, 126
Hanifa, Abu, 71, 110
Haque, Mrinal, 184
Hartog, Hendrik, 13
Hasan, Ahmad, 121
Hastings, Warren, 1772 plan of, 25,
    28, 30, 33
*Hedaya, The* (translated by Hamilton,
    1791), 27, 31
Herklots, Gerhard Andreas, 98
*Hidaya, al-*, 31, 62, 71, 72, 73
Hifazat-i-Islam (Protection of Islam),
    184, 186
Hindu law, 8–9, 23
    case law of colonial courts and, 53
    Company officials and, 27, 29
    customary law operating alongside, 37
    customary practices privileged over, 86
    East India Company rule and, 43
    Indian Law Commission and, 47
    *lex loci* and, 42
Hindu Law Committee, 172
Hindu Mahasabha, 139, 148
Hindu nationalists, 17, 139, 145, 149
    demonization of Islam and, 150
    destruction of Babri Masjid by, 1, 2
    electoral politics and, 3
Hindus, 8, 16, 114
    conflicts with Muslims, 107, 132
    high-caste, 17, 97, 103
    majoritarian politics and, 134
    Muslim law under Company rule
        and, 25–26
    personal law and, 172
    *sati* (widow burning), 35
    secular governance remade by, 20
    sexual politics of communal conflict
        and, 135–36
    socialism and, 159
*History of the Roman Law during the
    Middle Ages, The* (Savigny,
    1815–1831), 36
Hobhouse, Arthur, 127–29
Holyoake, George, 128
Hunter, W.W., 100
Husain, Maulvi Irshad, 120, 121
Husain, Sayyid Nazir, 116, 118–21
Hyderabad, Islamic economics in,
    160–65

Ilmuddin, 150–52, 153, 188
Imarat-i-Sharia, 82, 83, 84
indentured laborers, 102
India, colonial, 19, 182
    agrarian peasant communities
        in, 36
    ascendant Hindu majority in, 187
    global legal revolution and, 34
    secular legal governance in, 6
India, post-colonial, 20, 134, 152, 178
*Indian Journal of Economics, The*, 160
Indian Army, British, 93
Indian Civil Service, 100
Indian Contract Act (1872), 71, 96
Indian Law Commission, 16, 23, 61, 69
    custom and, 86, 100, 104
    *lex loci* and, 40–51, 58
    personal law and, 8–9, 51, 58, 132
    Rebellion of 1857 and, 52–53
Indian Law Reports Act (1875), 33
Indian Legislative Assembly, 133, 148
    Hindu Law Committee, 172
    Penal Code amendment and, 147
    Shariat Act (1937) and, 167, 168, 170
Indian Majority Act (1875), 53
Indian Succession Act, 55
inheritance, 6, 9, 19, 20
    cases under Company rule, 28
    customary law and female inheritance,
        88–93, 169
    economic-domestic boundaries
        and, 54–55
    Indian Law Commission and, 23, 52
    Islamic economics and, 156
    *lex loci* and, 42
    personal law and, 104
interest payments, 60, 65, 77, 163
*Intisar-ul-Haqq* [The Victory of Truth]
    (Irshad Husain, 1873), 120,
    121, 125
Iqbal, Muhammad, 142–44, 155, 161
Islam, 18, 26, 147
    economic thought and, 155, 156,
        166–67, 174, 182
    five pillars of, 31
    marginalized in Hindu-majoritarian
        discourse, 149, 150
    secular governance defined in opposition
        to, 16
    "spiritual democracy" and, 175
*Islam and Socialism* (Kidwai, c. 1912),
    157, 158
*Islam and the Theory of Interest* (Qureshi,
    1964), 164
Islamic law, 18, 72, 163, 169

British colonial views of, 3
four schools of Sunni jurisprudence,
    109, 115, 126, 127
Maliki, 63n15
as "Other" of secular law, 3
Shafi, 63n15, 125
Shia, 22, 23, *see also* Hanafi school;
    Muslim law; *sharia*
*Islami Ma'ashiyyat* [Islamic Economics]
    (Gilani), 163
Islamism, 177, 184, 186, 188
"Islamization," 153, 167, 177, 181, 187
*Islam ka Iqtisadi Nizam* [The Economic
    System of Islam] (Seoharvi,
    1939), 163
Ismail, Shah, 112, 113, 115, 116, 118
iterative performance, 15
*itjihad*, 109–10, 113–14, 117, 127
Iyengar, Srinivasa, 148

Jafri, Fareed S., 175–76
Jain, Girilal, 2
Jama'at-i-Islami, 165, 179
Jamaluddin-al-Afghani, Sayyid, 160
*Jamiat Ulama-i-Hind*, 146
Jevon, William Stanley, 161
Jinnah, Muhammad Ali, 150–51, 153, 168,
    170–71, 188
Jones, William, 22, 27
*Judoonath Bose* v. *Shumsoonnissa
    Begum*, 59n2

Khan, Abdul Kasem, 180–81
Khan, Ahmad Riza, 116, 117
Khan, Sayyid Ahmad, 54–55, 70, 115,
    116, 126
Khan, Sayyiduddin, 122–23
Khan, Zafar Ali, 144–45
Khilafat Movement, 83, 133, 145, 157
Khoja trading community, 49–50
Khomeini, Ruhollah, 165
Kidwai, Mushir Hosain, 157–59, 182
kinship, 13, 90
Kissinger, Henry, 176, 177
Koreshi, A.O., 170

Lady Justice statue, in Dakha, 184–85,
    186, 188
Lahore High Court, 137, 138–39,
    142, 145
Lajpat Rai, Lala, 16, 144, 148, 149–50
Lal, Sir Shadi, 145
*Land Tax of India, The* (Baillie,
    1853), 31–32
*Law and Colonial Culture* (Benton), 13

*Law Relating to Pardanashins in British
    India (Civil and Criminal), The*, 68
legal historicism, 8, 19, 23, 34, 36–37
legal history, 5–6
legal reform, 3, 6, 29, 35
    "Age of Reform," 23, 34, 38, 49
    in British-ruled India, 8
    global reach of, 34
    in India and Britain, 9
    *lex loci* and, 41, 48
    Muslims seen as resistant to, 2
    Rebellion of 1857 and, 51–53
*lex loci* (territorial law), 40–51, 56, 58
*Lex Loci* Report (1840), 42
literacy, 109, 120

Macaulay, Thomas, 40–41, 51–52, 101,
    132, 133
Macaulay, Zachary, 40
Macnaghten, William H., 33
*Madar-ul-Haqq* [The Axis Truth]
    (Muhammad Shah, 1869), 122
Maddock, T.H., 48–49
Mahmood, Saba, 18, 154
Mahmood, Syed, 70–73, 79, 126–27
*Mahommedan Law* (Ameer Ali,
    1892), 73
*mahr* payments, 69–74, 79, 84, 99, 126
Maine, Henry, 86, 89–90
*Ma'ishat-ul-Hind* (The Economy of
    India), 161
majority, age of, 53–54, 56
Malaviya, Mada Mohan, 144
*Manual of the Mahommedan Law of
    Inheritance and Contract* (Grady,
    1869), 32
marriage, 6, 9, 20, 31, 62
    conjugal rights in, 64
    customary law and, 90–91
    dissolution of, 4
    "domestication" of, 15
    *fatwas* on, 74–84
    governmentality and, 14
    Hindu, 26, 64
    Indian Law Commission and, 23, 52
    *lex loci* and, 45
    lower-class marriage customs
        demonized, 97–103
    *mahr* payments, 69–74
    *muta* (temporary marriage), 99
    Parsi, 64
    personal law and, 104
    religious and secular aspects of, 11
    "secularization" of, 53
    women's property and, 19

Married Women's Property Acts (1870s and 80s), 57, 66
*Marxism or Islam?* (Siddiqi, 1954), 176
Matrimonial Causes Act (1857), 52
Matrimonial Causes Act (1884), 64
Mawdudi, Sayyid Abul A`la, 165–67, 176, 179–80
Memon trading community, 49–50
Metcalf, Barbara, 75n47, 76
Metcalfe, Charles, 38
*Meyar-ul-Haqq* [The Measure of Truth] (Nazir Husain, 1865 or 1866), 118, 120, 122, 123
*Milap* (Lahore newspaper), cartoon in, 139–40
Mill, J.S., 161
missionaries, 39, 42
modernists, Muslim, 3, 115, 116
Modi, Narendra, 3, 185
Mohammedan Marriages and Divorce Registration Act (1876), 101
*Money and the Mechanism of Exchange* (Jevon), 161
*Moohummudan Law of Sale, The* (Baillie, 1850), 31, 32
Moonje, B.S., 144
*Moonshee Buzloor Ruheem* v. *Shumsoonnissa Begum*, 59n2, 63
Mughal Empire and law, 6–7, 16, 44, 107
    Arabic and Persian legal texts, 24
    crisis and decline of, 108–9, 131
    early British governance and, 24
Muhammad, Imam, 71
Muhammad, Prophet, 20, 113, 115, 140
    *bidat* and, 114
    censorship of books insulting the Prophet, 138–39
    press freedom and protection of, 141–47
    sexual politics of communal conflict and, 135–37
    socialist egalitarian ethos anticipated by, 158
    *taqlid* debate and, 116, 120
Muslim law: administered by Christian judges, 38
    age of majority in, 53–54
    case law of colonial courts and, 53
    colonial governance and, 8, 11
    colonial stereotypes of, 169
    colonial terminology and "Muhammadan law," 8
    communalization of, 23, 24, 49
    customary law operating alongside, 37
    customary practices privileged over, 86

early colonial legal developments and, 24–29
East India Company rule and, 24–33, 43, 56
economic-domestic binary and, 57, 58, 61–62, 74
excluded from criminal jurisdiction, 23
Indian Law Commission and, 47
inheritance and, 94
irrationality ascribed to, 3, 16
marginalization of, 40–51
portrayed as unified and static, 85
territorial sovereignty and, 44, *see also* Islamic law; *sharia*
Muhammad Shah, Emperor, 31, 122
*Musammat Rasulan and Zahooran* v. *Mirza Naim-Ullah Beg*, 72
Muslim League, 173, 178
*Muslim Outlook* (English-language daily), 142–43
Muslim Personal Law (Shariat) Application Act (1937), 20, 167–73, 180
Muslims: Ahmadiyyas, 153, 179, 187
    colonial officials' view of, 4, 15–16
    conflict with Hindus, 107, 132
    disputes over ritual practice, 20
    in Indian Legislative Assembly, 133
    intra-communal disputes among, 130
    liberalism and, 2
    at margins of secular governance, 18
    non-Sunni minorities, 19
    *Rangila Rasul* trial and, 137–41, 148
    sexual politics of communal conflict and, 132, 135–37
    Shia, 99, 114, 153, 179, *see also* Sunni Muslims
Muslim Women (Protection of Rights on Divorce) Act, 1, 186
Mussalman Wakf Validating Act (1913), 168
Mussamat Dowla, 94–95
Mussamat Mehrban, 94

nationalism, 135, 164–65, 187
Naujawan Bharat Sabha, 151–52
Nehru, Jawaharlal, 139
Nehru, Motilal, 139
*nika*, 98, 101
Non-Cooperation Movement, 133, 134
North-Western Provinces, 117
Norton, Caroline, 53

Objectives Resolution (Pakistan, 1949), 178–79

Orientalists, 3, 22
Osmania University (Hyderabad), 160–61,
    162, 164, 165
Ottoman Empire, 7, 83, 157

Pakistan, 152, 156, 182
    first constitution of, 20, 178–81
    Islamization policy, 153, 167, 177,
        181, 187
    as "laboratory of applied Islam," 173–78
    secularism in, 185–86
Pan-Islamism and Bolshevism (Kidwai,
    1937), 157–58
pardah (religious/cultural seclusion of
    women), 17, 65, 66–68, 136
partnership, 22, 28, 31, 77, 162, 164
patriarchy, 19–20, 60, 68
    control over labor and property, 87, 103
    customary law and, 89, 91
    Orientalized vision of, 67
    property regime and, 93
    ulama (religious scholars) and, 79
    upheld by colonial state, 64
    women observing pardah and, 67
peasants, 36, 87, 92, 102
Penal Code (drafted 1835, enacted 1862),
    51–52, 100
    amendment to criminalize religious
        insults (Section 295A), 132,
        145, 147–52
    "Of Offences Related to Religion,"
        132–33
penal sanctions, 97, 103
Perry, Erskine, 49–50
Persian legal texts, 24, 27, 29, 31, 33, 37
    lack of accessibility to wider reading
        public, 72
    shift toward vernacular publishing
        and, 118
personal law, 6, 7, 37, 51, 74, 181
    as anachronistic term, 33
    codification of, 171
    concessions to custom and, 86
    as core organizing principle of colonial
        law, 19
    domestication of, 51–53
    marriage customs and, 103
    Muslim law transformed into, 8
    narrative of eighteenth-century
        origins, 29–33
Pinhey, Justice, 64
Plowden, W.C., 55–56
Principles and Precedents of Moohummudan
    Law (Macnaghten, 1875), 33
Privy Council, 57, 70, 96

on conjugal rights, 62–64, 72
on immoral custom, 95
on Muslim women's legal
    capacity, 65–66
on pardah, 66
ritual differences and, 105
Ruheem case (first half) and, 57–59,
    62, 63–64
Ruheem case (second half) and, 65–68
Tajpore case and, 105, 127
on waqf, 168
property, 15, 70, 171
    marital, 19
    patriarchal control over, 87, 103
    transfer of, 52, see also inheritance
property law, 28, 33
prostitutes, 4, 17, 95–97, 100, 135
Public Worship Regulation Act
    (1874), 106–7
Punjab, 117, 170, 171
    British colonial goals in, 93
    female inheritance and custom in, 88,
        89, 92–93
    Rangila Rasul trial in, 137–41
Punjab Customary Law (Tupper), 90
Punjab Laws Act (1872), 91

Qanoon-E-Islam, or The Customs of The
    Moosulmans of India (Shurreef and
    Herklots, 1832), 98
qazis (judges), 7, 26, 75
    Cornwallis Code and, 28–29
    marriage customs and, 101
    office abolished as advisers to colonial
        courts, 52, 80, 82
Quran, 49, 50, 109, 113, 180
    changing historical circumstances
        and, 121
    direct consultation of, 116
    on division of estates, 168–69
    mandate on female inheritance, 87–88
    surah muzzammil, 163
    taqlid debate and, 119, 120, 123, 124
Qureshi, Anwar Iqbal, 161, 163–64, 165
Qureshi, Ishtiaq Husain, 173–75, 182
Qutb, Sayyid, 165

Rajpal, Mahashay, 132, 136, 137, 138, 145
    death of, 150, 151, 152
    trial and acquittal of, 153
Rangila Rasul (1924), 132, 134, 136,
    147, 148
    colonial legacies and, 153
    court case involving, 137–41
Rashtriya Swayamsevak Sangh (RSS), 134

Rawalpindi Conspiracy (1951), 179
reason, 15, 48, 55, 95, 188
    aql (human reason), 109, 115, 121
    Christian belief and, 10, 38, 48, 53
    English law and, 47
    evangelicalism and, 38
Rebellion of 1857, 23, 35, 54, 56, 115, 117
    domestication of personal law
        and, 51–53
Reconstruction of Religious Thought, The
        (Iqbal), 155, 161
religion, 16, 53
    as distinct social sphere, 5
    Indian religions seen as irrational, 61
    personal law and, 9
    in postcolonial societies, 21
    relationship with secularism, 15, 185
"'Religionism' v. Secularism" (Lajpat Rai),
        149–50
religion-reason binary, 4, 15, 20
    debate over taqlid, 115–24
    religious reform and meanings of reason,
        108–15
    secular governance and, 107
religious courts, 74, 75
rent, 31
Reza Khan, Muhammad, 25–27
Riba wa-al-muamalat fi al-Islam [Riba and
        Commercial Dealings in Islam]
        (Rida), 162
Rida, Sayyid Rashid, 162
Rittich, Kerry, 6
ritual, 18, 19, 104
    Muslim sects and colonial courts,
        105–6, 115
    prayer ritual, 115, 125–26
Roman Empire, fall of, 8, 37, 50
Roman law, 36
"Romantics," 36–37
Roy, Rammohun, 28
"Rubber-band" state, 10–15, 69
Ruheem, Buzloor, 57–69
Ruheem, Shumsoonnissa, 57–69, 84
Rushdie, Salman, 1, 153
Ryan, Judge Edward, 38

Sadiq, Shaikh Muhammad, 169
Sajjad, Abul Mahasin Muhammad, 82
sales, 33
Samee-Ullah Khan Bahadur, Moulvi, 11,
        72, 73, 74
Sanskrit legal texts, 27, 29, 37
Satanic Verses, The (Rushdie), 1, 153
Savigny, Friedrich Carl von, 36, 37, 49
science, 10, 89

secular conversion, 19, 23, 38–40
secularism, 1–2, 5, 16, 152, 185–86
    emergence of term in Victorian Britain,
        10, 128
    in Hindu majoritarian discourse,
        134, 149
    "indigenous" roots of Indian
        secularism, 6
    opposed along with Islam, 1, 3
    Penal Code and debate over meaning of,
        147–50
    persistence of, 187–88
    in postcolonial societies, 21
    relationship with religion, 15, 185
secular legal governance, 5, 7, 61, 131
    antagonisms with Islam, 16
    in Britain and in colonial India, 9
    colonial legacy of, 181, 183
    colonial parody of, 9–10
    concessions to custom and, 86
    defined, 4
    economic-domestic boundaries and, 67,
        69, 87, 103
    India as laboratory for, 106
    instability of, 11
    margins of, 18
    Muslim Personal Law (Shariat)
        Application Act (1937) and, 167–73
    nonintervention in religious laws, 83
    performative binaries and, 15
    secular nationalism, 135
    territorial sovereignty and, 107, 182
Sein, Judge Tarucknath, 60–62
Seoharvi, Hifz-ul-Rahman, 163
"separate-spheres" domestic ideology,
        9, 16, 17
sexual politics, communal conflict and,
        135–37
Shah Alam, Emperor, 25
Shah Bano case (1985), 186
sharia, 8n19, 11
    female inheritance and, 91
    fractured Muslim community and, 131
    as moral standard in non-Islamic
        state, 146
    in Pakistan, 175
    personal law and, 167–73
    Sufi practices and, 110, see also Islamic
        law; Muslim law
Sheikh Hasina, 184
shirk (polytheism), 114, 119
Shumsoonnissa, 104
Shurreef, Jaffur, 98
Siddiqi, Mazheruddin, 176–77
Sikhs, 112, 136, 137

Singh, Justice Dilip, 137, 138, 139, 145
*Al Sirajiyyah* (translated by Jones,
    1792), 27
slavery, 31
socialism, Islamic, 155, 157–59, 168, 181
social justice: Islamic, 20, 155, 156,
    178–81, 183
  Soviet Russia and, 174
social reformers, middle-class, 97, 104
Sorabji, Cornelia, 66–67
sovereignty, territorial, 8, 19, 24
  defined, 34
  *Lex Loci* Report and, 46
  Muslim law and, 44
  secular governance and, 107, 182
Soviet Union, 156, 157, 159, 174, 176
*Spirit of Pakistan, The* (Jafri, 1951), 175
*State in Its Relations with the Church, The*
    (Gladstone, 1839), 40
Stephen, James Fitzjames, 54
Stowell, Lord, 63
succession, 9, 23, 52, 83, 94
Sufism, 105, 109, 116
  Mujaddidi order, 120
  *pirs* (spiritual guides), 113
  *tariqahs* (paths or orders), 110
Sulaiman, Sir Shah, 73–74
Sunni Muslims, 153, 187
  conflict among, 107
  sects of, 20, 105
  social reformers, 99
Supreme Courts, 30, 35, 49

*tafriq* (divorce by decree), 81–82
Tajpore case, on ritual differences, 105,
    106, 108, 124–27
*Tanvir-ul-Haqq* (Illumination of
    Truth), 118
*taqlid* (following established authority), 3,
    20, 108, 128
  colonial law and, 124–31
  debate among Sunni schools of
    jurisprudence and, 115–24, 127
  *itjihad* contrasted with, 109–10,
    113–14
*Taqwiyat-ul-Iman* (Shah Ismail), 112–13
Tariqah-yi-Muhammadi (way of
    Muhammad), 112, 114–15
territoriality, 23, 37
Thanawi, Ashraf Ali, 83
*Times of India* (English-language
    daily), 1–2
Tiwana family, 169
Tjokroaminoto, H.O.S., 158
Travers, Robert, 25

*Treatise on Inheritance, Gift, Will, Sale and
    Mortgage, A* (Elberling, 1844), 32
Tupper, C.L., 90–91

*ulama* (religious scholars), 12, 78, 85,
    113, 114
  Gandhian Non-Cooperation movement
    and, 83
  Islamic economics and, 155
  Islamic social justice and, 179
  marriage customs and, 99
  moral authority of, 80
  Muslim patriarchy and, 79
  in Pakistan, 179–80
  *taqlid* debate and, 116, 119, 122,
    123, 124
United States, 176–77, 179
Urdu legal texts, 72, 112, 118, 155–56
*Urvat-ul-Vusqa* [The Firmest Bond]
    (Muhammad Shah), 122
Usmani, Aziz-ul-Rahman, 76, 78–79, 80
  *fatwa*s in absence of state-appointed
    *qazi*, 82
  Hanafi jurisprudence followed by, 81
  Imarat-i-Sharia and, 82–83
*Usul-i-Ma'ashiyyat* (Principles of
    Economics), 161
*Utilitarianism* (Mill), 161

vernacular legal culture, 12, 19
*Vichitra Jiwan* (Strange Life, 1923), 138
vigilante justice, 13
*Village Communities in the East and West*
    (Maine, 1871), 86
village councils (*panchayats*), 26, 74

"Wahhabis," 112, 114n30, 115, 117, 124
Waliullah, Shah, 110–11
*waqf* (charitable endowment), 31, 168–69
wills, 31, 55
Wilson, Jon, 27
Wilson, Roland K., 73
women: British, 68
  Hindu, 65, 66
  marital property and custody of
    children, 9, 17
  sexual politics of communal conflict
    and, 135–37, *see also* gender
women, Muslim, 16, 20, 186–87
  colonial officials' view of, 4, 15
  double "Othering" of Muslim women, 17
  Islamization policies in Pakistan and, 187
  marital obligations and, 62–64
  New Delhi protest with market scales
    (1995), 1

women, Muslim (*cont.*)
  property owned/managed by, 17,
    57, 65–66
  Quranic mandate on inheritance,
    87–88, 169
Women's Development Policy
  (Bangladesh), 186
World War I, 156, 157
World War II, 164

Yusuf, Abu, 71

*zakat* (charitable tax on wealth), 31, 158,
  162, 181
*Zamindar* (Urdu-language newspaper),
  144, 145
Zia-ul-Haq, Muhammad, 167, 181, 187
*zila* (lower-level) court cases, 33,
  59, 60